OWEN   78/1415

The hand made object and its
maker

The Hand Made Object and Its Maker

The Hand Made Object and Its Maker

by Michael Owen Jones

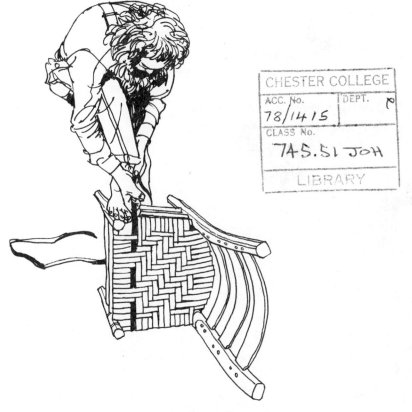

University of California

Berkeley · Los Angeles · London

1975

University of California Press
Berkeley and Los Angeles, California

University of California Press, Ltd.
London, England

ISBN: 0-520-02697-7
Library of Congress Catalog Card Number: 73-93055

Printed in the United States of America
Hand-lettered and designed by Dave Comstock

Preface

"In the chairmakin' business," said the bearded craftsman with whom I had been staying in southeastern Kentucky, "you make all kinds of different chairs an' different types of backs. I've made different types of chair seats. Chair seat like that chair you're settin' in there is a different chair." Charley was referring to a slat-back, panel-bottom, mule-eared "settin'" chair crossed with a dining chair which, like a rocker that he had made twenty-five years earlier, was a "mixed-up proposition."

"If it's a foursquare chair," continued Charley, "you've got to make a back in it to naturally go with that; or a turned chair, you got to make your back kind of go in with it." Charley no longer turns legs and stretchers for chairs, however, but shapes them eight-sided by hand using a drawing knife, a procedure that results in the manufacture of some peculiar objects, such as his two-in-one bookcase rocker, masterpiece of furniture.

"That eight-square postees like the chair I make today," he said, "you got to shape your backs kind of like these backs here in this chair is shaped to actually go in with it. That's the only thing about it, you got to kind of make your back go in with the postees," concluded Charley in explanation of his principles of construction and composition which he occasionally violated.

This book is about Charley and other people and about the many different things they have made and how and why they made them. I am concerned with individuals who make and do things and buy and use things in interaction with other people; I call attention to specific experiences and ideas of particular men which are related to, and often expressed by means of, the things they make; and I direct attention not toward great monuments allegedly genteel in nature serving to elevate the mind and spirit, but toward everyday things made for daily use which are appreciated for the skill and imagination required to produce them. The people I write about are known simply as "chairmakers"—and it is the chairs with which I am mainly concerned—although many of them have made baskets, musical instruments, and other furniture including tables and cabinets. Biographical information about the chairmakers is provided, and there are observations in regard to the manufacture, use, and evaluation of the objects. Methodological considerations are treated mainly in the first and seventh chapters, in both of which a framework for research is proposed. Throughout the book I raise questions about basic concepts and models employed by other researchers in their studies of what people make and do.

Objections to an examination of technical processes, creativity, and standards of excellence and preference might be made on the grounds that many forms of art in America, such as chairmaking, are so rudimentary and unsophisticated as to offer no field for investigation. In point of fact, however, any artist is a complex individual whose behavior is motivated by many forces, and the manufacture, use, and evaluation of any object presents a complicated subject for study which is difficult to analyze and comprehend. The challenge is to order and describe the activities in a meaningful way so as to attract the layman and also to assist other researchers concerned with similar questions about human behavior. Such goals require writing plainly without recourse to jargon which obscures issues, and they require setting aside, after a brief review, some of the pet theories, concepts, and models prevalent in several fields of study; absorption in them will only lead us astray from the events we study and inhibit our understanding of the activities of making and using things.

What is the organizing principle of this book? The central

problem is to discover a way to account for the nature of an object made by hand. Although several factors are considered, two points must be kept in mind from the outset. First, human beings have created these objects; many chairs are illustrated and much attention is paid to the physical quality of these things, but the end of research is to understand more fully human behavior. The goal of research concerned with people making and doing and using things is not "to promote understanding of culture," or to direct attention "to other aspects of culture, including economics, and also problems of cultural change," or "to teach others how personality is patterned in different societies and social classes." There is a great deal of difference between that type of perspective and the approach I take, which directly concerns what people make and do in daily life in inter-action with other individuals. Research into human behavior must begin as well as end with human beings and should focus on the individual, for an object cannot be fully understood or appreciated without knowledge of the man who made it, and the traits of one object cannot be explained by reference only to antecedent works of an earlier period from which later qualities allegedly evolved. Second, much of what has been called art, especially what has been labeled folk and primitive art, is useful in some way, which means that the object produced is as much an instrument to achieve some practical result as it is an end in itself (including not only drums and chairs but also masks, bis poles, and divination tappers). As a consequence the researcher cannot divorce what he calls artistic or creative processes from technological ones; the outputs of production serve not only what some people refer to as aesthetic ends but also practical purposes; and the evaluations of products admit considerations of both appearance and fitness for use. It is for this reason that terms such as "artist," "craftsman," "producer," "creator," and "chairmaker" are used interchangeably in the present study, that no artificial distinction is made between "art" and "craft," and that "to create" is used as a synonym for "to build" and "to construct." It is for this reason, also, that I criticize the methods of some other scholars.

I use one person and his works as the focal point of this book in order to develop these two points about the importance of the individual, and I examine several factors influencing the nature of the product, such as tools, materials, techniques of construction, designs learned from other producers, customer preference, mistakes, accident, and especially the craftsman's beliefs, values, and aspirations. The study begins with reference to one of Charley's most unusual creations, the "two-in-one bookcase rocker, masterpiece of furniture," and some analytical problems generated by its manufacture; in the latter part of chapter 1, I propose guidelines for finding answers to questions in general about designing everyday objects for practical use and about this man's works in particular. In the second chapter I return to this same chair in order to review when and how it and another strange chair were made, and to consider some aspects of originality, technical processes, and construction techniques, especially in useful design. The third chapter concerns the individual who made the masterpiece and other objects and the way in which his chairmaking, as part of his expressive behavior, is related to his problems, experiences, and beliefs as a man. Chapters 4 and 5, in which certain assumptions about style and periodicity and evolution are reexamined, focus on major qualities in Charley's works which can be accounted for by his conception of himself and by his relationship with other people. One theme that pervades these chapters concerning Charley and his chairs is that the grieving and the creative processes have much in common and sometimes are almost one (the search for structure and order, and the reaffirmation of self); and in the coalescence of the two processes lies part of the explanation of the origin of the two-in-one bookcase rocker and part of the explanation of why it is indeed, in Charley's life and work, a masterpiece. When viewed in this light, Charley's chairs no longer appear so strange or his behavior so peculiar.

Chapter 6 deals with other craftsmen in the area, some of their ideas, production techniques, and expressive behavior; this information provides additional insights into why individuals make the things they do, especially today when many people think that making things by hand is no longer necessary or common, and offers a comparative basis for later exploring questions about tradition, convention, conservatism, and originality in human behavior. The final chapter is concerned with methods of analysis and summarizes some features of this type of useful design in southeastern Kentucky which is known simply as chairmaking. I discuss some problems generated by relying upon constructs such as culture, group, and personality; I suggest ways of broadening the data base of research to avoid strictures imposed by the use of terms such as "aesthetics" and "style;" and I review several hypotheses commonly used to explain the origins of an object's traits and qualities, hypotheses that seem to be disconfirmed by the information on chairmaking.

This book probably should have been entitled "Untitled" in order to encourage multiple interpretations of its nature and contents, which is the principle subscribed to throughout the book in regard to methods appropriate for analyzing human behavior. Titles of books, like labels imposed upon people or objects, immediately establish a certain framework in one's mind which engenders the fixing of boundaries on what is perceived and limitations on what is imagined. Calling the book "Craftsmen of the Cumberlands," for example, generates one set of expectations, "Art and Artists in Context" another set, and "The Socioesthetics of Ethnocreativity" yet another. "Untitled" is of course a title; it is bound to be interpreted in many ways, which is why it probably should have been the title of this book. Certainly the method of analysis, illustrated by use in most of the book and described in more detail in chapter 7, has no formal title, because labeling it would be contradictory to its basic principle. After all, I am trying to expand the range of interpretations of human behavior, not restrict the inferences to be made.

My initial research, conducted during the summers of 1965, 1966, and 1967, received financial support from various sources. An award from the American Studies program at Indiana University directed by David E. Smith, a National Defense Education Act Title IV Fellowship in American Studies, and folklore research funds provided by Warren E. Roberts of the Folklore Institute enabled me to undertake the original observations and interviews. A doctoral student grant-in-aid for research from Indiana University and a Woodrow Wilson Dissertation Year Fellowship ensured the preparation of a written report on my earlier research.

I am indebted to Professor Warren R. Roberts who introduced me to the study of folk art and technology, who encouraged the original research project out of which the present study ultimately developed, and who offered helpful suggestions in the preparation of materials. To Professor David E. Smith I owe my gratitude for a number of kindnesses connected with my original investigations, from stimulating research to helping me obtain the necessary funds. Professors Roy Sieber, Richard M. Dorson, and John C. Messenger provided constructive criticism and helpful insights early in my work. To many other people, also, including Henry Glassie, Carlos C. Drake, Willard Moore, Robert B. Klymasz, David Bidney, and my wife Jane, I am indebted for information, insights, and encouragement.

In regard to the preparation of the present book I would like to thank my colleague Professor Robert A. Georges at UCLA and my friends Professor Bruce Giuliano at California State University, San Diego, and Professor Kenneth L. Ketner at Texas Tech University for encouragement and for the exchanges of views which contributed greatly to the development of this and other works. I would like to express my appreciation as well to the many students in my classes who not only tolerated my attempts to express some of the ideas in this volume but who helped me articulate them; and to some of my colleagues at UCLA, especially Professors Wayland D. Hand, D. K. Wilgus, and Inkeri Rank, for their support and encouragement of my research. I am grateful, too, to the Academic Senate of the University of California, Los Angeles Division, for having made available to me research grants to help defray the cost of preparing materials necessary for the project and a fellowship to provide uninterrupted time in order to consider more fully some of the ideas in this study. Finally, I wish to thank the many people in south-eastern Kentucky who answered my questions and permitted me to photograph the chairs in their possession, particularly the several craftsmen who revealed to me details of their lives and art. Owing to the personal nature of the information given to me, the names of these craftsmen and their customers as they appear here are fictitious, and the town and county designations do not reveal where the people actually live; in addition, I do not cite in footnotes several relevant essays in newspapers, magazines, and journals because they might make possible, even though the likelihood seems slight, the identification of people and places referred to in this book, and I have refrained from publishing certain photographs and have altered others for the same reason.

Contents

CHAPTER ONE

A Strange Rocking Chair

"I have Bin this month Workin day and nite on a Big Rocker," Charley wrote to my wife and me in late December, 1965, only a few months after we had met him and photographed him at work. Big chairs, although not typical in southeastern Kentucky, were scarcely remarkable for this craftsman, for he had been known for several years as the maker of rocking chairs at least five feet in height with seven or more slats, thick posts, and plenty of room in the seats. "This one is Made so different that hit dont look like iney chire that I Ever made," he insisted. "They are somtin strange about this Rocking chire   I don't Reley no what hapin   I just startied workin on hit   Seems to Be sometin Kidin me   so strang."

We were mildly curious but not really perplexed about this piece of furniture because we knew that while Charley has made some unconventional chairs they were — well—<u>chairs</u>; and a chair is a chair, so to speak. More puzzling was Charley's own bewilderment about the process of manufacture, for our impression had been that he fully conceived of the object before he began construction; the requirements of useful design usually preclude spontaneity in making the objects.

The chair disturbed Charley, though, because he wrote to my wife's sister about the piece shortly after he had sent a letter to us. "This one is a strang [chair]," he repeated to her. "I Reley dinton in tin to Make hit this tipe   Sem to Be somtin new about Ever day has got to Be Adied   Hit is so hevey now that I can't hardly lift hit." Weight was no surprise to us, however, because

Charley's big rockers are all heavy. There was no description of the chair, only the same reference to an unsettling feeling in Charley because "This Rocker is Reley strang Neve sen iney thing like hit in my hole life   hit Reley looks Like my Master Pece of furniture." He concluded his remarks about the chair with the promise that "I will Send you ale some pictures of hit sometime   A Bisnis man in New York wants some Pictures of hit and I gess they Will by hit."

No one in our family received photographs or further details. In another letter dated April 3, 1966, Charley mentioned in passing that he still had

Figure 1. Sassafras rocker with black walnut pegs made by Charley in November, 1965. Note difference in design of slats, with gradually rising peak in center, and the use of more elongated finials, in comparison with earlier chairs, e.g. figure 27 or 46.

the chair, and there was a hint that the businessman had chosen not to buy it. "Still have the Maste Pece," wrote Charley, "and lokes like I will get to Keep hit."

Curiously, the craftsman had not remarked upon the rocking chair he was supposed to be making for us which was similar to one we had purchased from him for a museum (figure 1); our rocking chair was to have seven slats, a seat of woven hickory bark splints, and pegs that contrasted in color with the wood of the chair. We learned nothing more about Charley's strange chair and nothing at all about the one we had ordered (except a brief statement in late spring that it was finished) until we saw Charley again at the end of August, 1966.

We wandered into Charley's workshop and found our piece of furniture crowding a corner of the room (figure 2); it was not what we had requested but the "masterpiece" that Charley had mentioned in his letters. This "strange" chair, which Charley presented to us as ours, is made of solid oak with black walnut decorative trim at the top; the heads of its walnut pegs are carved in a pattern of ridges and grooves. It has eight legs and four rockers. Five panels forming the back and sides create a strong feeling of enclosure. Shelves on each side of the chair are supposed to hold books. Beneath the lowest shelves are storage units, and the seat lifts up to reveal storage space below it. The shelves and the storage space partly account for Charley's calling the chair a "bookcase rocker," and because it has twice as many legs and rockers as usual it is a "two-in-one" rocker.

"That's a chair, hain't it?" asked one of Charley's neighbors. "New one on me. Yes sir, that's pretty — all that little stuff up here," he said, pointing to the decorative detail along the top of the chair.

"It looks like a privy to me," said a close friend of ours later.

"I think it looks like a throne," remarked another friend.

Most people who have seen the chair said nothing at first sight, perhaps because of shock, and little afterward owing to mixed emotions. But two other craftsmen in southeastern Kentucky declared the chair a work of art because of the elaborate construction and the extensive ornamentation.

"I think it's pretty," said one of the chairmakers named Hascal. "If I had that chair I'd set it up in my living room and set things in it. Put ivy vines on it, you know, to make it look kinda like a cliff."

"I think the people that bought that chair bought it for the looks," replied Beechum, the other craftsman, after a moment's reflection. "Now if I had that chair I wouldn't let nobody set in it. I'd fasten that

Figure 2. Charley's seventh two-in-one rocker, second bookcase rocker, and first and only "bookcase masterpiece" (December, 1965). It is made of red oak with white oak rockers and black walnut trim and pegs. There is storage space below seat and lower shelves. A visitor to Charley's shop queried, "Now what's it s'posed to be?" Asked a neighbor, "That's a chair, hain't it?" Charley's judgment was: "It don't look like it b'longs here yet; I b'lieve it come here too early or too late, one."

to the wall and put whatnots in it." Beechum also noted that the four rockers seemed to "fit the design of it" and looked "all right on the chair," although he had complained earlier that the extra rockers and legs on some of Charley's other two-in-one chairs are "kinda dangerous" and that "a man could hurt hisself on them things."

What was Charley's attitude toward his "masterpiece"?

"When I first saw it, I liked it pretty good," he said, but after having lived with it for eight months and having endured the puzzled stares and inane questions of neighbors and customers he was less sanguine.

"I'm kinda like other people," he said; "hit don't look right someway."

Charley suggested adding a leg rest in front, as he had done on a couple of other chairs, and black leather upholstery on the seat, back, and sides. Even so, "It don't look like it b'longs here yet; I b'lieve it come here too early or too late, one."

"If you don't like it," I asked Charley, "why do you call it your 'masterpiece'?"

"Cause, uh, it is," he said. "I never made nothin' like it in my life. There ain't nothing in the world like hit. That's why I call it my 'masterpiece.'"

Actually, Charley's remark is a bit misleading, for there were in fact many design antecedents for the chair in his forty-year career as a chairmaker, although we did not know that at the time, but the earlier works themselves are not an adequate explanation of the masterpiece's unusual qualities.

Regardless of one's own opinion of the chair, reference to the object at this moment leads us into a number of questions about the making and doing of things in everyday life and provides a way of introducing Charley, the main subject of this book. In addition the chair exemplifies the way in which even designing and making useful objects may be a mode of expressive behavior. Furthermore, the making of the chair is significant in the production of useful objects in that it represents, in some of its aspects, a rather rare occurrence in a type of manufacture which usually involves direct customer stipulation and the designing of objects that serve practical purposes: an object developing in form and design without the completely conscious control of the producer. Charley is by nature planful in his work; he would never, if possible, "just throw a chair together" or let the design develop of its own accord. Yet he wrote that he did not know what was happening to him or to the chair during manufacture. Apparently he had begun to depend upon intuition and sensation to guide him through much of the construction so that he could not, to his great distress, predict what he would have to do to the chair each day after he had begun work on it.

What happened during this time? What were the compelling forces over which Charley felt no control? Why did he make so strange a chair? What were his experiences as a man and as a chairmaker which led to the construction of this so-called masterpiece?

Other questions might occur to the reader. Is Charley's two-in-one bookcase rocker, masterpiece of furniture, folk art, and is Charley a folk craftsman (or artist)? No and no, respectively. No to both questions, because there is no distinct category of human phenomena or of human beings for which or for whom such a label as "folk" has been applied in a defensible way; at the very best, the term "folk artist" has directed attention toward the way in which an individual such as Charley learned his craft and now practices it, and, at the worst, the term "folk art" has suggested the product of a different and inferior intelligence. What is folk art and in what way does it differ from primitive art? There is no significant difference between what has been called folk art and primitive art, despite the widely held belief that folk art is the low art of high cultures whereas primitive art is the high art of low cultures. Neither folk nor primitive art exists as popularly conceived. So-called primitive culture and society are complex, as is the art produced therein which is primitive neither in the sense of being first nor of being simple or crude;[1] and there is in reality no social entity that can be called a "folk," for "folk" is a cognitive category that once required a value judgment by members of an educated elite who conceived of certain individuals in their own or in another society as backward and unsophisticated (though the judgment had positive as well as negative connotations).[2] Most of the phenomena that have been lumped together under the label of folk and primitive art consist of units or structures of expressive behavior learned and manifested primarily in situations of firsthand interaction; together they have been contrasted, for heuristic purposes, with the arts of mass production and mass media and with the so-called fine arts, even though folk and primitive art, as well as the fine arts, are not independent phenomena clearly distinguishable one from another. Attempted distinctions among these modes of production are an academic convention tending to obscure, rather than to clarify, the study of behavior. As is shown throughout this book, criteria usually employed to distinguish folk and primitive art from each other or from other kinds of behavior are not consistent or mutually exclusive; several qualities, such as the extent of conscious manipulation of materials, the degree of originality or conservatism, the range of skills and imagination, claimed to differentiate the folk or primitive artist from the elite (or "sophisticated") artist are obviously disconfirmed by research of individuals making and doing things.

For those people who have been exposed to the published literature on what has been called folk art there is another nagging question. Charley's chairs are unmistakably of his own manufacture, and the works of Aaron and other chairmakers in southeastern Kentucky are peculiar to them, just as the potter Ben Owen in North Carolina, the Pueblo potter Maria of San Ildefonso, the Yoruba potter Abatan, and the Asmat wood-carver Ndojoker have made objects uniquely their own;[3] sometimes these people have been called "folk artists" and the things they made "folk art." Furthermore, Charley's chairs are solidly built and their authorship is known. If Charley and these other people are called folk artists, then what does one do with the frequent allegations that folk art is impersonal in nature, anonymous

in origin, unimaginative in conception, and inferior in construction?[4]
One takes them with a grain of salt, suspecting the sampling
procedures, looking for underlying preconceptions that prejudiced
the writer, and assuming that comments were based on an examination
of poorly preserved, unrepresentative, and inadequately documented
museum specimens. One also begins to question the usefulness of
terms like folk, folklore, and art, and to doubt that there is a
distinct category of human phenomena which can or should be
labeled "folk art."

Perhaps the most vexing problem of all is: How does one find
a way to answer the other questions above? That is to say, what
techniques of data recording and analysis, what intellectual constructs,
what investigative schemes or frameworks, will guide the student
through the maze of problems presented in the study of objects and
will bridge the enormous gap in our knowledge about the making
of things for everyday use?[5]

Franz Boas had part of the answer. "We have to turn our
attention first of all to the artist himself," wrote Boas in his
analysis of North American Indian art; but in the almost fifty
years since the original publication (1927) of Primitive Art his
edict has seldom been heeded. Boas in fact was unable to comply
with his own demand because "unfortunately," as he admitted,
"observations on this subject are very rare and unsatisfactory, for
it requires an intimate knowledge of the people to understand the
innermost thoughts and feelings of the artist." And as Boas
realized, "even with thorough knowledge the problem is exceedingly
difficult, for the mental processes of artistic production do not
take place in full light of consciousness."[6]

Boas was neither the first researcher to call attention to
the individual nor the only person to lament the absence of
information about the producers of objects. In 1895, for example,
A.C. Haddon chastised museum curators who, in their zeal to bag
trophies, failed to grasp the significance of the objects or to

interpret their form and design. In his view, "There are still some 'collectors' (that is, purchasers of 'curios') who think that when they know where an object comes from, and, may be, what is its native name, they know pretty well all that is worth knowing about it." Haddon went one step further, admonishing that "we must not stop short when we have determined what a form means, or what is the original of a device. We have to discover why it was so. The reason for a motive, the meaning of its present form, have also to be sought."[7]

In accord with Haddon's view is the direction of the present volume: interpreting form, and discovering why it is so; to accomplish these ends we must examine not only the objects but also the makers of the objects and their interactions with other people. But why, one wonders, have there been so few studies during the past eight decades of individuals who make things? Haddon, as well as Balfour and Pitt-Rivers, implied very strongly one important reason, but it was Ernst Grosse in The Beginnings of Art (1897) who made that reason explicit. He wrote, with regard to what he called folk or primitive art, that "everywhere we search in vain for the individual artists; we see only the mass of the peoples, out of which no single figure is recognisable. In all these cases—and they form the immense majority—the problem of the science of art is solvable only in its second or social form," rather than in its individual form, despite Grosse's contention that "Individual manifestations are, for the most of us, far more interesting than social ones." The individual artist was to be found only in "civilized society" where his art serves "primarily for the elevation of the spirit" and not for "unification only," as among "modern savages."[8] Because of the assumption that the art of "primitive folk" was simple, static, and most like the art of "the first progenitors of our species," and because of the persistent belief that, in contrast with "our" art, primitive or folk art is "very uniform" and the artist is an undifferentiated member of a "very homogeneous people" or of "a small, relatively homogeneous society" who "presents, usually without question, the normative values of his culture,"[9] research has been devoted largely to relating the "aggregated character of the art groups of a period or a district to a whole people, or a whole age." Thus, Grosse writes (and many investigators seem to have concurred): "We shall consider the art of primitive peoples as a social phenomenon and a social function."[10]

There are other reasons, too, for the neglect of individual producers, although a satisfactory explanation must await the preparation of a history of folk and primitive art study. I believe it will be found that in some instances the theoretical framework of investigation has caused the researcher to lose sight of the individual, as in some studies by evolutionists, or has required the disregard of the individual, as in most examinations by diffusionists, or has relegated both art and artist to a position of secondary importance in favor of understanding the workings of culture and the values of a society, as in much of the analysis by functionalists. Seemingly all three approaches have been informed by the same organic model that developed in the nineteenth century, the first subscribers to which turned their attention to what they conceived to be folk and primitive art, that is, "the art of the most backward peoples, in the hope of gaining sufficient light to cast a glimmer down the gloomy perspective of the past."[11] This art has seldom been studied for its own sake or for the better understanding of human behavior; it has been studied for other reasons. Thus, little is known about the individual who makes things, and for most research the method of work is of the second type noted by Haddon, "an investigation of induction and interpretation where oral or written tradition fails."[12]

As a consequence of this situation, Boas and others have tended to rely heavily on an examination of objects to infer the nature of creative processes and to posit the existence of, but not to examine in detail, an aesthetic attitude.[13] The shortcoming of this inferential method, however, is that even if the alleged principles obtain we do not know who responds in what way how much of the time, nor do we know the depth of the response of individuals; in addition, we can scarcely guess at the origins of various designs in a work, or comprehend the way in which some special need in the individual precipitated the creation of a particular object, or ascertain the extent to which the product owes many of its qualities to direct or indirect customer influence. Such topics can be dealt with only when we can interview and observe the maker of objects, and the mental processes in manufacture can best be inferred from the producer's own comments and the way in which he handles his tools or inspects the work in progress, checking surface quality, balance, and the harmony of component elements. In other words, we must turn our attention to individuals and their behavior rather than to the objects, though the objects may attract us initially.

We tend to feel more comfortable in analysis when the subject under discussion is tangible, or visible, as in the form of a chair or a vase or a song text that has been written down, for then we can, we suppose, better understand it; after all, it exists in physical reality, it affects our sensibilities in some way, and it is not so elusive as thought processes. No one can deny that the objects are there. But is our subject matter just things, and may we content ourselves with the collection and study of artifacts or linguistic entities? My response to both questions is no, even though this volume contains many illustrations of chairs and a discussion of such objects.

Assume for the moment that someone shows the student of folklore an object or a typed copy of a song or story and asks, "Is this folk art (or folklore)?" The question is difficult to answer, for there are simply no distinguishing physical attributes that ensure immediate recognition of the object or the text as folklore or as art, as there are obvious physical traits by which horses may be distinguished from trees. The folklorist probably will not answer right away but will himself ask questions about who made the object (or sang the song); where, when, and from whom the producer learned his skills; and in what circumstances the object was produced. Only then will the folklorist be able to say, somewhat guardedly, "Yes, it might be folk art," or "No, it probably isn't folklore."

The object is not a very important consideration when attempting to answer such a question, and the question itself, like the answer, suggests doubt in regard to the existence of a unique and isolable mode of behavior distinguishable from other human phenomena. Nevertheless, most of the published research on art by different investigators elevates the object to special significance; there is little or no regard for the maker, the processes of production, or the circumstances of manufacture and use. The objects often are called art if they seem comparable in form to the researcher's notion of the fine arts, and the objects frequently are labeled folk art if they are simply or naively executed; these objects usually serve as the basis for tracing patterns of historical and geographical distribution, or of reconstructing a historical period, rather than as a vehicle for gaining insight into the nature of making things or the expression of responses to objects and activities.[14]

Granted, an object once produced, like the performance of a story or a song that has been filmed and tape-recorded, endures for some time so that people can see and use it; museums and archives are filled with such things. But the object was and is in fact only one part — the least ephemeral and most perceptible part — of a dynamic process of human thought and action. This manifestation of human imagination and this output of social interaction cannot be fully appreciated or adequately understood without a knowledge of when and how and why there was such a manifestation or such an output.

In a recent essay on storytelling events, Robert A. Georges object-ed to "the persistence of the premise that stories are surviving or traditional linguistic entities" and "the a priori assumption that the means of discovering the meaning and significance of these entities is through the collection and study of story texts."[15] Nearly a decade earlier Edmund Carpenter had claimed that "Eskimo are interested in the artistic act, not in the product of that activity. A carving, like a song, is not a thing; it is an action." Carpenter admonished that it is "senseless to assume that when we collect these silent, static carvings, we have collected Eskimo art."[16] There often are outputs of produc-tion, of course, but the "art-object as such is nothing," writes C. Nooten-boom. "It has value through the qualities it receives at the hands of a

man. This man . . . is the real object of the inquiry."[17] The output is
in one sense a manifestation of the production or the performance signaling
the existence of the process of production or performance; the output
sometimes precipitates an appreciative, pleasurable reaction, but so does
the making or doing; and the output, even when tangible in the form of
a pot or a chair, is not really static, for concrete things change texture
and surface quality with handling, color with aging or with changes in the
light striking them, appearance and soundness with use and the inevitable
restoration or repair. The output, as one aspect of the processes of
production and consumption, has received too much attention, with the
result that other parts of these processes have seldom been noticed
and have been examined hardly at all.

    Georges proposed a new conception of narrative and narration
not as story or art or linguistic entity but as "the distinct events within
continua of human communication," and he stressed the significance of
these "storytelling events" as "communicative events, as social experiences, and as unique expressions of human behavior."[18] Implicit in
Carpenter's statement is a more dynamic conception of the making and
using of objects which has not been fully exploited. Of central concern
would be not the object but the activity, the process of production or
performance and all that goes into each; and the process of consumption, use, response, evaluation, and all that goes into the appreciation of
production or performance and the formation of standards of excellence
or preference. Not story, but storytelling event; not pot or chair, but
pottery or chair production and consumption: what needs to be
examined is not object or entity so much as process and event. Of primary
importance are the producers and the consumers and their interactions,
of which the objects are in a sense only partial records of events that
in themselves manifest certain processes, and of which the objects are
outputs that may be subjected to use, thus precipitating the process of
consumption, including evaluation.

    The essay by Georges on storytelling events, as well as an unpub-
lished paper by Kenneth L. Ketner on the concept of story, is essential

in understanding the behavior that has been dubbed art,[19] in this case, "art" in daily life, despite the fact that the authors do not discuss at length the artistic element in storytelling events. It is, however, the characteristics of harmony, balance, and order in storytelling, singing, and so on which often facilitate the communication and social interaction with which the authors are concerned.

"Old Joe Peabody used to be an awful man at telling tall stories," a fisherman in Newfoundland told me. "I couldn't tell it the way he used to tell it. Anyone that is used to this can tell 'em in a different way from what I can, you know, make a lot of fun out of it. I'm, I'm no good to tell a story. You don't get no kick out of me tellin' a story. I don't know how."

Stories can be told rather "artlessly," as we know, but communication is impaired and social interaction impeded. Who likes to listen to a poor storyteller? Or who fancies noise?

"There's some people gifted with music," I was told. "There was a fella here . . . you had to dance to music he used to give, you had to dance — you couldn't help it! He could do anything with a 'cordian."

Or, for that matter, who wants to carry water in a heavy, lopsided jug, or sit on a chair that "has the rickets and cries" because it was fashioned of unseasoned pieces? "A good chairmaker," said Charley, "would have to make 'em slow and make 'em right. You can't just throw a chair together any way and get a good chair out of it." Another chairmaker named Hascal said of his friend Aaron, "He can make a chair so pretty you can see your face shinin' in it."

But this is not to suggest that storytelling or chairmaking is always or even necessarily conceived of as "art" by those who engage in it. "What do you think art is?" I asked a man with whom I had been staying in a Newfoundland village.

"I dunno," he said.

"Well, is it painting? music?"

Rather uncertainly he replied, "I'd say painting, drawing, stuff like that, wouldn't it be?"

"What about music and dance?"

"Music? and dances?" he asked; there's no art to that . . . is there?"

"I don't know," I said in all honesty; "that's what I'm trying to find out. What about storytelling like Mary Burrage — what about that?"

"I don't regard that . . ."

"What Mary tells is true, you know," interrupted his wife; "it's, it's experience."

"But," said the man slowly, "she's got <u>a way of tellin'</u> it, yeah."

While some behavior may not be called art, it nevertheless is taken to be something special, often because of the skill required which itself may generate a sense of satisfaction. "That crippled woman Mary, by God-damn, mister, you get her a-goin'," said the fisherman, shaking his head back and forth in appreciation, "she can tell ya. Some of 'em is true, too: funny stories." One of the men who had been to a wedding told this fisherman that "after the lunch everybody was tellin' stories, you know, and he said Mary started to tell about the crippled wedding. Well, Mr. Barrow said everybody in the place was groanin'.' Some of the women had to go to the bathroom! Oh, my son, t' hear her tell that you'd crow; she got a way of tellin' it . . . I can't do it."

For present purposes I am using the word "art" mainly in the sense of skill in the making or doing of that which functions as (among other things) a stimulus to appreciation of an individual's mastery of tools and materials apparent in what he has made; the output of that skill; and the activity manifesting the use of that skill.[20] Admittedly, for some arts so conceived, the aesthetic aspect is limited (for example, the "art" of defensive driving); and for some things that generate a contemplative and appreciative attitude, accident may be more important than skill (for instance, randomly sorted piles of yarn to be used for knitting or rug-making which in and of themselves may generate visual pleasure in the percipient because of the balance, harmony, symmetry, and centrality of their arrangement). As a general characterization, though, it would seem that what is most often taken to be art (whether actually called that or not) is something thought to be special (usually because of the skill required), generating an appreciative, contemplative response in the percipient.[21] Given this characterization, it is not difficult to understand why the practice of medicine has been called both art and science —indeed, the best practitioners engage in both at once — or to appreciate why gossiping is sometimes an art,[22] or to comprehend why some analytical models in the sciences generate appreciative comments like "beautiful" and "elegant."

Storytelling, then, is sometimes called art, or it is said to have an artistic-aesthetic dimension, but the art is not exclusively a story, a linguistic entity that is conceived to be the counterpart of written literature, which is one of the so-called fine arts; this difference is even more apparent in daily eating behavior between the meal that is served, which is the output of production and the result of performance admitting skill, and the recipes as "texts" on which preparation of the dishes was based. The Newfoundland fisherman was willing to concede that the activities of storytelling, music, and perhaps dancing with which he was familiar had an "artistic-aesthetic dimension" (my words, not his); that is, the activities depended on special skills he did not possess and generated an appreciative response in him when the storytelling or music was skillfully executed. (I do not mean to be facetious, but surely some of the women who wet their pants found Mary's storytelling to be "beautiful" or "pleasurable," or otherwise they would not have laughed so long and hard.) But storytelling was not art, compared with the fine arts ("painting, drawing, and stuff like that") which are allegedly genteel in nature, befitting the upper classes, serving primarily an aesthetic function, and tending to refine or elevate the mind. By excluding the element of art from his essay, and by emphasizing storytelling events rather than focusing on narratives as oral literature, Georges deals with storytelling for what it is primarily: a communicative process and social experience generated by the interactions of two or more people regardless of socioeconomic or educational status; it is simply not art in the usual Western elite sense of the so-called fine arts, a concept that itself is suspect. Yet it requires skill, generates an appreciative attitude, exhibits distinctive qualities in performance, reveals the presence of imaginative thought, and is subject to evaluation in terms of other people's standards of excellence. Storytelling, singing, and the production of most tangible outputs that we are concerned with are most frequently treated as art when skill is evident and the performance or output is considered to be special, but they are not comparable in nature or intent to what is conceived to be the fine arts because they tend to be learned and manifested in a somewhat different circumstance, that of face-to-face interaction primarily. That is why some commentators have remarked upon the routine quality of what they designate folk art production.

Several students of what they refer to as folk or primitive art have noted that, in the words of Edmund Carpenter, "art belongs to ordinary day-to-day experiences: the way a father addresses his son, decorates his house door, butchers a pig, dances, puts on his loincloth in the morning, or addresses his guardian spirit."[23] Or, according to Beatrice Blackwood, what the investigator is concerned with is the "ordinary members of the community, sharing in its general activities and making in the course of their every-day work articles for their own amusement and that of their immediate family;"[24] the behavior is learned as well as manifested in such situations, and some of these ordinary people, engaging in a very special kind of behavior, show extra-ordinary skill and imagination. "The making of pots can be viewed simply as the manufacture of ordinary objects for everyday use," wrote Patricia Altman, "or it can be regarded as something very special. This latter attitude is best expressed in the words of a Laguna woman," she continued, who said that "'some people do not think that pottery is anything, but it means a great deal to me. It is something sacred. I try to paint all my thoughts on my pottery.'"[25]

Communicative events and social experiences, and personal expression and practical problem-solving devices in everyday work situations, are what the folklorist or anthropologist is most often investigating. The production of tangible outputs in these everyday situations has sometimes been examined in terms of its artistic-aesthetic qualities, but what is produced is not merely an object nor is it the counterpart of painting or sculpture or architecture as one of the so-called fine arts. The Kentucky furniture makers were willing to concede that what they produced demanded special skills, for "you can't just throw a chair together any way and get a good chair out of it," and generated a special kind of appreciative, contemplative response, as "he can make a chair so pretty you can see your face shinin' in it." But furniture does not belong in a class of objects that are comparable to products of the so-called fine arts, supposedly genteel in nature and tending to refine and elevate the mind (although chairs or the making of furniture may indeed appeal to one's sensibilities). As Georges writes about storytelling, "Though it is possible to draw analogies between written narratives and the messages of storytelling events, the same criteria cannot be utilized to judge both, nor can both be subjected to the same kinds of study and analysis."[26] The skills in each are learned and practiced in somewhat different situations.

There is irony here. The student of folk or primitive art investigates what he calls "art," by which he usually means fine art; for example, one researcher, in a methodological essay on primitive art study, notes that the "term 'art' is used here only for the so-called fine arts."[27] The actual producers or performers and their immediate customers or audiences do not, however, usually conceive of their skills and activities in this way. As Ralph Altman admits, "the concept of art in our civilization today [a particular academic tradition of art study and the concepts to which the researcher has been exposed] has no true equivalent in any of the cultures with which we are here concerned. Our attitude toward tribal objects that we call art differs from that of their makers and users."[28] This difference in conception has resulted in some distortion of the nature of the making and doing and using of things in daily life, as in conceiving of and dealing with mask making as sculpture or the messages of storytelling events as oral literature (it may even be somewhat presumptuous and perhaps misleading to speak of pottery making as ceramics or the building of shelters as architecture), or in attempting to determine whether or not there is a "folk aesthetic." (Standards of excellence and preference vary but the appreciative, contemplative attitude seems to be universal, although seldom if ever does one find a codified system of criteria for evaluating the things that are made and done in everyday life; the search for such a system indicates the "fine art" orientation of the researcher.) Altman goes on to say, however, that "our discussion can make sense only if we consciously assume the right to designate objects as art subjectively regardless of the attitude their makers had toward them in this respect."

Do we have that right? Perhaps, if we avoid conceiving of the activities and skills and outputs in everyday life as comparable to, yet distinguishable from, the so-called fine arts. The behavior we study is not identical with what has been conceived of as the fine arts and cannot be judged or examined on the same basis, for the actions and objects usually designated as folk art are modes of behavior tending to be learned and manifested in a somewhat different fashion, and neither folk nor fine art is a distinctive type of activity or object with unique qualities, that is, a perceptual phenomenon whose characteristics can be listed or whose nature can be defined to everyone's satisfaction. Thus, while the right may exist to designate as art the making and doing of things in daily life, exercising that right usually results in misinterpreting the subject matter for study.

Attempted definitions of folk art have generally failed, largely because, it has been suggested, "Too many different kinds of art produced in too many different circumstances are involved."[29] The same researcher herself seems to conceive of folk art as unsophisticated art, mainly material objects, primarily in America and western Europe. And that is important, for definitions of folk art have failed, too, because of object or entity orientation among commentators who focus attention on the formal characteristics of a thing and who assume a priori that folk art, as a unique phenomenon with distinctive characteristics, is the inferior counterpart or debased imitation of the fine arts. Folk art differs from the fine arts, in their view, because of its less sophisticated formal qualities, which

stem from the low socioeconomic or educational status of those who
produced it or for whom it was intended.

The student of what is sometimes labeled folk or primitive art
chooses to study not that which is conceived of as fine art in Eurasia and
America or machine-made goods on an assembly line; rather, he investigates
those communicative processes, social experiences, and the making of problem-
solving devices occurring primarily in ordinary day-to-day experience which
are learned firsthand from others. For some researchers, however, the
term "folklore" or "folk art" has suggested that "folk" is a synonym for
backward, poor, or illiterate people, but this assumption ignores the
similarities in human behavior (all people tell stories and make things),
and it renders folklore a historico-cultural survival and the people who tell
stories and make things uncritical, unthinking, unimaginative dupes. It
has been said also, in an attempt to avoid negative connotations, that the
word "folk" refers to "a folk, not the folk," which is "a vitally integrated,
like-minded group," [30] or "any group whatsoever having at least one factor in
common;" [31] but not everyone who interacts with other people conceives of
himself as belonging to a group even though a researcher has labeled him
a group member, usually on a rather tenuous basis (most often, simply
being together in a particular place at a certain time); the designation by
a researcher of other people as constituents of a group overemphasizes
alleged similarities in their behavior to the disregard of individual differences. Moreover, vaguely implying that "folk" means "people generally" renders
the term inconsequential and thus of no use whatsoever which, on reflection,
is probably the best thing one can do. [32] Generally speaking, use of the
designation "folk" or "primitive" art has directed attention, though not
always effectively, to a process of learning and utilizing modes of behavior
and codes of communication in a situation of face-to-face interchange
comprising members of a small interactional network without "consistent
corrective reference to a fixed text or an officially standardized way of
doing things." [33] Furthermore, use of the designation "lore" has called attention
not merely to song texts or quaint old objects but to the units of expressive
behavior or the styles, designs, and techniques of a particular tradition, the

general category of behavior to which we tend to give an identifying label such as storytelling, chairmaking, dancing, cooking, or singing, and in which the process has been sustained sufficiently long for several individuals to have learned and utilized the behavior. In our activities in daily life in which we interact and communicate with others and attempt to solve various problems, objects and stories surely are not "passed on" or "handed down," an "item" is not "in oral circulation," and people are not "active" or "passive" "bearers of tradition;" instead, as Ketner has noted, "an ability is learned or is demonstrated according to a teacher's guidance or an audience's appreciation, subject to social approval."[34]

What about originality? The presentation of a new form or conception, or the act of investing something with a new character, which is obviously present in much of the production or performance in which one is engaged, is simply the clarification of potentialities inherent in the raw materials (whether clay, sounds, collard greens, or body movements) into activities or objects that some people take to be more completely satisfying than the materials themselves;[35] it is for this reason that skill is so important. Singing and dancing or baking and serving a cherry pie may be a communicative event and a social experience, but if the behavior is not engaged in with skill then communication and interaction may be impaired or prevented, thus suggesting the desirability for the researcher to examine the attention to structure, order, harmony, and similar qualities in performance if he is to understand the activity. The manufacture of pots or chairs is industry resulting in outputs serving practical purposes, but one must also consider the decorative quality of objects, the pleasure inherent in making things, and the appreciative response to the outputs of production in order to account for the remark by Aunt Sal Creech: "Weaving, hit's the purtiest work I ever done. It's a settin' and trampin' the treadles and watchin' the pretty blossoms come out and smile at ye in the kiverlet."[36] This is not to contend that what has been called folklore is "artistic communication in small groups," because such a characterization exaggerates the importance of the artistic and aesthetic dimensions of the behavior and thus diminishes the significance of other qualities and functions.[37] Finally, no matter how appealing they may be, the outputs of production are only the precipitants of research, for they fall between production and consumption in a continuum of behavior; the end of research is the same as the point at which we begin, namely the individual whose behavior we seek to comprehend (which will then help us explain the nature of the product if that is important to us). The study of the manufacture and use of objects as unique events manifesting processes of thought and interaction, and the examination of human behavior in production or performance in terms of skill in the making or doing of that which functions as (among other things) a stimulus to an appreciative response to objects and activities, should make possible a fuller understanding of the things that people make and do.

One final question needs to be raised and answered. If the modes of expressive behavior generally called folklore and folk art (meaning a diversity of expressive structures learned and manifested in face-to-face interchange) are common in social interaction and not limited to the past or to poorly educated people on a lower socioeconomic level of society, then why do many folklorists, anthropologists, and art historians have a penchant for investigating the traditions with the longest history of continuous development among the (allegedly) most isolated people? Instead of studying Charley and other southern mountain chairmakers, why not examine the behavior of street artists in San Francisco or the candlemaking, leatherworking, tie-dyeing, and stained-glass window making that are being practiced by people in Los Angeles and other cities? Some of us do. Eighty years ago the English folklorist Joseph Jacobs contended that "folk-lore need not be all survivals. We ought to learn valuable hints as to the spread of folk-lore by studying the Folk of to-day;" and "after all, we are the Folk as well as the rustic, though their lore may be other than ours, as ours will be different from that of those that follow us."[38]

Consider an instance of contemporary urban tie-dyeing. A young college-educated housewife in Los Angeles learned to tie-dye T-shirts; she relied in large measure on the instructions that accompanied a bottle of commercial dye, though other sources of information about textile work were available.

With experience in this part-time activity the housewife made her own discoveries and began to evince a unique style; her primary outlet was a
department store with whose customers she did not interact or share much in
common, yet her first clientele consisted of friends and family. Another woman
(my wife) learned to tie-dye from her and from the same set of instructions,
containing sample designs and knotting techniques; she, too, accepted only
some of the suggestions and made her own discoveries and inventions. My
wife then taught some of what she knew about tie-dyeing to her two nieces
(and recently to several other women), but all three of them still had occasion
to refer to the instruction sheet for ideas and to ensure mastery of technique. The nieces and other family members were the "consumers;" my
wife's direct interaction with them resulted in the production of objects
evincing certain qualities expressive of herself and of the attitudes
and values of those with whom she interacted directly. The two girls,
who live in another state, have now taught a dozen of their teenage
friends how to tie-dye—with only infrequent reference to the printed
instructions—resulting in the production of objects with characteristics
expressive of their shared experiences. One of these days in the United
States we may have a well-developed tradition of tie-dyeing learned firsthand and practiced in many small interactional networks, each with its own
special identity and particular set of values; indeed, we have several already,
in spite of the fact that for many people right now print seems to be a major
source of such information and is often considered the great leveler in American
society. In the instance cited above, then, tie-dyeing is an example of behavior
analogous to other kinds of behavior usually referred to as folk art which, in its
present incipient stage, involves to a great extent the primary process of
face-to-face communication and interaction and the attendant units of
expressive behavior which interest the folklorist, even supposing the process
has not been sustained for a long time among these people.

   In answer to the question about neglect it might be argued that
analysis of more recent activities in urban areas is complicated by the
influence on behavior of sources other than firsthand ones, not only in the
learning process but in consumption as well, so that we do not always have the

opportunity to study in depth the dynamics of the primary interactional processes. Charley, Verge, O.P., and other Kentucky chairmakers, however, have also borrowed ideas from mail-order catalogues and have appealed to the tastes of consumers they do not personally know. Another explanation is that those researchers who conceive of folklore as surviving "among backward peoples, or retained by the uncultured classes of more advanced peoples,"[39] have no use for studies of behavior closer to home, such as tie-dyeing among college-educated women in Los Angeles. And, it is often more interesting, more convenient, or more desirable to examine other people's behavior than to look at our own; while my wife and her tie-dyeing activities among nieces and neighbors have served as a source of many insights, I find it easier in print to review the behavior of individuals now remote from me, and I suppose other researchers do, too. Finally, and this is the only defensible position of the four, in order to evaluate past research and the models and concepts built upon it, it is desirable to examine behavior and circumstances which will be recognized immediately by other scholars as similar to those treated by themselves or by earlier investigators, so that critical remarks which I make about assumptions and interpretations cannot be dismissed simply on the grounds of a different data base.

Some of the many modes of behavior in the United States today which many scholars would probably accept as an appropriate data base are chairmaking in southeastern Kentucky, pottery production in northern Georgia, the weaving of rugs in New Mexico, the manufacture by hand of surfboards in southern California and Hawaii, the cooking and serving of food in the home, and the building of sand castles on beaches. It should be noted, however, that in many of these traditions designs do not always come directly from other people and that there may be at least two major consumer publics: the local people with whom the producers interact and share some values in common, and an outside clientele whom the producers do not know and seldom meet and for whom they may make a rather different product. Navaho weavers, Pueblo potters, and Eskimo carvers have long been influenced by whites; not all the owners of sorghum mills actually like the molasses they make by boiling juice from the stalks; some manufacturers of plastic pails include instruction sheets explaining how to build sand castles. That which has been conceived of as folklore and folk art or technology — the process of learning and using modes of behavior in firsthand interaction among people which is usually called "folk," and the designs, techniques, and expressive structures generally known as "lore" — are present in most of our activities much of the time, but they are not in a readily isolable form. The foregoing suggests that what has been called folklore is not truly unique and does not exist as a separate entity; we are concerned with behavior and learning processes in certain circumstances. It suggests that the use of the term "art" creates as many problems as it solves. And it suggests the desirability of speaking in a straightforward manner of making and doing and using things in everyday circumstances.

Several of the men mentioned in this book, such as Courtney, Morris, and Coy, may not be of much interest to the folklorist as chairmakers because they have made only a few chairs to pass the time or to furnish their homes with make-dos; they have learned little about the craft from others, though that is their major source of information, and they practice it rarely. Charley commands attention not only because he is talented but also because he has engaged in an occupation of making things by hand, taking into account many individuals who learned techniques and designs from other men, several of whom devoted much time and energy to making new discoveries and inventions that contributed significantly to the historical development of the production of chairs in a specific geographical area. For this reason, among others, the present volume focuses on Charley and his behavior. Let us return, then, to Charley's seemingly strange chair and what led to its creation.

Figure 3. Charley splits a "bolt" with a hickory maul and the edge of an ax (once the split is started he uses a dogwood glut): ". . . takin' it from the stump it takes one week to make a settin' chair and a month to make a rocker."

Figure 4. "Hewin' out the slats" for a settin' chair: ". . . it's a job to split it out—hew it out—and then dress it with a drawin' knife."

Figure 5. "Shavin' posts," showing Charley's technique of "controlled shaving."

Figure 6. Slats and posts are cooked to make them pliable for bending.

Figure 7. "Breakin' a post" before putting it into a post press.

Figure 8. "Posts" or chair legs after being driven into post press to dry.

Figure 9. In the process of "mortisin' the back posts," each mortise requires about twenty-five strokes with hammer and chisel.

Figure 10. Charley
checks angle to drill
stretcher holes.

Figure 11. Determining
the proper length of slats.

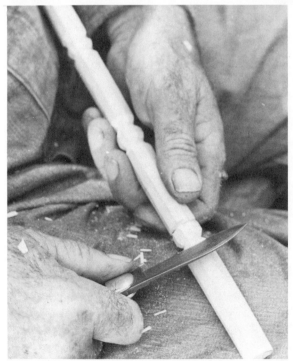

Figure 12. "Layin' off the rounds"
or "postees," that is, marking
the stretchers or the legs for
"notchin'," which corresponds to
turnings. Charley leaves the marks:
"It really looks nice on a chair—
pencil mark or a mark caused by
a chisel or a knife."

Figure 13. "Notchin' a round."

Figure 14. Assembly of the back of a settin' chair. The craftsman uses a maul so as not to scar the wood; he judges the fit by the sound.

Figure 15. "Barkin'" or "bottomin'" a chair: "My uncle Oaklie taught me to do the barkin' but I had a long time a-learnin' it." Charley uses "notch lockin'" to hold the strips of hickory bark together, but most chairmakers tie the ends of bark together instead.

Figure 16. Charley checks to be sure the chair is level by placing it on a table or against a windowpane.

Figure 17. A rocking chair is made the same way as a settin' chair up to the point of affixing rockers and arms; Charley makes a tenon on end of front post to fit into armrest.

Figure 18. Driving armrest into back post with a hickory maul.

Figure 19. It takes ten to fifteen minutes to carve each peg for a chair; on a settin' chair Charley has "to use twelve pegs an' hit takes a right smart time," but it takes longer for a rocking chair, which has about forty pegs.

CHAPTER TWO

The Bookcase Masterpiece and the New Design

"Now what's it s'posed to be?" asked the visitor to Charley's workshop.

Charley informed him that it is a rocking chair that holds books—hence, a bookcase rocker. "That's nice, real nice," said the man, without much conviction.

All of us were uneasy, Charley because this was not the chair we had ordered, my wife and I because it was not what we wanted or could really afford or perhaps even fully appreciate, and the visitor, who was as surprised as we were at the nature of the chair. After an embarrassing pause in which none of us could think of anything to say the man asked, "How much time you got involved in that?"

Charley explained that this chair was one of the few he had made for which he did not have to cut timber in the hills and dress it entirely by hand (figures 3-19); therefore, despite its complexity, the chair required less time than one might expect. During most of his productive career, said Charley, "takin' it from the stump it takes one week to make a settin' chair and a month to make a rocker." Most other chair-makers can produce the same kinds of chairs in a fraction of that time owing to the use of different techniques of construction and more modern tools. This chair, made of wood purchased from a lumber company, required a month or so to build.

There was another pause. The man finally said, "Boy, that's excitin'," and hurried out of the room.

Another man who knows Charley well examined a stack of photographs in search of Charley's chairs, which he claimed he could recognize easily. He made many mistakes, confusing works of Aaron's with those of Charley's and failing to identify many of Charley's earlier chairs because he had focused attention on ornamentation rather than on form and technique; but when he spotted the bookcase masterpiece he proclaimed it Charley's chair because of the pegs and the strange design.

"It's kinda pretty," he concluded.

"Maybe," I granted, "but it's not very comfortable to sit in."

"Well, I think it's pretty and probably more for lookin' at than to set in."

Such a remark would have disturbed Charley. On one occasion I showed him pictures of a stool and a chair made by Hugh, who works in a coal mine and dabbles at chairmaking (figure 20). "He ain't no chairmaker," said Hugh's neighbor; "he jest pranks around with it."

"That's completely handmade but that back's bound to a been worked out on a bandsaw or a jigsaw," noted Charley. Hugh copied the stool, which is of northern European design, from a picture in a magazine and used a jigsaw to form the back. But the stool is poorly made, uncomfortable, and unstable.

"Looks to me like hit's jest somethin' to look at, not to use," complained Charley. "Looks to me like it's useless. That's good-lookin' an' it'd be nice in a home jest to look at," he admitted, "but I al'ays said, somethin' or other that's made oughta be useful."

Other craftsmen felt the same way, and that is why the bookcase masterpiece posed a problem for them. In this area most chairs made in the past or in the present are rather plain and simple in appearance; their simplicity facilitates their primary purpose of use and corresponds with the values of many people in regard to home furnishings—the absence of ostentatiousness and the striving to obtain status symbols and objects for prestige enhancement. (Some ornamented dining and rocking chairs recently made by Aaron and Charley, however, are an index of the socioeconomic status of several customers.) Even Charley said of one of his other complicated works, "It's too expensive for a poor man like me." But this so-called chair is a bookcase that surrounds one and moves with one's own motion, a throne that rocks, a privy that won't sit still, just something to look at, or an anomaly whose purpose cannot be divined. Characterization of the chair depends on who is examining it and on what he associates it with, given his past experiences. Ornament and exaggerated attention to appearance override utility, thus confusing the issue.

Both Hascal and Beechum declared the chair a work of art to be chained to the wall and not sat in; at least that was their first impulse. "I think the people that bought that chair bought it for the looks," said Beechum. But neither man, like Charley, could quite accept the proposition that a utilitarian object should serve no practical purpose. They came upon the chair unexpectedly when flipping through about thirty photographs of different chairs and for a moment said nothing at all. It seemed that as chairmakers they had suddenly lost their frame of reference as they stared at this creation. After stating initially that the chair is a

Figure 20. Stool made by Hugh in 1966; he copied it from a magazine illustration. Charley was critical: "Looks to me like hit's jest somethin' to look at, not to use . . . I al'ays said, somethin' or other that's made oughta be useful." A neighbor remarked that Hugh "ain't no chairmaker; he jest pranks around with it."

work of art just to be looked at, these men had second thoughts. No, if Hascal and Beechum owned the chair themselves they would not just look at it but use it in some way, perhaps to hold pretties or whatnots; the former are useless things such as flower and pine cone arrangements or found objects or the miniature corn sleds Beechum made, and the latter are objects whose purpose is not clearly apparent, or small, useful things too attractive or expensive to be used often. Either way, whether a work of art to be gazed upon only or an ivy-covered cliff or whatnot holder, the chair was still not conceived of exclusively as a chair.

Charley had intended it to be a chair, or so he said (it is also a symbol of other things which he is aware of though reluctant to discuss), but he admitted that it did not look quite right. "It come here too early or too late, one," he said.

Why did it "come here" at all? The many factors accounting for the creation of this chair may never be completely known, because no one was with Charley during the month or so in which the chair was built. In addition, Charley never would tell us much about the circumstances of manufacture because of our mutual embarrassment. Yet it is possible to ascertain to a great extent the effects of precedence on the making of the chair and to speculate with some degree of authority about the reasons that the chair is of this form and design, for we have considerable information about Charley's experiences and his procedures in chairmaking.

In all probability the form of the chair was clear in Charley's mind at the beginning of construction: like a few of his earlier chairs, it would have eight legs and four rockers. Specific elements of design, such as the shelves and the enclosed seat and perhaps the panels, developed in part because of unanticipated technical requirements in construction but also because of a particular need in Charley at a time when his private world was invaded by a mass of curious outsiders. And the decorative trim, or at least the inscription on the walnut inserts, was added last, probably for economic reasons.

The manufacture of the chair was precipitated by Charley's desire to create something clearly indicative of his great skill, as well as something special for my wife and me; we were among the first individuals to aid Charley financially and to satisfy his need for someone to convince him that he is a talented artist. A later impetus for the creation of this strange design was the possibility, owing to sudden national publicity shortly after he had begun work on the chair, of attracting additional attention to himself and of increasing the sales of his works by producing a unique object that would be displayed in a department store; but the businessman who expressed interest in Charley's works bolted when he saw a photograph of this chair, thus leaving Charley with no alternative but the first one, that of selling the chair to us although it was not what we had ordered.

In addition, however, there was a trend in many of Charley's works in the mid-1950s and the early 1960s toward the production of bigger and bigger chairs with an increasing sense of enclosure and with a larger number of elements that Charley designated as "antique." During this time Charley's marital problems intensified, his sales decreased, and he was forced to move from one house to another farther from the protective mountain hollows and closer to the open highway where "that traffic jest aggravates me to death." The characteristics of Charley's later works, epitomized by the bookcase masterpiece, can probably be attributed to the man's desire at times to isolate himself from other people and from the world around him, to establish a feeling of security, and to escape into the past at a time when he was free of economic and marital problems. Even his body image — the long hair and beard, the overalls, the bare feet — harks back to an earlier age, as do some of his chairs to which he gave such names as the "old-timer," the "Li'l Abner chair," or the "George Washington chair;" and his comments about other men's works often dwelt on whether or not the objects had an old-fashioned appearance. As we will see, Charley, in attempting to adjust to a series of major losses, has on occasion been nostalgic about the past, and his identification with an earlier time has been expressed in several modes of behavior, including chairmaking, although other qualities characterize some of Charley's furniture. Some of his expressive behavior is related to the process of grieving, and the grief finds its resolution in the act of making things, a situation that is basic to understanding the origin of this seemingly strange chair and why it is indeed a masterpiece for Charley. Some of Charley's chairs, then, express the same feelings of fear, despair, and distrust which were common themes in his conversations, in many letters, and in a song he composed during the summer of 1965, only a few months before he built the bookcase masterpiece; but the song, a couple of letters, and the chairs also reveal a search for structure and order in his life and a reaffirmation of self.

These are rather strong contentions if one assumes that useful design and so-called folk art are not forms of expressive behavior but simply conventional tools impersonal in nature. It can be argued, however, that even the most simple work of individual manufacture is an expression of self, although in only some instances is this expression as apparent, or as significant, as in Charley's case. In the remainder of this book we will examine Charley's ideas and behavior in more detail, trace the development of these two qualities of enclosure and antiquity, and discuss the way in which several craftsmen's work procedures, notions about themselves, and products are entwined. But first, what happened in 1965?

In the summer of that year a short article on Charley appeared in a regional magazine. At the urging of Warren Roberts (who was then guiding my studies), my wife and I drove to southeastern Kentucky in mid-August to visit this craftsman. We did not stop the first two times our car crept past his house. In the yard stood a barefooted man in dingy blue overalls whose long hair and beard fluttered in the wind. Flanking him were two boys brandishing boards, their jerky movements indicating that something might be wrong. Coal dust smothered the grass and clung to the siding, for Charley's home was once a coal company office and weigh station. The only bright spot was a sign on the house, lettered in orange, proclaiming it the home of "hand Mad Furnitur/

maker of the C . . . chaires / wey Make Iney thng / ar hit Cant B Mad." As Charley explained about his sign to another visitor in 1967, "That's the first un I ever made; done a bad job on hit. Messed hit up so you can't hardly read it." A similar sign adorned the house's north side.

The building consisted of one room on the upper level in which seven family members slept (eight the next year) and three rooms — kitchen, living room, and workshop — on the lower floor. In 1967, when Charley built a workshop outside at his wife's insistence, the small room inside used as a workshop was turned into the kitchen and the kitchen became a dining room. It was also in 1967 that Charley picked up a brush and coated the new dining area a dark bluish purple with maroon trim and painted the kitchen in horizontal bands of red, yellow, and shocking pink, which he set off with red curtains.

We spent a week interviewing Charley and photographing his tools, work procedures, and the objects he made (including a "settin' chair" we ordered for a museum), and a few more days trying to track down some of his earlier chairs, especially a couple of two-in-one chairs.[1] We also recorded a song of his own composition which expressed the fears of a lonely man who would never endure his struggles or return to his "ole Kentucky mount'n home," a strange remark, we thought, because we assumed, erroneously, that he was "at home." Interviewing was not always easy. Charley was cooperative and lost some of his nervousness as the days passed, but when he talked he dipped his face down and mumbled into his beard or turned his head aside to avoid direct eye contact. That first visit was exciting and trying, exciting because of Charley's obvious skill, imagination, and sophistication in his work, and disturbing because of the tension between Charley and his wife Rose ("my wife don't think much of this here chair-makin'," he told us soon after we had met him), and because of Charley's poverty, the mental and physical retardation of his three sons, his difficulty relating to other people, and his apparent depression.

When we returned to Charley's home in late November, 1965, to pick up two smaller chairs he had made for us (figure 21, chair on right) and a six-slat rocking chair ordered by a museum (figure 1), we requested him to make a rocking chair for us which we would get at a later date; although we wanted a sassafras one like our two chairs and the museum rocker, he suggested red oak as he had a supply on hand. It was to be one of Charley's "eighty-nine-dollar rocking chairs" in accordance with his current price schedule. At that time he said he would make an ordinary mule-eared "settin' chair" for $12.95 (he had rarely received as much as four dollars each for such chairs); a dining chair with four slats in the back instead of three, and the seat seventeen to nineteen inches from the floor instead of fourteen or fifteen inches as in settin' chairs, for $18.95, although he has never made such a chair; a more expensive dining chair with "notchin'" or decorative elements and "knobs" or finials for $29.95; a rather plain rocking chair with four slats for $59 (the highest price he had ever got for earlier ones was $18); a five-slat rocker for $69; a six-slat rocking chair with a brace in the back for greater support for $79 (he made only one and called it the "Li'l

Figure 21. Different designs for settin' chairs used by Charley: (left) chair with single pegs (c. 1960); (center) redbud chair with black walnut double pegs and slats notched at ends (c. 1961); and (right) sassafras chair with black walnut pegs (November 1965). The last chair is more of a dining chair.

Abner chair" for reasons to be explained later); and a larger rocking chair with a "better rock," a seat of narrow hickory bark splints, seven curved slats, and extensive ornamentation for $89. He also said he would make a two-in-one rocking chair with seven slats, eight posts or legs, four rockers, and woven hickory bark seat for $269, although the most he had received for any one of the four chairs of this type he had made was $75 and the least was $30; a "bookcase rocker" with eight posts, four rockers, leg rest, and woven back and seat for $500, of which he had made one and eventually made a second, the first selling for $100 and the second for $269 (or $169; he said both on different occasions); and other kinds of furniture and musical instruments for various amounts.

These "Sears and Roebuck prices," as several people called them, were not very meaningful before the fall of 1965 because no one in the barter system ever paid Charley much for his chairs, and they meant little after the summer of 1965 because people who read newspaper articles erroneously thought that he made only seven-slat rocking chairs and they ordered only this type at whatever the current price was (which later increased and differed according to the wood, walnut being most expensive). It was also impossible for other people and for us at the time to conceive of the difference in chairs correlated with the various prices.

Now about Charley and our

Figure 22. Sassafras rocking chair (c. 1961), made by Charley, is one of a set of four; it sold for $18. "It's sort of an honor to have a chair like that, I guess. I guess I should take better care of it," said the owner's wife who leaves it out in the weather; her husband did not want the chair anyway but he was able to get rid of only three of the set.

relationship with him: How do I put it tactfully? Charley seems to feel greatly indebted to others who have helped him, probably because throughout his life he suffered unpleasant treatment, from rejection by his parents to the spurning of him by the girl he intended to marry, the woman he did marry, and then his second wife. He has admitted lacking close companions and friends owing to his eccentric behavior and marked inability to relate to other people. He still retains deep reverence for a young journalist on a local newspaper who published the first article on Charley in the spring of 1965; it resulted in other regional and national essays, all of which provided many additional sales at higher prices for Charley, which he wanted at the time. As a gesture of appreciation for the help that the young writer had given him, Charley presented him with a settin' chair and for several months considered making some miniature settin' and rocking chairs for the man to use as paperweights; but sometimes Charley has blurred vision and cannot make out small details, so he never built the model chairs. My wife and I, along with the young journalist and another writer, were among the first people to spend much time with Charley and his family and, with a few other people later, to show genuine interest in and appreciation of his creations. We have the distinct impression from letters and interviews that Charley intended to make a special chair for us as a gesture of appreciation (and at no extra cost) — he said as much when we were with him in November — despite the fact that repeatedly we asked for an ordinary rocker.

The settin' chair Charley made in August was unusual in its own right (figure 23); he knew it was to go to a museum and therefore he made it "special" by using small double pegs of black walnut in each slat to contrast with the white oak of the chair, and he curved the "top seat round" in back for greater comfort; neither trait was common on such a chair at this time. And the two chairs he made for us were supposed to have been simple settin' chairs, but instead, they were dining chairs with "knobs," "notchin'," and double pegs (figure 21, chair on right). He asked only the settin' chair price, though we gave

him the full amount for dining chairs before we left at the end of November.
(One might suggest cynically that Charley had found an easy mark for
more expensive furniture; that sounds quite out of character, however,
even though economic motivation has been important in the creation of
some of his more complex chairs.)

When we left Charley's home on November 28 we took the sassafras
rocking chair for the museum and the two sassafras dining chairs for
ourselves, and we requested that a rocker be made for us. In the letter
my wife's sister received right after Christmas Charley wrote, "Well I
startied on a Big Book Case Rocker the last of november." He had had
no order for such a chair or for any other chair except ours. "This one is
a strang I Reley dinton in tin to Make hit this tipe." Interestingly,
he began his letter with the remark that "Well you said you were related
to Jane and Mike Jones Well no Wonde you all are so good and kind
[both families had sent money and boxes of food and clothes for
Christmas, including a pair of new boots for which Charley thanked us
profusely in his letter] They are the tops if you ask me the Best I
ever met." After our visit a year later Charley wrote to us on September
11, 1966: "We awal shere Enjoied you all So much after you left we just
walked around and around for a few days funny nothin never Bothered
me this way Before hit are somtin like a famliey having some one in a
famliey levin for a new home are Ware are somethin." And his wife Rose
told me in 1967 that when we had left the preceding August "Check
hated to see you go. He went out there an' sat down by the side of the
house an' didn't hardly move all day."

Thus it seems probable that Charley wanted to create a chair with
some special qualities as a way of repaying us for the attention and the
orders for several chairs he had received, and also to make a chair befitting his self-image as a master craftsman. There was no other conceiv-
able reason, according to the information we have, for starting to work
on a "Big Book Case Rocker" of red oak at the end of November.

But then in early December a short article appeared in a national
paper. As a result of this publicity Charley was suddenly inundated with

Figure 23. An oak settin' chair made by Charley in August, 1965. The double pegs of contrasting color were not ordinarily found on settin' chairs at this time, but this was a "special" chair made for a museum.

requests for information about prices and for photographs of his chairs; and he received orders for rocking and settin' chairs regardless of what they looked like or cost, although he had none on hand.

"Lettres Went to Comin in froum East South North West Wantin to no if they Culd Buy a Laddre Back Rockker and they said they Engoid Redin About me in the . . . news papre   I never herd of this news papre . . ."

Just like the chair he had commenced to build, "Ever thing is so strang   I try to ancer Ever Lettre and tele thim that I dinton have iney [chairs]." The only chair under construction was the strange one, and so, "I tole thim about this one and to day I got a lettre from New York Bisnis sain they had made arrangement with [the local bank] to go in to [London] and see thim at the Bank   they said send thim some pictures of the Rocker and hit sise   I will haft to get a Poride Camery I gess."

One of the first requests for chairs came from Martin Loughhead in New York City who wanted to purchase a full year's production from Charley plus any chairs he had on hand. Charley tried to explain to him about the bookcase masterpiece he was working on, and Loughhead agreed to buy it for $300. He sent a check for this amount to the bank in London and made arrangements with the executive vice-president of the bank to handle the transaction; this much is clear from statements made later by Charley, in addition to information in the letter from Loughhead dated December 22, 1965, which Charley still had in August, 1966. Before he would close the deal Loughhead wanted a picture as he could not visualize the chair from Charley's remarks. He also wanted Charley to sign a contract binding him to sell a year's production of chairs to Loughhead; later Charley claimed that the businessman refused to offer the full price he was asking for the chairs. Charley bought a used Polaroid camera, took pictures of his masterpiece, and sent photos to Loughhead. Perhaps because he was suspicious of the man's motives and because he felt Loughhead was not offering enough money for a year's supply of chairs, Charley demanded $479 instead of $300 for the bookcase rocker. The businessman refused to buy it or pay any more money for a large quantity of chairs. After their disagreement Loughhead ordered a seven-slat rocking chair, but to my knowledge

Charley never made it for him. Within the next year two other business firms, one in California and the other in Indiana (an insurance firm), offered to buy a year's production of furniture, but Charley refused them both.

After his disagreements with the businessman in New York, Charley still had the bookcase masterpiece; all the specific orders coming in as a result of the nationwide attention were for seven-slat rockers and modified settin'- dining chairs, since only these types were depicted in the article. During the late spring Charley indicated to us in a letter that our red oak rocking chair

Figure 24. Charley's first two-in-one rock- ing chair (late 1961) sold for $50. It marked the first notable use of notchings corres- ponding to turnings on the posts or legs. It was allegedly created because Charley "couldn't sell the cheap chair, so I just thought up that kinda chair." The owner later had the chair sanded and varnished by another man for $50.

Figure 25. Charley's second two-in-one chair (early 1962) sold for $75. Made of red- bud or mulberry, it is about fifty inches tall and has eighty or ninety hand-carved pegs with grooved heads. The elongated finials were unusual at a time when most of Charley's chairs had mushroom finials, and Charley claimed the chair marks the first use of spokes under the arms since the '30s.

Figure 26. Charley's third two-in-one rocker and first "bookcase rocker" was made late in 1962 or early in 1963 of black walnut with hickory bark splints. This chair, known as the "mayor's chair," has a leg rest that extends in front; the lids of the basket arms lift up. It was sold for $100 to a politician who intended to give it to President Kennedy, but the assassination upset the purchaser's plans. The chair is now in a department store basement. "The only reason I make a chair like that is you find people that's interested in somethin' differ'nt, you know."

was ready and we could pick it up anytime; apparently he had once again
decided to sell the masterpiece to us at the cost of a seven-slat chair. For
the first few days we were with him in August he refused to consider more
money for the chair and said repeatedly that if we did not like it or want it
he would make the chair we had ordered ten months earlier. We finally over-
came our initial shock and managed to suggest that we thought the masterpiece was a brilliant creation; by the time we left in early September Charley
had agreed to accept at least $200 from us for the masterpiece, whereupon
we promptly ordered another chair, this time one that would have only four
legs and two rockers.

Several features of the masterpiece itself, as well as of its manufacture,
warrant comment now. In the first place Charley had built several other
two-in-one rocking chairs since 1961 (e.g., figures 24-28), but all of them
had been made from logs he had hewed out himself. The masterpiece was
the first rocking chair, to our knowledge, which was made of pieces of
wood purchased at a lumber company, and it required a somewhat different technique of construction.

Previously Charley had cut the timber in the hills, split the logs with
a hickory maul and a dogwood glut, and then roughly shaped the planks
into posts and slats with a hatchet. Next he smoothed the pieces on a
drawing horse using a drawing knife, and then cooked the slats and posts
in boiling water for twenty minutes and an hour, respectively, in order to
make them pliable. These pieces were driven into presses in which they dried
with the proper curvature. Charley then dressed the slats and posts with
his drawing knife, measured the proper places for stretcher holes using his
hands and fingers as a guide (two hands with thumbs overlapped equals
twelve inches, one hand with thumb extended equals six inches, and the
width of a thumb is one inch), and morticed the posts with hammer and
chisel. After assembly the chair was bottomed with a seat of woven hickory
bark splints, armrests were shaped and added to the chair, and rockers were
pegged into place. (See figures 6-19.) The procedure is similar for all
chairmakers except that most others use a drawing knife and horse only
to shape the stiles on the back posts of settin' chairs, and they usually turn

rounds and posts on a lathe (figures 29-36); since Charley refuses to use a turning lathe, his chair parts are not rounded but octagon shaped. Glue and nails were unnecessary — and so were most of the pegs though they were used for decorative effect — because of the differential seasoning of the chair parts: slats and rounds or stretchers are seasoned the most while the posts are less well seasoned so that the wood of the legs shrinks around the other pieces, and "when that wood's dried it's jest like hit growed thataway." On a rocking chair the trick is to have the feet more

Figure 27. Charley's fourth two-in-one rocker, made of black walnut in late 1963 or early 1964, sold for $30. "I was real sick that winter," said Charley. "I guess if a man gets to where he needs the money real bad, he has to give in to 'em." There is more curvature at a higher point in the back posts than in current chairs. The pegs in the rockers fill in holes mistakenly drilled by Charley.

Figure 28. Charley's fifth two-in-one rocker, of black walnut, was made in the winter of 1964-65. The rockers are too small because Charley ran out of wood. The chair signals one of Charley's first uses of pegs that contrast in color with the rest of the wood.

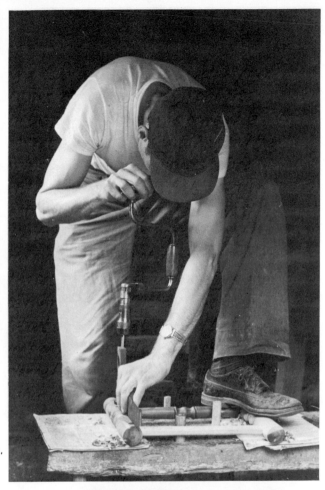

Figure 29. Aaron oils a post or leg
as it spins in place on the lathe.
Aaron worked with Verge and Verge's
son Hascal, as his early chairs indicate.
Later he improved. "He can make a
chair so pretty," acknowledged Hascal,
"you can see your face shinin' in it."

Figure 30 (top right). Aaron uses
a square to align stretcher holes
in post.

Figure 31. Slat press and tub for
cooking slats; posts are not
usually cooked or bent.

seasoned than the rockers and the tops of the front legs more seasoned than the ends of the armrests which fit over them, and the middle section of the legs less well seasoned than the stretchers and slats which fit into the posts. [2]

The bookcase masterpiece was not made that way. It is almost impossible to hew lumber that has been sawed and kiln dried as the wood has already been cut partly with the grain and partly across the grain; a hatchet or a drawing knife will not follow the grain at all. Charley used the boards he had bought from the lumber company for the panels in the back; he shaped the posts eight sided, using a drawing knife so they would look like his; and he had the rockers sawed out of a board at the lumber company, the corners of which Charley rounded off with a saw and a rasp. The seat consists of three planks pegged and glued together and then hewed out with a hatchet. The inserts along the top edge of the chair in back between the panels are of black walnut; they were probably added last because they are not structurally necessary but do contribute to the overall design. Charley has carved an inscription on these inserts indicating that the chair was "Made / Buy / [Charley] / C—'s / Hands / Engle Mill / Old, Kentucky." It is uncommon to find a signature on chairs in this area; perhaps it is a sign of conceit since this chair is Charley's "masterpiece of furniture," but it may have been added also because Charley erroneously thought the chair would be on display in a department store owned by Loughhead (that was not Loughhead's kind of business at all though Charley thought it was) and thus everyone would know who created the chair and where he lived and some people would order chairs from him.

The vast number of pegs (about two hundred), several with decorated heads, may have resulted from our indirect influence and again suggests that the chair was created for us. In November, 1965, I had expressed amazement to Charley at the decorated pegs in the two-in-one rocking chair owned by Phil Banks (figure 25); each of the eighty or ninety pegs has been carved with grooves and ridges. I was astounded by the nature of the chair itself and by the details of construction,

Figure 32. "Skinnin' bark" is usually done on Sundays during spring and summer.

Figure 33. "Peelin' bark."

Figure 34. Rolling strips of hickory bark into "hands."

Figure 35. The top half of the bark is removed and then discarded by most chairmakers in the area, like Aaron, but Charley uses the whole bark.

Figure 36. "Bottomin'" a maple settin' chair. Beechum, like most chairmakers, did not cook or press the slats but put them into the chair green.

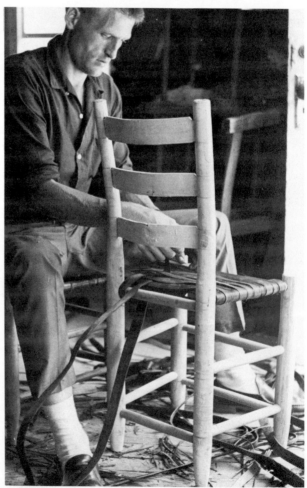

including the pegs about which Charley said, "Ain't too many people notices that;" many customers misunderstand the function of the pegs and think they are bolts, while others ask how "those little round things are stuck on the chair."

Is it possible that such a chair as the bookcase masterpiece is the result of spontaneous creation? I doubt it, although spontaneity of sorts is often involved in chairmaking: the details of an object may not be clear in the craftsman's mind, the material itself requires some revision of the mental image during construction, and the hand cannot possibly carry out precisely the idea inside the producer's head. Normally Charley has not only the product rather well in mind but also an image of the tools and techniques to be utilized in objectifying a particular idea. A look at his notebooks for orders reveals the detailed knowledge he has of the object before it is ever constructed, for he and his customers have written such specifications as the following order:

Paid in advance $75.00 for
a rocking chair like ———'s
in solid black walnut with
hickory bark woven seat.
Front posts bent outwards
Seat size — inside measure —
Front = 21"
Sides = 16"
back = 18"
High back with seven slats
Rockers = 2½"
balance same as chair I saw here

Ordinarily the customer would have received a chair made according to these specifications, but in this instance Charley had to alter another six-slat rocker to make it a seven-slat one so he could fill the order within a reasonable length of time (figures 37, 38). This brings me to the subject of the "new design," which probably helps explain the way in which the bookcase masterpiece developed.

Late in the evening of July 1, 1967, as we sat on his front porch, Charley told me that several of his chairs had appeared to him at night just before he went to sleep, and that later he thought about the forms and designs until they were well formulated in his mind. He imagined his first eight-legged dining chair of a decade earlier several months before he actually made it (figure 39), and more recently he had even conceived of a way to make a table with eight serving places and with a circle in the center representing a lazy Suzan. If he made such a table with a

Figure 37. Six-slat black walnut rocker made by Charley in early 1967; in July, 1967, he redesigned the chair, using seven slats instead of six (see figure 38).

Figure 38. Seven-slat rocker (photo by Charley), originally designed to have six slats.

Figure 39. Charley sold his first eight-legged chair (1953) for $2 or $3 to a man who bought it because "it was so odd and everything; I could see the sturdiness of it, the oddity, and that's why I wanted it." Another chairmaker said of the legs in back: "That's a useless thing to have on a chair; it could be dangerous."

Figure 40. Charley changed his design and created a seven-legged armchair in 1953, which he sold for $5. In 1954 he made six more like it.

revolving platter, he said, "A body wouldn't have to say, 'Pass me this, pass me that.'"

I asked him about the bookcase masterpiece.

"I've been a-thinkin' about that kind a chair for five or six years," he replied, ever since making his first two-in-one rocking chair. "I said the next one I was gonna make it outa solid walnut an' put a place on it for books and a pipe rack and also a place under the seat for books. I thought I could make a chair like that with a removable seat of hick'ry but it wouldn't work on account a the side pockets wouldn't a had nothin' to rest on." The first bookcase rocker (figure 26), antedating the masterpiece by three years, had been made with back and seat and armrests of woven hickory bark, whereas the masterpiece is of solid wood.

On the following Friday, July 7, as Charley finished altering the six-slat rocker into a seven-slat chair, the germ of an idea sprang up in his mind, and in a sudden flash of inspiration he knew that he could make yet another kind of chair. A more complete image of this new design (figure 41) came to him that night as he lay in bed in a semiconscious state; he was unable to sleep all that night, he said, for this design was the first major new one he had thought of in two years (since the masterpiece which was followed in 1966 by the special "California rocker" [figure 42] which owed much of its form and design to the customer's influence).

Charley explained the chair to me in great detail two days after his dream. It was to be a laminated rocking chair consisting of alternating pieces of dark and light wood. Initially his mental image was of a chair with one post dark, the other light, and one arm rest and one rocker dark with the opposite member light, but he rearranged the details in his mind as he spoke so that the conception was of a chair in which even the posts had sections of wood alternating in color with each other and with the slats, and the arms and rockers were not of one piece either (figure 43). He could probably make the chair of scraps of wood so it would cost him nothing for materials, he explained excitedly (although as it happened there were few scraps he could use and he had to cut up some good pieces), and he had even figured out how to join the separate pieces of post to one another. He would shape eight sided with a drawing knife two pieces of black walnut, say, about eight inches in length, drill a hole perhaps an inch deep in the top and bottom of each piece, and insert doweling in each hole; then he would make two more pieces from light wood, say sassafras, in the same manner and connect them to the walnut pieces using glue and pegs that would contrast in color with the wood they were driven into. The only features he was uncertain of were the arms and the rockers (figure 44): Would the thin pieces of wood glued and pegged together be placed horizontally or vertically before the

Figure 41. Charley's "new design" rocker which came to him in a dream on Friday, July 7, 1967. He made the chair in August, using alternating pieces of sassafras and black walnut; the final product is not quite the same as the original vision. The basic procedure was the same as that used to make a seven-slat rocker out of a six-slat rocker.

Figure 42. Charley's first "Ford rocker" or "California rocker," made of red oak in 1966 (photo by Charley). The chair was named in honor of a Californian who provided Charley with a sketch showing how the chair was to be made, but the final product is not quite what was ordered.

arm and rocker forms were carved out of them? For awhile his mental construct was without arms and rockers, but finally he decided they should be horizontal for greater solidity; during actual manufacture, however, he made them vertical for appearance's sake.

And what about the finials? He had forgotten those. In his mind they, too, would be made from pieces of wood alternating in color, but as yet they had no clearly defined form. No matter, he thought; he could turn them on his new turning lathe, the one he had just bought with an FHA loan but had not used, and make them any shape that happened to develop without definite planning. Or, as an alternative, he could make them octagon shaped without ornamental turnings; he preferred the former but had to leave the image of turned finials fuzzy in his mind because he did not know quite what they would look like. Later he turned some finials from the laminated wood, but he

Figure 43. Charley finishes the assembly of his "new design" chair in August, 1967, using glue because of the type of construction. Usually no glue is used, as the differential rate of seasoning of chair parts holds the chair together.

threw them away (figure 45) and used instead simple carved finials of solid walnut to cap the final sections of posts of sassafras with the black walnut slat between.

In Charley's mind the seat of the chair was of ordinary woven hickory bark, but this concept was not in keeping with the rest of the chair. No, he would have to have a checkerboard pattern, he explained, which he could easily make by using fresh hickory bark for the woof and, for the warp, bark soaked in the creek until it had turned dark. Eventually, however, Charley used very narrow bark of light color; he did not weave a checkerboard pattern after all.

The new-design chair, like the bookcase masterpiece, was unusual as a whole, but half a dozen or more antecedent experiences served as a basis for its generation. The immediate source that provided the

Figure 44. The armrests of the "new design" chair were made of laminated pieces of walnut and sassafras.

Figure 45. Turned finial that Charley chose not to use on his new design, at least not on the first version of it shown in figure 41.

essential technology was the technique of turning the six-slat rocker into a seven-slat one (figures 37, 38). Charley had made a separate section consisting of two pieces of post about nine or ten inches long with a slat between them; he shaped the finials of the six-slat rocker so they became dowels about three-quarters of an inch in diameter; then he affixed the separate section — with finials at one end and notches at the other — to the top of the six-slat rocking chair. That night he had his dream.[3]

Charley had been trying to think of some way to use waste pieces of the wood he had been buying at a lumber company, beginning with the manufacture of the masterpiece. In early June, 1967, he had settled on a design for a bedstead with a checkerboard veneer of black walnut and sassafras squares, about two and a half inches wide, glued and pegged onto a supporting frame; he gave up the idea because of the time and work required, although he did make a small trivet by way of illustration. And in the late spring of that year he made his wife Rose a dining table of alternating pieces of walnut and sassafras; he had intended the

Figure 46. A baby rocker of black walnut and hickory pegs made by Charley in August, 1965; he sold it for $35. A cheap version sold for $18. The chair is one of the last examples, for several years, of the use of mushroom finials, and it is an early instance of using contrasting colors of wood for decorative effect (see also figure 47).

Figure 47. Black walnut rocker made by Charley in August, 1966, marks one of the last times, until he moved to the Midwest, that he used wood hewed out of timber; most rocking chairs for three or four years after this one were made of lumber purchased from a lumber company. The price of such rockers rose from $79 to $100 and then to $125. Now they are much more expensive.

table to be entirely of sassafras but, as he did not have enough boards on hand, he used a few pieces of black walnut.

The use of contrasting pieces of dark and light wood was an old idea. Charley had utilized the white outer wood on black walnut for decorative trim on many earlier chairs, particularly in the arms (figure 46) and in the slats, which often had a band of white at least half an inch wide along the lower edge (figure 47). The hickory bark seat also contrasted with the rest of the chair when made of dark wood. Most chairmakers, including Charley, when making a chair or a stool of black walnut, usually make the rounds and sometimes the slats of hickory for greater durability, because black walnut is a rather fragile wood; Charley's first child's rocking chair was of this type as was a black walnut settin' chair he made in the spring of 1964 and sold to a man in Rising Sun.

The idea for a checkerboard seat came from another source. Early in the summer, in June, 1967, Charley and I had gone to another small town to try to find someone who would sell Charley hickory bark for seats. We met another chairmaker named Verge who told us that he and his son Hascal and the chairmaker Aaron had made a chair for President Kennedy (presented to him by the dean of a local academy and by state politicians in order to attract attention to themselves and the school). The chair was of spotted walnut. In order to accentuate the decorative quality of white spots on dark wood, the men wove a seat of light and dark hickory bark in a checkerboard pattern; the light bark was taken fresh from the tree, whereas the dark bark had been soaked in the creek. Charley did much the same thing before making his new design by rebottoming an older chair, using some of the old bark along with fresh splints. He talked about this kind of seat for the new design but did not make it because he was appalled at the poor quality of the bark and felt that the fine chair he was making should have only the best bark of the narrowest width.

The new design was not perfect, as Charley realized after construction. The pegs were not properly seasoned — they were dowels purchased at the lumber company — and eventually some of them fell out, and the back was too tall and too heavy for the chair. None of the joints were really secure because the many peg holes and the holes for rounds removed much of the hickory dowel inside the pieces of post, and because these pieces were not properly seasoned but were held in place with glue. Two of the joints broke. Charley said that if he made another chair of this sort he would turn a projection on the end of one post, then drill a hole in the end of the other section of post and insert the projecting piece into that hole; hence the joints would be stronger. In addition, arms and rockers would be of solid wood but alternating in color: one rocker dark, the other light; one arm light, the other dark.

As the idea of the new design developed into an actual chair (we paid Charley $150 to make it because he would have had no other opportunity to make such a chair at that time), alterations were made for technical reasons and for appearance's sake. The masterpiece required revisions, too, and construction of unpredicted elements, partly because of technological problems (such as how to make the seat) but also because of Charley's need to enclose space around him and add accoutrements necessary to withstand a prolonged siege, or to prove to himself that he was a master craftsman (themes I return to later). In neither instance was production wholly spontaneous.

Students of what they have called primitive art, such as Franz Boas, Ruth Bunzel, George Mills, and Ralph Linton, have contended that the artist knows from the beginning exactly what he wants to make and "continues with unwavering constancy until it is attained."[4] Yet many commentators have characterized what they call folk art as spontaneous and unselfconscious.[5] Which tendency obtains? Neither, in that there is nothing unusual about creativity in what has been called folk or primitive art except that the sources of designs and techniques tend to be directly from first-hand interactions with others; and both, in that these two extremes in conception and manipulation may be found in all production, depending on the individual, the medium in which he works, and the particular circumstances at the time of production (or performance).

Consider another chairmaker named Aaron who tends, when possible, not to plan the work in advance but to develop designs in the fields of

decoration not only by imagining a visual image but also by actually manipulating the raw materials (figures 29, 30) until design elements
emerge; he chisels designs into the post rotating on his homemade
electric lathe, selects patterns that are most pleasing to him, and then
duplicates the decorative elements on the other chair parts before
constructing a chair (the planful operation). Once he finds a pattern
that is acceptable to him and attractive to customers, he follows that
design until boredom compels him to alter the visual appearance of the
chair again. Only once did Aaron make a drawing of design patterns for
slats and posts, but he found no satisfaction in sketching designs and
trying deliberately to translate them into wood (although two other
chairmaking brothers I heard about but never met are said to follow
this procedure); rather, Aaron's only successful development of ornamentation resulted from unplanned chisel work on the chair legs. This
seemingly spontaneous manipulation of raw materials is limited to decorative details, however, and does not extend to form. Aaron has made
several minor modifications in the form of a rocking chair but only one
major alteration — changing vertical panels in the chair's back to horizontal slats (figures 48-50) — and this was a deliberate change intended to
divest the chair of an alleged commercial quality typical of factory-made
chairs.

   If he had his choice, then, Aaron would do nothing but turn posts to
create new designs. But since economic survival depends on building
chairs, he cannot spend all his time at the lathe turning designs for the
pleasure derived from this simple act. Like Charley, he is still a chairmaker
who must construct utilitarian objects serving a practical end; thus,
before the actual manufacture of a whole chair Aaron knows what the
intended object will look like, what size the product and the separate
component parts will be, and what decorative designs the chair will exhibit.
Not every chair, however, will be quite the same as envisioned. As Aaron
remarked about one of his rocking chairs, "It ain't the prettiest one I ever
made," by which he meant that the grain and the color of the pieces of
walnut did not match as he had expected, although the chair's form and

ornamentation corresponded with his initial vision.

Another basic question needs brief attention: the existence of unique discoveries and inventions in what is supposed to be a conservative, conventional, and traditional mode of behavior. In the words of Stith Thompson, for example, "the characteristic feature of the folktale is that it is traditional. It is handed down from one person to another, and there is no virtue in originality."[6] Such an assumption is based on a conception of folklore as necessarily static rather than dynamic (and as text that can be handed down); a new discovery does not render the behavior or output of production nonfolk, however, because what researchers have called folklore actually refers to a process of learning and utilizing modes of behavior in particular circumstances, rather than to static texts or objects. Part of the originality in what people do is knowing when and how to employ the proper modes of behavior and codes of communication on the appropriate occasion in an acceptable fashion, as evident in the existence of

Figure 48. An early black walnut rocker made by Aaron in 1962. The notch in the top slat became Aaron's trademark. Charley deemed it a "good-lookin' chair if they was a few improvements in it"; he listed nine.

Figure 49. Black walnut panel-back rocker made by Aaron (1963 or 1964). Its separate elements are more distinctly formed than in earlier chairs.

Figure 50. Black walnut slat-back rocker made by Aaron in June, 1967. Aaron switched to the slat-back design because he felt his earlier chairs looked too much like factory-made rockers. He said his chairs are "kinda pretty but they don't set too good, 'specially the dining chairs." Said Verge, "I like that chair, but for myself I wouldn't have them rings and nubs."

initiation rites that test the aspirant's knowledge of the lore.[7] Originality
is also manifested by individuals who, while employing well-known expressions,
formulas, motifs, or design elements, engage in a performance or in the
production of objects unique to that occasion: "the folk-singer, however
much he be keeper of a tradition, is never for a single moment dominated
by it," wrote Phillips Barry. "He learns his songs and in his interpretation
of them does exactly what he pleases with them."[8] A young man, highly
skilled in using nonverbal "lines" (elaborate routines intended to change a
situation of physical copresence to one of comingling between a male and
a female) to which he has even given names, remarked: "These aren't the
ordinary lines; these are definitely original because I created them. But
it really isn't fair for me to take all the credit. You see, when I was
younger, the guys in my crowd gave me advice; so I picked up a few ideas
there. Then, of course, sometimes we heard their older brothers talking,
you know, behind closed doors. So I took the main ideas from both and
. . . I created something different."[9] And that is typical of human
behavior in daily life.

Many examples of original works are examined in chapters 4-6 of
this book, but individuality obtains in the technological dimensions of
production as well as in the visual and more expressive aspects of chairmaking. Each producer is unique in his values, aspirations, abilities, and
needs; all the instruments, procedures, special lore, skills, and socioeconomic arrangements required for technological processes differ from one
craftsman to another. An example of unique discovery that may become
part of the procedures of other individuals was suggested in a conversation between Charley and his maternal uncle Oaklie, from whom he
learned much about chairmaking, though it is apparent that the
student discovered something about getting bark which his mentor
did not know.

"I always cut a hick'ry tree down an' let it lay there two or three
days, week maybe, 'fore I take the bark off of it, when the sap's up . . . ,"
said Charley to Oaklie.

"You do?"

". . . an' that makes all the water dry out in there. An' then I go back and take that outside bark off, an' it holds that color — you know, when you first take the bark off, it holds that same color."

"Is that right?" exclaimed Oaklie. "Well, I'll be damned."

"It don't change color," Charley continued. "Take a fresh pole out here in the hills, and take the bark off it, and, uh, in a few minutes it changes color."

"Oh, yeah, yeah, uh-huh."

"But if you let it lay there two, three days, or a week, and then pull that outside bark off it, hit don't change color."

"Yeah? I never thought about that."

Charley went on to explain — to Oaklie's amazement as evident in such expressions as "I never did try it," "I never thought about that," "You can?" "I'll swear, I never thought about that, sure wouldn't," and "I'd never of thought of that" — that if the log lay for several months in winter it was unnecessary to use a drawing knife at all to peel off the outer bark, and that he discovered the technique by accident one winter when he removed a strip of bark from a pole several months after he had cut it down. As he indicated to his uncle, Charley had learned how to skin bark more easily than permitted by the more common technique, and to ensure that the bark remained light in color rather than darkening, both problems that other chairmakers have not solved with complete success. The technique has become traditional for Charley, meaning that he has done it this way several times and may do it this way again, and, owing to the number of precedents he has established for himself, he is able to communicate the idea to other craftsmen with a great deal of authority, but he is not bound to this procedure and often does things differently. "Tradition," then, is the ideas communicated from one individual to another which serve to establish precedence for the procedure; what the individual does with the ideas and the skills that have been revealed to him is his concern, and his own discoveries and inventions may become "part of the general tradition" by being communicated to others who accept them and then communicate them to yet other individuals. The element of precedent may be important as a technique of persuasion, for ideas often must be demonstrated as satisfactory in order to be accepted. Conceptually, the diachronic dimension is more important than the synchronic in the use of the term "tradition," as it is the history of precedence which is emphasized. Precedence provides some evidence that assumptions and procedures are valid, because it establishes that similar means were used in analogous situations in the past in order to control the environment. It is this element of precedence which suggests to many researchers the importance of conservatism in behavior. Although individual discoveries and inventions at the moment of inception are not normative for other people, they may become so for that individual who is himself relying on tradition to some extent, and his ideas may be taken as traditional by other people at some time in the future.

"Convention," too, is processual, and it is not a norm or a standard from which each individual deviates, even though use of the word tends to encourage the researcher to stress conservatism in behavior. It is the synchronic dimension that is given special importance conceptually in using the term "convention" to refer to modes of behavior to which individuals tend to conform in the present to facilitate communication and inter-action, to control the natural and social environments most effectively in order to promote survival and enjoyment of life, and to solve practical, everyday problems in an effective way. It is conventional, for example, that chairmakers use summer bark in the seats of chairs, although Charley said "I don't like summer bark at all," and whenever possible he uses winter bark obtained in the fall. Specific details of convention, such as the best loca-tion of timber or the best height and diameter of trees or the best time of day or day of the week for getting bark vary from one set of circumstances to another and from one individual to another; only the steps taken in getting bark remain fairly constant and are generally agreed upon by craftsmen.

What the foregoing suggests is the desirability of employing dynamic models of human behavior, which is difficult to do when words like "tradi-tion" and "convention" are used; it also explains why the concepts of "ur-form" and "variant" in folklore study seldom have utility and why "tradition" and "convention" must be used with care. "'Barb'ry Allen' as I sing it has got seventeen verses," an Arkansas singer told a collector, "and if you hear somebody sing it with more or less than seventeen verses, it ain't right."[10] To an individual aware of only a few of the multiple manifestations of a common theme, his own expression may be the norm from which other individuals deviate. Many researchers in different fields, however, have erroneously conceived of each performance as a variant of a norm in which the term "variant" does not mean simply being different from others of its kind or class but, in a narrow sense, indicates a discrepancy; that is, they conceive of a variant as a certain kind of behavior or mode of expression which is less perfect than the ideal norm to which it is related but from which it deviates. For example, Stith Thompson suggests that the chief interest of the folktale scholar is to "establish an approximation to an original form which will sufficiently account for all the available variants,"[11] assuming in principle that there must be a nonchanging standard in human behavior to which individuals should conform but from which they usually deviate. Each example of the telling of a story, or the singing of a song, or the making of an object is not a variant of a static norm because being processual, it is obviously dynamic; and the activity itself is but an event manifesting this process, an event that can be dated in time and localized in space, an event that, of limited importance by itself, when taken together with other events is significant as a manifestation of one or more processes. The process itself can never be adequately described, for all we have are a few records of a few events giving evidence that the process exists. This is the real lesson that has been learned from decades of historic-geographic diffusion research in which events manifesting processes of human thought and interaction and expression were mistakenly treated as variants of a static norm. And it is because of this static model that some people have contended that there is no originality in what they call folklore; a more dynamic model, based on the study of individuals and their behavior, convinces me that there is much original thought and expression in what people make and do in daily life.

It is apparent that the particular method of creation varies from one situation to another, depending on the craftsman's values and ability, his emotional state at the time, and the problem that needs solving (the last point is especially important and is developed further in chapter 4). An individual without orders to fill may have occasion to experiment with new forms or patterns that will appeal to a certain clientele, as Charley once did when he sawed a crosshatch pattern on the front posts of a settin' chair. But an artist who must manufacture an object according to stipulation by the customer cannot rely wholly on intuition in constructing the product, because, as the chairmaker Verge said, "You gotta make it how the customer wants."

Charley's new design was not exactly what he wanted; and his bookcase masterpiece was not what we wanted, though apparently Charley wanted it for us. Both chairs began with an inspiration and a dream, developed into a more detailed mental image, and finally ended with spontaneous modifications during the actualization of the mental vision. One reason the new design was precipitated was that several people, including Charley himself and a local newspaper publisher who promised him "a good write-up" if he made another unusual chair, expected Charley to be innovative in his chairmaking, and this chair, despite its faults, certainly reveals imagination. But in what ways might the bookcase masterpiece be expressive of Charley's needs and conceptions of himself, and what were the precedents for it? There should be enough information in chapter 3 to suggest the way in which this man's beliefs and experiences are related to the things he makes.

CHAPTER THREE

It All Ended Up the Wrong Way

"You know, I had it all planned and all; studied about it an' studied about it. When I come home on the furlough, what I was gonna do was take my wife back with me when I went back to the service," said Charley, who did not have a wife at the time.

The year was 1944 and Charley was, as he sang in a song of his own composition two decades later, "a soldier boyee, a long, a long ways from my ole Kentucky mount'n home."

"I guess I was cravin' a woman, if the truth is known," he admitted. "I was 'bout thirty years old, hadn't never been married before, an' didn't know too much about a woman a-tall."

Charley was sitting on the edge of his chair, head bent forward and hands cupped together between his legs. "I was shore gonna get married now. I had it all planned out to get married, but I was tryin' to plan whether to take her back with me or not." As he stared at the rotting boards of the porch he shook his head back and forth. "It all ended up the wrong way," he mumbled.

Much of what has happened to Charley has ended up the wrong way, according to him. He attributes most of his problems, including poverty, marital discord, mental and physical illness, and the retardation of his sons, to experiences in the 1940s when he was plucked from the protective mountain hollow where he was born and raised and dropped onto one of the fog-shrouded islands in the Aleutian chain for two years, seven months, and twenty-eight days. But Charley's problems really began when he was a child. He was a loner who kept to himself and spent most of his time making things, partly because other people would have little to

Figure 51. Charley, about 1944, when he was stationed in the Aleutian Islands. "Now I'm a soldier boyee, a long, a long ways from my ole Kentucky mount'n home," he finally sang twenty-one years later.

do with him. He tried to help his uncle build chairs when he was young, but Charley was a slow worker and his uncle was an impatient man. "Oaklie used to swear at me when I was a kid if I didn't get that bark when he shot it through there."

Charley was often taken advantage of by his uncle and his brother. "Steton never did have to work," complained Charley's wife; "somebody else [meaning Steton's brother Charley] always kept him up." As for his Uncle Oaklie, "You couldn't put any faith in him," Charley admitted to me once in a moment of candor; "you couldn't depend on 'im." On one occasion while Charley was in the hills peeling bark his uncle and his brother took all his chairs to town and sold them for forty cents each to buy liquor. Another time they took the money that Charley had been sending home to his mother while he was in the army so they could get drunk and then pay the fine after they had been thrown in jail. After their mother died Steton tore down the cabin that Charley had built for her when he was about twenty, found the first two chairs that Charley had made on his own, and apparently sold them for a few dollars; at any rate, for the past several years Charley has been asking about the chairs but his brother will not give him any straight answers. Those chairs have a special meaning for Charley.

Because Charley was born on September 4, 1913, "Thirteen is my lucky number; I never worry about the Friday the thirteenth," as if it really mattered. But as Charley told me several times, "I never work on Sundays 'cause it's bad luck an' I got enough a that."

Charley attended school for only a few weeks at a time because he was shuffled back and forth between families in two counties, finally reaching the fourth grade when he was seventeen. He felt embarrassed in the classroom because of his age and dropped out of school to make chairs full time; he did not learn to write until he was in the army and retrieved discarded letters to copy.

"I was borned on Kings Creek, Letcher County," he said in August, 1966, as we drove deeper into the hills of southeastern Kentucky in search of the graves of his mother and her father Hat. It was Charley's third trip "home" in two decades. He had insisted on returning the year before with the young journalist to find the burial sites of his kin and to stand once again on top of Pine Mountain above the fog and far from the noise of cars and the sight of people; and he had been in the area half a dozen years earlier trying to find his runaway wife.

"Is that where you were raised, too, on Kings Creek?"

"Nope. Left there when I was a boy. We went to Poor Fork. My dad and mom, they separated when I was a little bitty young un, 'bout eight years old, I guess. I was just startin' to school on Poor Fork when they separated.

"Dad got the four kids," said Charley, but he never kept them. "He give the school teacher money to buy us clothes with. All I got was an ole hat out of it." Charley laughed nervously.

"Two weeks later Dad got us and walked back to Kings Creek to his mother's. Grandma put up with us about two or three days when here comes Mom. Grandma made Dad give Mom the two least uns and Grandma took the two biggest uns. Mom had a time raisin' us two little fellas," said Charley, referring to himself and Steton.

"Then when I was 'bout ten years old Dad come up and got me and took me home to his other wife. I stayed three or four months, but they had three kids and she had two of her own an' I was right in the way. Then Dad took his wife and kids to homestead in Oregon and then he up an' left the land, woman, and chillun there. He left them jest like he did Mother."

The upshot of Charley's remarks was, "I couldn't say which — Letcher County or Harlan County — I was mostly raised up 'twixt both them counties."

There was no malice in Charley's voice as he reviewed the events of his youth; it was a straightforward narrative occasionally punctuated with a nervous laugh at the most serious points. But the war left a bitter taste in his mouth and a disease on his skin.

"Been botherin' me ever since that winter when I was overseas," said Charley about the patches of redness under his beard and hair and over much of his body. "That last winter I was over there, buddy it got down to sixty below zero."

He laughed, but not because he found it funny. "Them Aleutian Islands. An' I b'lieve my soul I got frostbit one way or another an' it never will be right no more.

"Or maybe it's them shots they give me or somethin' or other. They give me so many shots I always think 'at they caused it. Some people can't take them shots, they're elergict to them. It hurts 'im. An' I al'ays felt worser ever time they give me one of them shots."

Again he twittered. "Don't b'lieve in 'em myself. That's the reason I won't get these chillun vacinated or anything on account a when Donny was a little baby they started him in on takin' shots in town at the health department an' he got in such a shape he had to quit. Couldn't give him any more shots."

Donny is Charley's oldest son who cannot walk or speak but lies in bed making buzzing sounds; when he was a child like the youngest boy Al, however, he seemed all right, but as the years passed his condition deteriorated, as has that of Charley's two teenage boys. Charley does not know why three of his sons are physically and mentally retarded. He tends to blame himself and the war, though, because the boys are nervous and so is Charley, and Charley's nervousness was worsened by his army experiences; in fact, he spent several months in a hospital and was finally given a thirty per cent certified disability discharge because of his mental state.

"Know what caused it?"

"The nervous condition? Zactly what really caused it was the isolation over there in the 'Leutian Island, really 'bout what caused it. I al'ays really was kinda nervous on the edges since I was a child. But I don't know just what if it wasn't the isolationist over there in them 'Leutian Islands. You know, there was nothin' much over there, not a thing."

Charley also claims to have weakened eyesight, a cataract, impaired hearing, a disease resulting in a strange taste in his mouth and missing teeth, and general aches and pains caused in some way by his military service in the Aleutians. "That's where my eye started botherin' me — that last year I was over there. 'Bout every year it takes a spell and starts botherin' me." He also worries about his hands which he said had been "bothered" by medicine given him in the army. "I'll betcha one a these days my hands'll get completely stiff," he said, flexing the fingers on his right hand but staring at two fingers on the left hand which would bend only far enough to form hooks. Charley's paternal grandfather had been crippled with arthritis as a young man and could make few chairs.

When he was in the Army Charley was trained for nothing in particular but did everything in general. "First they have you doin' one thing an' then another'n." Mainly he peeled potatoes, cleaned latrines, washed pots and pans, greased army vehicles, and stood guard duty late at night in the snow, which covered the ground from September to June. "No matter what the company commander tells you to do, you got a do it."

And that is what Charley did for more than two years without a break. No wonder he was "cravin' a woman." But his wife Rose was third choice. They scarcely knew each other and seventeen years separated them in age, but they had grown up in the same general area; they had one other thing in common: both were despondent when they decided to get married. By counting on his fingers Charley ascertained that they had first met in September or October of 1945 and were married in London shortly afterward.

"I married oncet before I married Rose. Didn't last, though," said Charley. "I come home on a furlough after I come back from overseas. They give us a furlough to come home and I got married." He laughed again because he was serious. "That's as long's it lasted — two weeks.

"When I went back in the service an' they put me in the convalation hospital there in Fort George Wright there at Washington, kept me till October the twenty-seventh [1944], I was give a discharge. I come back home an' the first place I went was, I got a taxi out a Cumberland an' went up to her house an' she'd backed out on me.

"I was tryin' to get her to live with me for several months afterward," said Charley about his wife Sarah; "couldn't get her to live with me no more. I met Rose an' we come to London an' we took a notion to get married. She'd been married, too, before. She already had a young un. It was just a baby somewhere aroun' a year old." The child's name was Annie Mae and her father had deserted the mother and child.

"Why did Sarah turn her back on you? Was it because she was only fifteen and you were over thirty, or was it that her mother just didn't like you?"

"I don't know. But I al'ays thought it was the mother's fault the reason she wouldn't live with me. I think all her mother was after was 'llotment from the gov'ment. When I went back in the service I made her out a 'llotment and the gov'ment paid her $50 a month. She just drawed about two checks. I b'lieve that's what her mother was after an' she found out I was bein' discharged an' comin' home, why she talked Sarah out a livin' with me then. I really didn't love the girl when I married her."

"Why did you marry her?"

"I just married her too quick. I just been over in the 'Leutian Islands all that time an' I just — I knowed her all my life an' ever'thing — but I never thought a bit 'bout marryin' her than I did a flyin' when I come home on my furlough. I didn't even think about it."

Sarah spread rumors to the effect that Charley was a poor lover and perhaps impotent. Charley claimed he had had no previous sexual experience, but as he said, "You could tell she'd been pranked around with 'fore I ever pranked around with her."

Originally Charley had intended to marry his first cousin. The initials M.W. are tattooed on his arm but the ink has faded over the years. "I's figgerin' on marryin' her when I come home on furlough," said Charley, "but she was two or three months pregnant an' she wasn't but about, uh, sixteen. An' she thought enough of me she wouldn't marry me. Boy, I guess I'd a blowed up all over the place if I'd a married her an' found that out later. She might a been 'fraid to marry an' then I'd a found out . . . I guess I'd a whipped 'er maybe . . . I don't know jest what I would a done."

It was at this point in the conversation that Charley said everything had ended up the wrong way. "I was in bad shape when I come home on a furlough. That last winter was when it hit me. My eyes bothered me. I was in a bad shape when I come home from a furlough. An' when I went back after my furlough, doctor sent me to a convalation hospital at Fort George Wright in Washington. I stayed there till October 27, 1944. I'll never forget that date."

Nor would Charley forget his experiences in the early 1940s and later. In fact, in the late spring of 1965 he composed a song entitled "My Old Kentucky Mountain Home" which ostensibly related to 1944;

it is roughly set to the tune of "Man of Constant Sorrow," a song that
Charley mentioned several times as one he vaguely remembered from his
youth. The song that Charley sang for my wife and me on August 21, 1965,
as he plunked on his homemade guitar or banjo into the face of which
he later scratched "My Old Kentucky Gourd," is as follows:

I was born and raised in old Kentucky mount'n home.
Now I'm a soldier boyee, a long,
A long ways from my ole Kentucky mount'n home.

Fer, oh, fer o'er the deep blue sea,
Whar the sun hardly ever shines,
I get to wonderin' about my ole Kentucky mount'n home.

Whar the sun shines so brigh',
Whar the whippo'wills are so lonely and lonesome,
And I wonder if they ever think of me.

At night when I lie down a-lookin' up at heaven,
With a prayer in my heart,
To God I pray if thy will,
Oh, if't thee go through this war,
So that I can go back to my old Kentucky mourt'n home.

Whar the sun shines so brigh',
Whar the whippo'wills are so lonely and lonesome
After the war is over.

Now the war is over, so I thank God in heaven
That I'm now on my way
Back to my ole Kentucky mount'n home.

The place where the sun still shines so brigh',
And at night the whippo'wills are so lonely and lonesome
Place whar I was born and raised.

Four years later Charley would use some of the same phrases and images in letters to us after his wife left him for the third and final time. But in 1965, when he first sang the song, I misunderstood and thought that it had been composed twenty years before, a few months after Charley's service in the army. Consequently I asked, "Were you thinking about makin' it up while you were in the war?"

"No. No. No, I just thought about it, sayin' this war's a-bein' a long ways from my ole Kentucky home — <u>mountain</u> home. I just mumbled that, studying about it, you know, an' so I just took a notion about four months — it's been about four months countin' from now. I had that five-string banjer an' I just got to beatin' on hit, an' kinda thought up that song. It's not been over four months ago. I ain't got it completed yet — all of it — just a few verses of it."

"And this is the only song you know?"

"That's the only song I know. And, uh, hit's a quar song."

Just like the bookcase masterpiece he would build a few months later, Charley's song was "queer" or "strange;" in other words, it was of great significance to him but he was reluctant to explain how or why.

"Now the story in the song relates to when you were in the Aleutian Islands?" I asked him at the time, taking the song's content literally.

"That's right. The sun hardly ever shines up there. It'll be, uh, sun'll peek out a minute an' all at once here comes a rollin' fog, just rolls 'er away."

In the years that followed Charley sang the song only twice to other people, at their request, and he never added any more verses to it. He did not have to add anything because he made the bookcase masterpiece instead and because each major work of this sort — directly relating to the grieving process — attended to the emotional problem at that moment.

Still curious about the song, though, I asked Charley two years later, on June 24, 1967, "That song you made up, how long was that on your mind before you made it up?"

"That hasn't been but about three years ago. I thought about it a lot. You know, you hardly ever see a morning here in Kentucky but what you don't have sunshine. That is, now, <u>back up on top Pine Mountain where</u>

I was raised at. Always the sun shines bright in the mornin'. And, uh, that's where I really made that song up, based on that country back in there" (emphasis added).

Charley never returned to Pine Mountain to live after the war. Once Sarah had spurned him he headed for London to marry Rose; they lived many places, near the highway and in hollows, but always kept ninety miles of twisting road between them and Pine Mountain.

"Down in these valleys," said Charley, "you know, early mornin' it'll be fog, but there in that mountain you look down an' see the fog down under thar. Just like lookin' out over an ocean . . . You can look out over that fog thar early in the mornin' when it's kind of a cool night, an' that fog's all settled down thar in the valleys an' you can see back over the top of it — just see the backs of them hills over in there's all you can see. Just like lookin' out over an ocean." He laughed again, but the laugh was edgy.

"You'd like to go back there an' live someday?" I asked rhetorically.

"Yeah, I'd like to live back in there an' go back in there where my gran'pa is [that is, Hat's grave]; course, all them buildings is burnt down an' gone now. If I could lease that I'd go back in there an' build that back jest like it was when me and Mother had it. Don't guess they'll ever lease it to me. It b'longs to the wildlife — act'lly, guess it b'longs to the state."

Obviously the words of the song express the loneliness and despair of a man who longs to return home, a man who is afraid he will never again see his "old Kentucky mountain home where the sun shines so bright" that he asks for divine assistance to see him through the present trouble. One can understand the way in which a southern mountaineer, or anyone else for that matter, never before away from home and kin, would react to being in the army on some desolate island in the midst of a war; there would be shock and fear and a desire to return home, and then withdrawal and an idealization of life in the past before the disruption. In such a situation a man might well compose a song expressing his feelings as a way of dealing with his grief and of adjusting to his loss.[1]

The song was not composed, however, until twenty years after the end of World War II, suggesting that Charley had never fully adjusted to the events at that time but continued to be disturbed by them. The setting of the song is generalized: no specific war is mentioned and the narrator does not identify his present location, only that it is a very long way from his home. As Charley intimated, the early morning fog in the valleys where he has lived separates him from Pine Mountain like an ocean, and like the sea during World War II. Apparently a global conflict among nations is not the only sort of war one must struggle through; Charley has had other battles to fight since World War II, but as soon as he won one of them he had to confront another, and some of them he may have lost.

There have been additional problems since 1944 to which Charley has attempted to adjust, as evident in his behavior in the 1960s. Many of Charley's letters and conversations, his body image, some of his chairs, and the song indicate an identification at times with an earlier age and an isolation from his problems and from other people who might have caused those difficulties or who certainly will generate further frustrations for him. By isolating himself socially and geographically Charley can, he apparently feels, reestablish and maintain his mental stability; interacting with other people often upsets him and external pressures are partly responsible for his losses, requiring the expenditure of much emotional energy which in turn enervates him physically. As part of the process of grieving and as a function of his dislike of interacting with other people, Charley has attempted to erect protective barriers, real and symbolic, and he has sometimes developed a nostalgia for and an idealization of the past when he was free of other responsibilities, was living among his own kinfolk, and had not suffered the hardships to come. In order to isolate himself in 1965 or 1966 Charley would have had to live in a secluded hollow on top of Pine Mountain, far away from the highway in the valley where he then resided, for there on the mountain he could be in full control, and there on the mountain could be found his most pleasant memories, made more golden by the passage of time and by comparison with the unhappy events that occurred after Charley left the mountain twenty-five years ago.

What else happened after the war? First of all Charley married a woman whose values and aspirations and needs are the opposite of many of his own and with whom he has frequently been in conflict. It was at Rose's urging that they moved to town and that Charley tried to find a "decent" job instead of making chairs. So Charley tried his hand at several occupations, but employment at each task lasted only a few days or weeks.

"When I first come back from the army, why, uh, I got a job in the Blue Diamond coal mines. I don't know just how many shifts I did work up there. I never was used to that, never could work in a mine, but I thought I'd try it. Them fellas was makin' good money when I first come back from the army. Doctor couldn't hardly decide whether to let me go to work or whether to not. Finally I talked 'em into lettin' me have a paper and sign it lettin' me go back to work."

After all, Charley had a wife and child to support and an apartment that he could not afford, so he had to have a job whether or not he was fit for it emotionally or by training. He loaded coal onto a conveyor belt.

"How long did you work at that?"

"I don't know how many shifts . . . I didn't work a week I don't think. Might a worked a week at it. Couldn't take it. I'd get them cramps in the back of my legs . . . I got so sore I couldn't go down a hill to save my life. Had a go down back'ards.

"That's the first job I undertook. Then I signed up on that unemployed. Then I got me a job workin' for that newspaper up there, workin' as a janitor an' a caster. I'd do a little castin' work and a little janitor work—I'd have to sweep the floors. I was just a handyman around."

"You enjoy that?"

"Nope."

"Why not?"

"I don't know. I never was used to that type of work. But I's always could do anything, you know."

Charley worked as a janitor for four or five months but was fired because he did not always appear on Saturday when the Sunday paper was printed. Then for a few months he had a job in the Pepsi-Cola bottling plant loading cases of pop onto a truck and sweeping floors. He quit.

"What did you do after that?"

"We lived over there in London, had an apartment over there — two-room apartment — an' I had a work at somethin' so I signed up on unemployed an' in just about a week or two I got a job with the power company settin' light poles in that there 'rural areas,' puttin' up power out in the country — what they call 'rural.'"

Charley's job was to help carry the heavy transformers. "Sometimes you'd have to pack 'em hunnert, two hunnert yards to where they'd go on a pole." He enjoyed being out of doors for a change but it was simple-minded work requiring nothing but manual labor; he was often on the job for ten or twelve hours because of the distances the workers had to travel, and of course he had to punch a clock. There were also financial problems.

"We had a move out of that apartment. I didn't make much money then, 'bout seven dollars a day it paid. An' the only apartment I could find was fifty dollars a month an' I couldn't pay that much. So I bought a few pieces of furniture an' moved out on Main Jett's Creek," said Charley, who then tried to laugh about it. "I started makin' chairs when I moved down on Jett's Creek. I couldn't get a ride back and forth an' stay on my job an' I had a give it up."

"Have you been a chairmaker ever since then?"

"Been 'bout twenty years an' I've done nothin' but that. Boy, we've seen it pretty hard sometimes. I've worked many a time all night long and packed it off the next day just to get enough to do us a day or two." Again Charley twittered nervously.

"Did you ever think about getting another job?"

"Yeah, I tried to get a job around a few times. I'd get burnt out a few times tryin' to make chairs. Bad job, I'll tell you. I've heard it all my life, a chairmaker never has nothin'." He laughed again as one does at a bad joke just to be polite. "I've heard that all my life, a chairmaker never has a thing to set on. That's about the way it is here, ever' time I get one made pretty an' I wanna keep it I al'ays sell it—somebody talk me out of it."

Chairmaking is the only occupation at which Charley is skilled and the only work he enjoys, for it provides the opportunity to develop and present to others the images with which he is chiefly concerned. During the many days and nights I lived with the family in 1967 I saw Charley wander around the yard from one piece of work to another, usually oblivious to the presence of others, preoccupied with the visions in his mind to which he was trying to give physical shape. Often he did not realize that cars had driven into the yard or that someone was standing in his shop or that others were talking to him, and he gave little attention to his relationships with the world outside himself or with his wife.

"A body gets to doin' somethin' an' he just don't wanna change," said Charley in explanation of why he is a chairmaker. "My wife," however, "don't think much of this here chairmakin' business." For many people whom I met in this area, Rose included, handicrafts are too much a reminder of an older way of life characterized by poverty and deprivations which they seek to escape. This is one reason that some of Charley's nephews and younger cousins who learned chairmaking from him prefer to work in the coal mines or to pump gas at a service station instead of building furniture. Rose eventually replaced handmade furniture in their home with the more desirable plastic and chrome table, chairs, and cabinets, and the Early American-style sofa and end tables (which soon fell apart). After all, "A body has a right to have somethin' aroun' that you kin enjoy. The other stuff wasn't fit to set on."

"I understand you haven't always been happy with Charley as a chairmaker," I said to Rose late one evening as we sat on the porch enjoying a few moments of cool air after a summer storm. "Sometimes you thought he oughta be something else?"

"I don't know. Sometimes I thought he ought to be, I guess." She chose her words carefully. "But that's what he's always liked."

"You have anything particular in mind you think he oughta do?"

"No, he thinks it hisself more so than I do," she said and then chuckled for my benefit. "He thinks that I think he oughta get out an' work." Smoke drifted lazily from the end of her hand-rolled cigarette and hung in the air until a sudden gust of wind blew it away.

"She gets tired a-lookin' at me day after day after day after day," said Charley, who tried to laugh it off. "I bet that's it."

"He thinks that," Rose mumbled.

"Well, it does. People ought to be away from each other at least oncet a year awhile. Man an' wife should. Body gets tired a-lookin' at one another year after year after year. . .

"I 'magine!" he added quickly. "Hit never bothers me much, though," he said in all honesty, for he pays little attention to what happens around him. "But it bothers her. I'm sure it does."

"I couldn't go away and stay an' work," protested Rose who struggles to care for three retarded children, a young son and daughter, and an infant girl.

"No, I never said that. I said it bothers you 'cause it — we — have to look at one another all the time. I said it never bothers me, but it does you. That's what I said," repeated Charley, growing a little threatening as he raised his voice for emphasis.

We were huddled very near one another because the porch was small and because we could scarcely hear ourselves above the noise the children were making inside the house. The breeze had died in infancy, the heat crept in again, and the air felt sticky and close.

I noticed perspiration trickling down Rose's neck like a small riverlet picking its way among the parched channels of what had once been rich and fertile ground. "You get tired of looking at Charley?" I asked her.

Rose laughed, rather sadly it seemed to me, and eyed her husband. "No, I don't get tired a-lookin' at 'im."

"I can go away and stay a night or two an' you're pretty well pleased t' see me come back." Charley's eyes struck mine. "When I went down to Lexington — stayed down there with Lester a few nights — she was pretty glad to see me come back," he boasted as he clapped a hand

Figure 52. The chairmaker Charley and his wife Rose and three youngest children in July, 1967. "He truly is an artist in his craft," said a customer; "he reminds me of a saint who gained sanctity by doing the common things uncommonly well."

on the arm of his chair. Lester is their third son who slipped on the ice and broke his hip the day before Christmas in 1966 and who now cannot walk at all. A bone in his leg deteriorated at the same time that his mind began to crumble.

"I guess that was the first time I'd stayed away from home in a long, long time," said Charley. His remark was like an echo from the distant past, for we all knew that Rose had twice run away from their stormy marriage, leaving some of her children behind in her haste and hiding from Charley for six months the second time.

Rose's temper broke. "I b'lieve he thought I art t' went up an' stayed wit' 'im but I didn't have no chancet to go an' stay wit' 'im; they wouldn't a let me kept the baby in thar," she snapped. "An' he had a better way t' go 'n I did." Her eyes flashed. "I wouldn't care to go down thar an' stayed wit' 'im if I'd knowed they could get 'im t' walk a-tall, but I don't see no chance t' it."

Charley was stunned for a moment. "Well," he said slowly, "I'm gonna hafta take 'im back if he don't start walkin' by July the tenth or whenever it is." He did not know the date because it was Rose's responsibility to care for the children, not Charley's. After a pause to recover his sense of indignation Charley turned on her sarcastically and accusingly: "Now, of course, if you don't want 'im to walk I won't . . ." In fact, Charley never took him, and Lester never did walk. Charley rigged a contraption to lift him off the ground to free his limbs but he had to beat the boy to get him into it and then Lester dangled helplessly, sobbing and flailing his arms and legs, for he could not understand what he was supposed to do; both of them finally settled for a wheelchair.

Rose tries to discern Charley's feelings and she is concerned about his welfare — although Charley often refuses to believe it — as evident in her comments about Lester's cripplement. "Jest like I say, Mike, hit'd be worth more to Check to git him t' walkin' than all that work out thar, wouldn't hit? Stay thar an' make chairs . . .," she said derisively. "You know, in just a few days, if he could get 'im t' walk, it'd mean a whole lot to 'im. It would Check and it would Lester."

To Rose, Charley is simply "nervous," which says everything and nothing at once, but she refused to elaborate on her diagnosis. "He jest gets excited. I'd jest rather not talk about hit. He wouldn't like me to talk about hit."

Charley apparently did not have the patience or understanding or compassion to help Lester overcome his fear of walking again, to encourage him to exercise his legs; and Lester's mental and physical state had degenerated to the point that he could not and would not help himself. Although six years younger than Donny he was already in a similar condition. Whatever it might have meant to Charley if Lester could have walked again, it was less important to him than his chairmaking.

Charley's responsibility is the making of chairs, and nothing must interfere. Why care for the children, tend a garden, saw firewood, fetch water, buy groceries, share experiences with his wife, or even spend time hunting raw materials? From Rose's point of view, Charley's seeming disregard of other duties proves that "Check, he always wants the easy way out." But to Charley his work impatiently awaits him, and his task in life — his goal, his reason for existence — is to create things and give his ideas to others who seem, unfortunately, not to accept or appreciate them. As he trudged through the streets of town one day I saw him mocked and aped and I felt the sting of barbs aimed at him. Sometimes it seems that chairmaking, instead of being his salvation, is really a cross for Charley to bear.

Charley has put much of the blame for their marital disharmony on Rose who has, he feels, neglected him, made fun of him, rejected him, and in all ways possible hurt him by her words and actions. One cause of his nervousness or irascibility, however, is other people and anything that might divorce him from the one thing he loves.

"I can't stand big, big crowds," said Charley; "at times I can put up with 'em pretty good, but times I feel like runnin' and hidin'." A crowd usually consists of one or more strangers. Several times when we were with other people whom Charley did not know his hands shook, his eyes looked frightened, and he coughed and shuffled his feet and circled about like a caged animal. Only when he was working on a chair did he seem to be at ease; only when he held a drawing knife in hand like a scepter was he in control of the situation.

Often he remarked, "Traffic just aggravates me to death," but since the early 1960s he has lived on a major highway exposed to strangers from the outside world. He is especially annoyed by people who stop at his house to stare or take pictures. "Some ask you to take a picture; some of 'em just steal it. They honk their horn and get ya t' run out, then bing! they snap a picture, and whoosh! off they go. Them people aggravate me t' death. Guess I won't get to do nothin' all summer."

Why live by the highway, then? Mainly because of Rose's demands. At first they lived in town, then Charley moved to a hollow for two or three years. Rose insisted they move to the highway, which they did, but after two years Charley could not take it any longer and moved to another hollow. When isolated Rose "don't git no chance to visit people," which she needs, so she ran off for a week to live in a shack near the highway until Charley agreed to move there permanently. Shortly afterward Charley grew a beard and discovered the basic technique with which he made several armchairs and settin' chairs with seven and eight legs. In the mid-1950s Charley's will prevailed and he and Rose moved back to a hollow for half a dozen years. Eventually Rose ran away for six months, but Charley finally tracked her down at the home of some relatives near Cumberland. Rose agreed to return. After one of the children was born when Rose was home alone on a snowy night, without even a midwife in attendance, she said that that was enough isolation. Rose forced Charley to move near the highway again in the early 1960s, after which he grew another beard and began building chairs with a strong sense of enclosure epitomized by the two-in-one rocking chairs.

Charley is the consummate artist. He can create a world of his own in which he is in total control — sometimes. Unfortunately, however, people and some of the forces in the world external to his own are not easily held in check. He reigns supreme over his old hand tools, which are rather an extension of himself. He has even employed such expressions as "controlled shaving" to describe the power he has in manipulating the drawing knife when working a piece of wood; and he is able to use a knife or an ax with such skill and precision that one is unaware that the pieces in a chair have not been sanded.

New objects seem to excite fear in Charley, however, perhaps because they conceal unknown dangers and maybe even a life principle of their own which cannot be dominated. For example, in the spring of 1967 Charley bought a garden plow to make gardening easier. Neither of us understood how the plow worked, Charley could not start it himself, and he had put the belt on improperly. We got the engine running but Charley did not exert enough pressure to hold the plow in the ground as the blades turned. When it started bucking in the air Charley dropped it and ran for the house. Eventually he had to pay a fourteen-year-old neighbor

Figure 53. Shaping an armrest, made on a jigsaw, with an ax to fit one's arm; the thin shavings indicate the craftsman's control.

Figure 54. Cutting a walnut plank from the lumber company on his new electric saw (bandaged fingers indicate earlier mishaps), Charley said: "Spect I'll cut my hand off one of these days."

boy to plow the garden with his machine.

Charley had used power woodworking tools briefly in the early 1940s, and in 1966 he spoke with enthusiasm about buying some equipment to make his work easier and to enable him to make cabinets, tables, and chests. In 1967, with an FHA loan, he was able to purchase a lathe, a drill press, a jigsaw, and other tools. But the scream of the saw terrorized him as much as the snorting, bucking plow. As he ran a board over the saw he screwed up his face, with tongue clamped in the corner of his mouth, while his shaking hands, propelled by rigid arms, pushed the plank into the blade. After a few minutes' work Charley's shirt was stained with perspiration. He tried to plane the board but it jumped out of his hands. Charley looked at the board and admitted that it had a "whole lot a humps and bumps. Take a whole lot a experience to cut without 'em. I'm nervous anyhow."

"Spect I'll cut my hand off one of these days," he muttered. One Sunday while he was sawing firewood with his electric saw, a small block of wood broke off the plank and shot upward at Charley's face. He threw his arms up and the block cracked a knuckle. Wild-eyed and trembling, Charley ran to the house, doused the wound in turpentine, and tried to wrap it in a rag, but he could not hold his hands still enough. While Rose bandaged the finger Charley rocked back and forth on his feet, moaning low in his throat.

Later in August Charley got his beard tangled in the drill press. The event so frightened him that he defied fate, risking his future as a chairmaker, and shaved. "I b'lieve I'm broke up now. I'll never get another order. I said I'd never get it shaved off." Indeed, his business steadily declined during the following two years. Charley was no longer sure it was wise to buy the electrical equipment; nor was Rose, who remarked about his nervousness when using the machinery. "I don't know what in the world is gonna happen if I die. I still have to pay for it," lamented Charley. "I never thought of that till too late." The equipment was a financial burden, Charley could not make chairs faster, the work did not seem easier than it had when he used the old equipment and techniques, and he had not been able to meet the challenge of control presented by the machines.

Charley had also tried unsuccessfully to impose his will on his wife Rose. A congenial environment for Charley is an isolated hollow where he is in control of his world, but Rose needs other people. In addition, Rose has social mobility aspirations manifested, among other ways, by her demand to reside near the highway or in town, which is more expensive and prestigious than living along a creek or on a ridge, by her rejection of Charley's furniture and her stipulation that their home be furnished with expensive factory products, and by her currying the favor of her oldest daughter Annie Mae and her son-in-law who, without children and with their fabulous annual income of $5,000 from coal mining, are free to socialize, go to movies, travel, and buy consumer goods at will. The daughter dresses rather grandly but Rose wears rags without even a bra or a slip, much to Charley's moral indignation. When Charley criticized her appearance Rose retorted, "I jest wear what people give me." Charley, seeing Rose's daughter as a threat to his own home, has taken steps to alienate her. He has enraged the woman and her husband in an effort to force them to leave; during one visit to his home Charley kept them awake by working on chairs in the house all night, and he accused Jim of theft, contended that Rose wanted to run off with Annie Mae, and alleged that Rose and her daughter committed the unforgivable crime of making fun of Charley behind his back and laughing at his appearance.

Charley desperately wants Rose to love him, but he also wants her to be subservient to him; he wants her to take care of the children by herself and do the mundane chores while Charley immerses himself in chairmaking. He, in turn, seldom extends love to others, at least not in the form of affection physically displayed. Sometimes he bought dresses for Rose and pop and candy for the kids, but often he was subject to violent displays of temper, hardly in proportion to the provocation, during which he struck out physically at the children and verbally assaulted Rose whom he accused of plotting to leave him saddled with their offspring or even of mistreating them, especially the retarded ones. In July, 1967, for example, Clifford had a muscle spasm in the neck which for several days Charley, without evidence, maintained was the result of Rose's having beaten him with a broom; I expressed my doubts and Rose vehemently denied the charge, so finally Charley attributed the spasm to Clifford's unfulfilled sexual desires. Whenever Charley talked with Rose the conversation soon developed into criticism of her and the things she did, such as her handling of the children, the meals she cooked, the way she dressed. Even Rose's last pregnancy was entirely her fault. Charley wanted their marriage to be a pleasant one but mainly on his terms, which included his dominance and the submission of others. Charley yearned to believe that his wife loved him, but doubt, causing him to challenge her feelings and demand that she convey her love verbally, disturbed his well-being. Frequently he expressed fear that Rose would leave him, which in fact she did.

Charley could not shape Rose, as he shaves and trims the planks of wood for his chairs, into the image he had for many years sustained. It was Rose who was to blame for their marital problems: she "has hert me so meney times," Charley wrote in 1969, and "is never goin to Chang her Way are hit semes to me that way." As far as he could discern Rose had no reason to leave him, despite a financial setback the last winter they were together: "Bisonis has Bin Bad this Winter But she had a nofe I no." If there was food on the table and a roof over her head, what more could Rose ask for, Charley seemed to be thinking. It may not have occurred to him, or perhaps he refused to believe, that his freedom to travel and to be among other people, culminating with trips to folk art fairs in several places, reinforced Rose's own feelings of deprivation and subservience.

Neither Charley nor Rose always understands the other person or is able to resolve satisfactorily the mutual antagonism that sometimes has arisen because of a conflict in aspirations, values and behavior. Rose likes the company of others, but Charley would prefer to hide in a hollow. "Check, he talks about Pine Mountain all the time. What he sees in that place I don't know; if he ever goes thar hit'll be by hisself, that's fer shore."

Charley is satisfied only when he is at work; he engages in chairmaking regardless of the absence of financial rewards or status, while Rose demands a few of the consumer goods and modern conveniences, which they cannot afford, available to other women. Charley's duties begin and end with his art, but Rose has to attend to the home and care for six children, several of whom are retarded. "Hit's jest like takin' care a three babies, an' Check, he don't do nothin' 'cept make chairs."

"Check, he always wants the easy way out," so he detaches himself from family and the world to devote himself to objectifying his images. But Rose has to handle all the domestic responsibilities, and "Whar thar's jest one to wait on 'em, boy hit keeps a body busy." And, "Hit's a job t' keep up with you fellas, I swear t' goodness it is; if hit ain't one a ya needs waitin' on, hit's the other'n." The only solution open to Rose, it seemed, was to leave Charley to his chairmaking while she went in search of a better life.

In a letter dated March 4, 1969, Charley informed us that a few months earlier Rose's aunt had visited the family and the two of them talked Charley into going with the aunt to a sawmill where the woman left him. She then took Rose and all the children. As Charley wrote, "they dinton Leve me very much this time, But a Brokin Hart and Wered mind   I Love my familey very Much But she has hert me so meney times   Cant take much More   she is never goin to Chang her Way are hit semes to me that way." Charley added: "I ame afraid she Will destroy thim kids   I cant do iney thing about hit   Bisonis has Bin Bad this Winter But she had a nofe I no and Every Body around noes that to Be True."

A few weeks later he wrote that "hit Shere lookes Bad for me   gess Will louse Every thing that I have in this Wourld for the Way I fele will not Be Able to make hit much longer   my head is in Bad Shape and Semes to Be getin Worse   Ame Getin Totry whin I get up in the Morning." In the first letter he had also mentioned a general malaise: "Have Bin sick and very Puney all this Winter   I ame all alone." As he said in the second letter, "there is no one But God to ask for help and am Shere he is With me all the time and makes me fele Betre to no that he goin to Stay With me   he has the Pour that no man one this Erth Haze are have I."

Charley then mentioned offhandedly having been at work on several rocking chairs which he would finish in the near future, and added: "thin I dont no Just hoap God Can Help me Some Way shere Wesh you were here hit Shere is Afful Lonely at times." Significantly, perhaps, he was writing to us on Easter morning. "Well to day is Ester Sunday and Shere is a Butiful day Clere and Brite Ame Sitin here trin to Rite this lettre." At that point he used a phrase from his song and reiterated his hope that he was being looked after. "Shere hoape this lettre Reches you all Happey and Well as for me Just lonely and Lonsom But Hopin that tomarow Will be a Betre day and a happey day are What Every God wats for me to have good or the same Will say so long for now   your frind."

Most of the stages in the process of grieving over a loss are apparent in the letters. There is a feeling of shock at the event that has occurred and the gradual comprehension of the loss over a period of time, followed by an emotional release when the depth of the loss is fully realized. Charley sought an explanation of the loss first in respect to himself and his possible contribution, but he finally concluded, as one usually does, that it was not his fault, that even his financial failure was not the cause; it was Rose's wantonness, and it was she to whom he directed his hostility and resentment. There is mention of physical distress, generated by emotional anxiety. Panic is obvious in predictions that Rose would destroy the children and that he would lose everything in the world. Nostalgia for the past is apparent in wishing that we were there and in his opening line in the first letter: "ame thinkin About you all to nite   Were goin thrue some ole lettres of last yere." Finally there is an apathetic return to life at the end of the second letter. Usually, of course, that stage would be followed by a successful readjustment to the loss and a reaffirmation of reality, a stage that Charley has come close to reaching each time. But has he always attained it?

Half a year after Rose left, Charley went into hibernation; he stayed in bed day and night for several months, getting up briefly twice a day to relieve himself and to eat from one of the cans of pork and beans with which he had stocked the cupboards. His only companion was a stray cat. He had built himself a raft on the polluted water near his house, furnishing it with sofa, stove, refrigerator, and tools, for he contemplated floating down Stinkin' Creek dumping his problems behind him like so many tin cans as he neared Pine Mountain. He hesitated, however, because he hoped Rose might return or perhaps we would arrive. While he was wrapped up in his dreams one night a tornado struck, picking up Charley's workshop and smashing it down in anger upon the little raft, which sank. Trembling, Charley called some relatives in the Midwest to come for him immediately.

Now he claims that these same relatives have turned against him, leaving him vulnerable once again. He keeps correspondence to a minimum and refuses to accept mail orders for fear "they"— those who are "after him"— will discover his address; the few chairs he makes are priced many times higher than in earlier years, and these the customer must pick up himself. From childhood Charley has had difficulty relating to other people; he fears those inanimate objects that refuse to be held at bay; he worries about the future of his children now that they are not underfoot; and he is concerned that his own health is failing or that he may be injured. Because "there's too much meanness in the world not to have a gun," Charley used to cradle a loaded revolver in a box under his bed at night, then lock it in a suitcase during the day only to put it back under the bed again each evening; according to a recent report from a friend of mine, he still does. Apparently nobody loves Charley, from his first cousin pregnant by another man to his first wife with her slanderous remarks to Rose who has "hert me so meney times." Even his mother, no longer alive, whose hard edges have softened in Charley's memory, had bounced her boys from one relative to another.

When we took him back to Pine Mountain in 1966 we could not find the graves of his mother and her father. But Charley located the spot where the house had been and found the oak tree that was a sapling near the cabin door when he left a quarter of a century before. It stood proud and high, deeply rooted in the soil. Charley tried to put his arms around the tree but it had grown much too large for that. So he scratched a toehold in the ground at the base of the trunk and tucked his arms next to his sides with thumbs crooked under the straps of his new overalls. The sun splattered bits of light through the leaves, dappling Charley's face and shoulders as he stood like a sentinel on his mountain next to his tree. It was almost perfectly still, except for a rooster crowing on a hilltop a mile away. Charley felt the freshness of the air about him; he saw the highway far below where tiny people inched along in little cars; he heard voices faintly in the distance. He sank slowly and deeply into quiet reflection, his eyes glazing over as his attention turned inward to the only world that really mattered, the realm of images and ideas. A fly buzzed nearby. Charley paid it no heed until it touched him, its incessant nagging finally bringing him back to the present. We wanted to go. Charley left reluctantly but the sky was graying; a cloud of fog had rolled in, filling up the space below the mountain; and we had a long way to travel that day to return home to Charley's family whom we had left behind in a valley far away.

In his song and in his dreams Charley is thrust into an imaginary hollow on top of the tallest mountain in Kentucky, where he is surrounded by the familiar, and controllable, things of childhood: objects that he has recreated in his mind as he would have to reconstruct them in reality, since most of the tangible things in his youth — including his first chairs and the log cabin he built for his mother — have been destroyed. But if he cannot escape physically to Pine Mountain or into the blurred past, then Charley can for a few moments retreat into his fantasies or, as a way of dealing with the present, into the comforting enclosed space of his two-in-one rocking chairs that "hug you." More constructively, he can rebuild himself as he creates strange chairs challenging his skill and his identity.

After his wife left him for the third time Charley was shocked into realizing that once again he was engaged in a battle in which he was "lonely and lonesome," with no one at his side to help him through the conflicts of life or to guard the flanks and protect him from unseen enemies. Only with God's assistance, Charley said, might he be able to adjust to this most recent catastrophe, though Charley told me several times that he has never been devout (maybe God caused the oak tree to grow but Charley had planted the seed). Charley's appeal to the Supreme Being was weak, the plea of a man who was temporarily desperate, perhaps, but not of a man who could give himself up to someone else or relinquish all control to another power. Charley is himself a creator and a wielder of authority. As some people have said in print and in person, Charley is the "king of the chairmakers" and Charley knows it; he has known it for years, and he has said as much in the chairs he has built, but until recently few would listen to his message.

Charley still holds his raw materials in a gentle embrace as he shapes them, once again using hand tools which are extensions of himself and with which he caresses his loved ones. He can express his feelings and emotions in the things he makes, but he seldom displays affection for people or for those things in the world which seem beyond his control and inferior in importance to his immediate concerns; the more strongly he attempted to dominate the objects in his environment, the more enslaved he became to them. Freedom was withdrawal. The day would come, however, as he mistakenly thought it had on several occasions in the past, when Charley might step forth in the world of men bathed in the glory of his brilliant creations.[3] With his wife gone again for the third and apparently the last time, Charley now has only himself and his work, with nothing to divorce the two. And of course he has memories of suffering which link him to Jesus, as manifested in letters and in his sculpture in wood of the tormented Christ upon the cross which Charley erected in front of his house. Beneath this figure of the bearded Son of God, blood dripping from the crown of thorns, is a plaque with an inscription warning of the Savior's return as He descends from a cloud high above man.

While Charley's unique personal qualities have been instrumental in the creation of some remarkable objects, they have also led him into situations he could scarcely handle. It is perhaps unfortunate that a man so sensitive to images, ideas, and the intrinsic qualities of raw materials has been so aloof from other human beings and so indifferent to their feelings. But if he were a different man, his chairs, too, would be of some other kind.[4]

There remains, then, only the task of examining his chairmaking in more detail and noting some of the forces that gave shape to it, and perhaps of considering whether the bookcase masterpiece came too early or whether it came too late.

CHAPTER FOUR

Make It Look Older, More Antique

"The backs don't look flared," said Charley about two chairs made by Aaron (figures 48,50).

It was a hot afternoon in August, 1967, and Charley was sitting in the shade of his porch, taking a break from work in order to plan his next step in manufacture of a chair. I interrupted his thoughts by handing him a stack of photographs of chairs I wanted him to examine. His task was to group the chairs according to the individuals who made them on the basis of the photographs alone, as I never told him who the craftsmen were, and to evaluate them, discussing whatever points he found significant; he tackled the job with considerable interest and skill.[1]

Eventually Charley singled out two rocking chairs by Aaron, one made in 1962 and the other only a few weeks before our conversation. Charley criticized the earlier chair extensively and then compared the two, noting that the "backs don't look flared," a feature that disturbed him because he usually bent the back posts of chairs outward and backward to increase the comfort and improve the appearance.

"Only thing I think is better lookin' twixt them two chairs is the backs," continued Charley. "The slats make it look older, more antique, more like a rockin' chair oughta look." It was the more recent of Aaron's works which had a slat back, whereas earlier rockers were vertical or panel back like some of Charley's earliest (and latest) chairs.

After a brief pause Charley complained again about the legs in the back. "I don't like the posts straight like that," he said.

A major characteristic in some of Charley's works in the middle 1950s and especially the 1960s is the use of features he conceived to be "antique." Even his body image harks back to an earlier age, as do some chairs to which he gave such names as the "old timer" (figure 55) and the "Li'l Abner" or "George Washington" chair (similar to figure 56), and his comments about other men's works often dwelt on whether or not the objects exhibited an old-fashioned appearance. In chapter 3 I suggest that sometimes Charley has been nostalgic about the past, and that this identification with an earlier time is expressed in several modes of behavior including conversations, letters, and the song "My Old Kentucky Mountain Home." It is apparent in many chairs, too.

But other qualities are also evident in Charley's furniture. This chapter might well have been entitled "The Unique and the Antique," because certain traits peculiar to his chairs from the beginning made it possible ultimately to express a sense of both enclosure and antiquity, and the very elements Charley designated "antique" are in fact unique to him and his works.

At this juncture an admonition is in order. "It is of course impossible to define any style of art since it is of its nature without fixed limits or precision," wrote Ruth Bunzel more than thirty-five years ago. Her remarks are certainly true in Charley's case, but they have been disregarded by many researchers who try to fix the

Figure 55. Charley's only "old timer" (early 1963; photo by Charley). The seat is twenty-four inches from the floor so that an arthritic woman could more easily sit down, but she died before Charley could sell her the chair. "That was the most beautiful chair," said Charley, "I mean for a reg'lar rockin' chair, I ever made." Because of the high seat and the footrest, which extends from below the seat, the chair "made you set away up high like a King or some 'un."

Figure 56. One of half a dozen chairs made by Charley (late 1965 or early 1966) under extreme pressure (photo by Charley). The simplified designs and techniques of construction were necessary for speed; Charley used designs for more simple chairs he had made earlier in his career. The chair shows the influence of the Li'l Abner comic strip.

limits of an artist's "style"(a collective term like "group" or "culture" or "personality," whose use seems to force one into fixing limits) and establish precise boundaries of periods of productivity. "It is equally unrewarding," she added, "to describe individual works of art, the essence of which is untranslatable." [2]

It seems to me, however, that one can mention certain tendencies at particular times in an artist's career and explore how they relate to his needs and values and to his relationships with other people, including customers. Space limitations prohibit the inclusion of all information about works of Charley's (or those by other men) which were located and photographed, or all the data concerning the circumstances of their manufacture and use; such a situation is regrettable, for it is conducive to excluding objects that simply do not fit neatly into the patterns the investigator thinks he has perceived. Because I do not subscribe wholly to a theory of evolution in art as an explanation of the traits of objects, however, I shall not limit discussion to the qualities of enclosure and antiquity in Charley's works or suggest greater regularity than actually obtains in this man's productive career. The results may be somewhat confusing, as seemingly there are contradictions in the artist's remarks and behavior; discussion cannot follow a simple chronological scheme, and multiple traits must be examined. Thus a review of the same chairs at different times from dissimilar perspectives is necessary; only in this way can we actually gain an understanding of this man and his works.

"A theory of style adequate to the psychological and historical problems has still to be created," contended Meyer Schapiro more than twenty years ago. "It waits for a deeper knowledge of the principles of form construction and expression and for a unified theory of the processes of social life in which the practical means of life as well as emotional behavior are comprised."[3] There is still no adequate theory of style, and the reader should not expect to find one articulated in this chapter, although it is hoped that the book itself will contribute to the generation of a method that will help account for the nature of the object produced.

What I want to make clear in these two chapters is that individual style is anything but clear. The analysis of objects and behavior, is, as Bunzel implies, far more complicated than might be assumed from an examination of some art historical literature, where individual or group styles are neatly lumped into periods that are alleged to have evolved from and to lead to other periods (again, the use of the term "style" seems to encourage the propensity to fix limits). Such an evolutionary model has been employed in another major study of an individual in which a Yoruba potter's works are compartmentalized into four periods, each conceived of as "a unit of development." This method was used in order "to restore the art of Abatan to the flow of development" which presumably could be accomplished by considering "the traits that distinguish one period from another."[4]

This procedure in art historical research is to be avoided for several reasons. Its practitioners tend to assume by necessity that later works will be superior to earlier ones, but this assumption is often invalid owing to senility, emotional paralysis, inadequate talent or interest by the producer, or the influence of faulty consumer standards; this truth is tacitly admitted by the researcher who writes that "neoclassicism is possible at any time," meaning simply that in regard to any particular object made at any time in his career, rather than at the end of it, the producer has satisfactorily solved the problem at hand and has achieved perfection of form and design. In addition, this method of analysis is dubious because proponents assume "stylistic succession" when in fact there are irregularities caused by personal problems or consumer influence; these irregularities are accounted for within the evolutionary model as "transitional works linking Periods I and II," which is itself an admission that periodicity is an artificiality only vaguely corresponding to an individual's productivity; it also indicates that using the term "style" requires establishing boundaries where behavior is really fluid. Furthermore, researchers engaged in such a "developmental analysis" claim predictability, which actually occurs only with hindsight during a present review of past production, as in the claim that the "siting of hatching predicts the future: later, in the art of Abatan, these same areas are embellished with impression." Characteristics of objects that do not fit the evolutionary model are dismissed as inexplicable, but the model itself is not questioned: "It is clear, first of all, that aesthetic choice is unpredictable and that an old style may reappear without warning at any time." [5] Or even worse, in some of the literature the objects and their producers are explained away as mutants or misfits, rather than as a next and necessary step in the evolution of the tradition, until long after the objects have been produced, at which time they are then conceived of as having been part of the regular and smooth flow of past events.

"The dangers inherent in the construction of style-evolutionary theories are obvious," writes Ralph Altman in criticism of methods suggested by one researcher for studying what she terms ethnological art. Altman goes on to say that the "question whether a given object belongs 'to the beginning, the climax, or the end of the development of a particular style' seems to imply the assumption of periodicity and may lead to the construction of evolutionist sequences. I do not understand what artistic merit has to do with that." Altman also complains that "Ideas of unilinear or cyclical evolution belong to this category [of obsolete tools and obstacles to research], since they keep us from evaluating, for example, the effect on art of the individuality of the artist and of a multiplicity of external forces or pressures." [6]

An individual's skill may develop, certainly, and the solution to one problem may require refinements or may suggest to him another, related problem for further treatment; but this is development in a psychological sense and does not imply evolution in art analogous to biological adaptation and survival. We do the producer a disservice if we imply that his behavior was guided by a preordained plan. The explanation of the many traits in objects, then, is more difficult than usually imagined because of the fluidity and elusiveness of these qualities from one object to another, and because of the many factors other than an antecedent work which influenced the producer and the act of production. We are fortunate indeed if we can discern general tendencies in an individual's productive career; although some of these directions may be more evident than others at particular times, periods cannot be fixed because works evincing other qualities are produced virtually simultaneously, as in Charley's case.

In Charley's remarks quoted at the beginning of this chapter the emphasis was in fact not on antiquity — though his concern for old-fashionedness marked much of his expressive behavior when I was with him — but on flaring the posts outward and backward which is not directly related to a propensity for making things "look older, more antique," or to a sense of enclosure corresponding to a desire to isolate himself from others. The dramatic quality of flaring his chair posts outward and backward, however, is sometimes (either at the time of manufacture or later when reminiscing about the chairs, or both) an expression of aggressive self-certainty as a chairmaker, which made possible the manifestation of other, rather undramatic qualities at different times in his work. In a few chairs the dramatic and forceful qualities of large size and bold curvature are also a reflection of Charley's desire or need to build his own world and the things in it, and paradoxically, as we shall see in chapter 5, the qualities of enclosure and old-fashionedness made possible the creation of large, forceful forms. In addition, however, the curving of posts outward and backward is often indicative of Charley's desire simply to make comfortable chairs, and it is not really a dramatic gesture; furthermore, the small, simply made, cheap chairs are just as indicative of his skills as are the massive forms. It is Charley's many interests and unique skills as a craftsman with which we must begin if the nature of his chairs is to be understood.

"When I was about the size of Al," said Charley in reference to his youngest boy, "I was makin' chairs outa cornstalks. I made little horses and I made little people. Used to make little dolls outa rags and use empty shotgun shells for boots." Somewhat to Charley's chagrin, his four-year-old son was not interested in doing any of these things.

I asked Charley why he had become a chairmaker.

"Well, I don't know. When I was a boy big enough to make anything I was always makin' somethin' or other outa cornstalks—little log cabins: I built 'em outa cornstalks—things like that that I couldn't . . ." He never finished his sentence but said, "I guess I just inherited it from other ancestors. They was all makin' chairs by hand, makin' ever'thing by hand them days; they even made the shoes they wear by hand. Just about ever'thing they made it, couldn't buy 'em them days, you know."

Charley's maternal uncle Oaklie and Oaklie's father Hat made chairs, as did Charley's paternal grandfather Pike and Pike's brother Hiram. But Charley was different from his ancestors. Pike made only a few chairs, mainly for his own use, and the other men worked rapidly, lacking the patience to "shape 'em out by hand" the way Charley does, because making chairs meant making money. Economic incentives have been important to Charley, too, as we shall see in chapter 5, but his primary concern has been that of fulfilling to the best of his ability the requirements of useful design, especially those of access and appearance. As a result many of Charley's chairs have an organic quality and an aggressiveness suggesting power, strength, and self-assurance as a craftsman.

"Them days they made 'em awful small," complained Charley about the chairs of his kin in the past. "They jest barely made 'em big enough you could set in 'em; then you'd be settin' partly on the rounds. And the rockin' chair was almost completely square all the way around. The back and the front was about equally the same size them days. The rockin' chairs they made in them days you couldn't rest in one hardly—they didn't space their backs in 'em, they didn't put the right bend in 'em to rest your back."

Typical of his grandfather Hat's work, for example, is a settin' chair of maple and locust made on a foot-powered turning lathe about 1925 (figure 57). Hat's chair is small; stiles are present but ambiguous in nature; there is little curve to the slats and none to the posts; and there are no shoulders on the ends of the stretchers. Such traits indicate speed in production with only minimal attention to considerations of practical use. In

Figure 57. Settin' chair made by Charley's grandfather Hat (c. 1925) was sold for $1, but Charley bought it back in August, 1966, for $5. Said Hat's son Oaklie, "Buddy, when he threw one together, hit was together." Charley commented, "They weren't comfortable, but. . . it'd be good an' stout. They didn't make for the beauty part, they made for the lastin' part."

Figure 58. This early settin' chair, which Charley made about 1935, was whittled with a pocket knife. From early in his career Charley's tendency has been toward a broader, more comfortable chair with back posts flared outward and backward, and toward more sharply defined stiles. Charley's works are unmistakable.

appearance the chair is a closed form, its simple rectangles suggesting stasis rather than tension or movement.

In contrast, one of Charley's earliest settin' chairs, whittled from white oak and locust about 1935 (figure 58), is larger, has curved slats and back posts that are bent backward and out, exhibits sharply defined stiles, possesses a total of twelve rounds instead of the eleven common in the works of other chairmakers, and is more dynamic visually. There is a sense of wholeness about the chair (if one mentally restores the top slat which was broken sometime in thirty years of hard use). Continuity is emphasized and there is centrality

Figure 59. This baby rocker made by Charley's grandfather Hat (c. 1907) was rebottomed by Charley's uncle Oaklie in 1966. The woman who owns the chair said she "wouldn't take fifty dollars for that chair 'cause it was made by Hat."

of movement, an energetic thrust in the curving biomorphic lines. Most of Charley's chairs seem to grow upward from the ground, like organic forms boldly pushing outward into space, in an emphatic declaration of presence.

Charley attributed the shortcomings of his ancestors' chairs to inadequate financial remuneration. "They had ways a bendin' em, you see, same as I do. They, uh, but most of the sales they'd get 'cause they'd be straight an' they'd sell 'em cheaper. An' the bent chair that was curved in the back postees [of which I never found an example], they'd be more espensives, they'd charge more for them."

"Them days they didn't get over two to five dollars apiece for a settin' chair," Charley concluded. "An' maybe three to six dollars for a big rockin' chair," though none of his ancestors ever made big rocking chairs as Charley would do. "They couldn't get more for a rockin' chair or a settin' chair them days like they can these days."

What Charley did not note was that he received about the same amount of money for his chairs, too, until the 1960s. Although there is the implication that Charley's kin could have made chairs of higher quality, greater comfort, and more attractive appearance if they had been able to obtain higher prices for them, it is more probable that they were limited to customers unable or unwilling to pay more than a few dollars for a chair and that they were primarily interested in economic gain rather than in the pleasure of making things. Charley was somewhat different and so were his chairs.

"The chairs that I make is completely differ'nt, all the way round, than what they used to make," he said. "I can put in the wide bark, or the nar' stuff or the real nar' stuff. They had one reg'lar size they'd make." His kin, he said, "would never fool with makin' a little bitty nar' chair," that is, a chair whose seat consisted of very narrow hickory bark splints. For Charley, however, a bottom of narrow bark in a chair "really makes it comf'table to set in and it really makes it purtier." And these two qualities—comfort and beauty—have been of most importance to Charley, consciously in chairmaking, although he does not like some of his own chairs because they are neither comfortable nor attractive.

"Chairs they made them days," said Charley, "the back postees—I call 'em—they come straight up, an' they tapered off and get really small up at the top, an' nine times outa ten they turn on the turnin' lay a little knob up thar on top." An example is a chair made by Charley's great-uncle Hiram about 1905–1910 (figure 60), whose seat and rockers Charley repaired in 1967; it has barrel arms, a few turnings nicely placed on the arms and on the front posts above the seat, and small, rounded finials at the top.

Several of Charley's earliest rockers are interesting by comparison. The oldest chair of Charley's which he and I could locate, built in the early 1930s (figure 61), was a panel-back rocker made of square pieces; spokes under the arms were employed in the 1960s on his two-in-one

Figure 60. Rocker made by
Charley's great-uncle Hiram
(c. 1905-1910); the rockers
and the seat were restored
by Charley. Other chairmakers
liked the chair but agreed
that the "bark's too wide for
the chair."

Figure 61. The rocker on the
porch, one of Charley's first
rocking chairs, was made in
the early 1930s; Charley said
the spokes under the arms
were not used again until he
made his two-in-one rocker
thirty years later, but other
design elements were used
continuously.

rocking chairs, and he made other chairs with square posts, as in 1963 (figure 62), because they are easily and cheaply made and are readily sold at a low price (and hence do not fall into periods).

"Why was the first chair made with square posts?" I asked Charley.

"Easier to make thataway. You got a take more time to make it to eight square, you see, an' I guess it just come easy to make it thataway."

"The first chair I ever made was completely foursquare—the postees," he continued. "Course the back wasn't slat back, they was panel back: two crosspieces and then one big center piece in the back and two little nar' pieces on each side next to the post was the first chair I ever act'lly made by myself." His first rocker, then, did not look "antique."

"Did your uncle make one like it, too?"

"No, no, I just thought that up my own self a-makin' that. You take a square post thataway, an' put slats in it — called a 'slat back' you know — hit don't look right a-tall to make the back look

Figure 62. A panel-bottom and panel-back chair made (c. 1963) by Charley. It is a "cheap chair" made with nails, a type Charley frequently built because he could sell it more easily.

like that. To make it look right, for a foursquare post, you got to have a panel back, you got to have two crosspieces an' one big piece in the center an' two nar's on the side of hit."

"Were the pieces bent?"

"The two crosspieces were bent; if they wasn't bent they was carved out to fit your back the way I made 'em."

On Hiram's chair, however, the slats are just barely bent and the posts not at all.

"Were the posts on your chair bent, too?"

"Yes sir, I bent the back postees down 'twixt the seat an' the back of hit. The postees was gen'lly hewed out in a crook or bent, but I always bent 'em 'twixt the seat an' the first crosspiece in the back. That's where I bent 'em at or carved hit out to fit 'em."

"When did you change the design to the slat-back chair?" I asked, revealing my own mistaken notion that different qualities of an individual's works fit neatly into specific time spans; I did not know then that Charley continued to make panel-back chairs as well as slat-back ones (and, rarely, bark-back rocking chairs).

Charley never answered directly because the question was not mean-ingful to him, but he reminded me that "in the chairmakin' business you make all kinds of different chairs an' different types of backs," as he did throughout his career rather than during certain periods. Then he repeated some of his own principles of composition and construction which he sometimes violated, as in the last rocking chair he made before being drafted in 1942 (figure 63). This white oak rocker has barrel arms like Hiram's chair and has neither bent posts nor curved slats despite Charley's

Figure 63. The last chair Charley made before being drafted in 1942 was of white oak with turnings only on the front rounds or stretchers; the design is a bit daring for chairmaking in southeastern Kentucky

contention that he always bent or carved both; the seat is bigger than in Hiram's chair; the armrests are placed higher, which is typical of Charley's work; there are more slats than are usually found on chairs made by other men, which again is common in Charley's creations; and close attention is paid to the decorative quality of the chair, especially in the front, the position from which it is usually viewed.

A panel-back rocker that Charley made about 1935 and sold for $2.50 corresponds more closely to the technical and compositional principles he stated, and it evinces a feeling common to his works despite later changes in form (figure 64). The posts and panels are indeed bent, the seat is roomy, and there is evidence at this early date of originality in construction and design. The chair is, in Charley's words, "a mixed-up proposition," as it consists of maple panels, four-sided back posts, turned oak front posts with extensive ornamentation, hickory rounds, and hickory bark seat. He claims he did not have enough materials on

hand to make the chair of one wood or one design, but he proceeded anyway, as no other chairmaker would have done; in fact, Hascal identified the chair as Charley's because of its unique composition and construction. The only

Figure 64. A panel-back rocker (c. 1935) consists of maple panels, ash back posts, oak front posts, hickory rounds, and hickory bark seats. "A mixed-up proposition," said Charley who made it.

118

criticism came from Charley himself:
he thought the bottom stretchers
were too close to the rockers (as
in Hiram's chair).

Charley made many other
chairs in the next thirty years,
all of them possessing a quality
peculiar to him which few people
have been able to articulate: a
propensity for the unusual and an
adeptness at chairmaking are
the tendencies suggested most
often. Perhaps the epitome of
the traits most often found in
Charley's works is a rocking chair
(with matching love seat) of mulberry with hickory pegs, made
about 1954 or 1955 (figure 65).
Charley used only an ax and a
hatchet to make the chair; he
did not turn pieces on a lathe
or even shape them with a
drawing knife. Only the two
slats at the top of the chair have

Figure 65. Charley's favorite chair (c. 1954 or 1955), made with an ax and a hatchet. Owing to narrowness at the back, it does not tip over backward. Pegs, arms, outward curve of front posts, and outward and backward flare of back posts are typical chair traits Charley manifested throughout his career.

been pegged, as the arms go through the posts at each end of the bottom
slat; the arms are rather thin and have been pegged from the top in
order to hold the ends securely in place on the front posts, both of which
traits characterized many but not all of Charley's rocking chairs until
about 1965.

Tackett, the chair's owner, said: "It's got great balance and it just
fits your back perfect; been in use here about ten years." The chair "sets
good," he said, and he was impressed by the fact that it would not tip
over backward because the rockers are extremely close together in back

with only four inches of space separating them. "Now that man ain't foolish," said Tackett; "I don't know how much education he's got, but he sure can work with wood."

The chairmaker Verge remarked, "That looks like a comf'table chair to set in an' I like the looks of it. It don't have no rings." His son Hascal disagreed: "I wouldn't make one or have one like it. I don't like them square posts or bent posts," which Charley prefers to turned pieces. Beechum told me he likes "that rocker but the arms are a little high," a trait typical of most of Charley's work. It was also Beechum who identified the chair as Charley's, citing several elements common in his chairs.

"I think Charley made that rocker," said Beechum: "Way the posts is bent, an' it's wide in the front and nar' at the back; way he's got them pegs in there, and all them rounds, and the posts and rounds has got eight sides." And that characterization suggests the essence of Charley's works, which is why this chair appealed to Charley.

In August, 1966, I asked Charley what his favorite rocking chair was.

"My favorite chair in a rocking chair would be — the one I like best — I don't know just which one it was. But it's not the one I've got now, an' it's not the one I made the mayor. I b'lieve that the chair that I like besten myself is the one you looked at, took pictures of at Fred Tackett's."

"Why do you like it the best?"

"I like the shape of it, the way it's made. It's my favorite chair of any of the rest of 'em."

"Do you think it's better made than the rest of them?"

"No, no, it ain't no better, but I just like the design of it. I like the shape of it, the design. It's no better than the others but I like the design of it."

By "design" Charley meant not merely appearance but fitness for practical use, too. In 1955 he made four sassafras settin' chairs which he sold for $3 each to a man who owns a nearby grocery store (figure 66); Calvin Manning kept one which his wife, now dead, varnished and

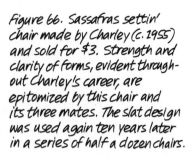

*Figure 66. Sassafras settin'
chair made by Charley (c. 1955)
and sold for $3. Strength and
clarity of forms, evident throughout Charley's career, are
epitomized by this chair and
its three mates. The slat design
was used again ten years later
in a series of half a dozen chairs.*

left in the bedroom of
their home beneath the
store. (After I photo-
graphed and tried to buy
the chair in 1966, however,
Manning left it outside in
front of the store appar-
ently for passersby to see.)
The chair is unmistakably
Charley's work: the
attention to details such
as shaping the feet so
they would not puncture a linoleum floor and "notching" the slats at the
ends to produce a striking decorative effect; the use of a large peg at
each end of the slats; and the propensity to bend the back posts both
backward and outward at a rather exaggerated angle. Charley told me in
1965 that "that's a beautiful chair there," but it is also a technical failure,
for the seat is too high and the posts are not flared outward far enough
to provide the comfort he feels is required in a settin' chair.

"Why would it not be good as a settin' chair?"

"The way it's curved and the way it's bent an' ever'thing."

"It wouldn't be comfortable as a settin' chair?"

"Huh-uh, it wouldn't be comf'table as a settin' chair. Cause a settin'
chair, you're gonna do a whole lot a settin' in it. An' it takes a real comf'-
table back in hit. Course a dinin' chair, you don't set in them too much."

Hascal was dissatisfied with the chair, too. "The slats are too high,"

he said. "There's too much space between the seat and the bottom slat.
It's got pretty slats and pegs. If it had one more slat at the bottom it'd
been perfect. It's a neat-lookin' chair all right. It has that extry round
but that's nothin' to criticize a chair over—it don't hurt no more than
it helps."

Ordinarily chairmakers put two, not three, stretchers in the back
of a chair—the seat round and the bottom stretcher. Only Charley, from
the beginning of his career, insisted on including a middle round in back
which he contended added strength to the chair, although Hascal disagreed. The problem of structural soundness is probably a moot question.
The visual effect of the 'extry round,' however, is to render the chair
more "complete" in appearance, more "whole" as it were, which is obviously important to Charley who did not simply make chairs but built
a separate reality for himself, a total world in which he felt comfortable.
He often photographed himself sitting peacefully in one of his chairs
(including the bookcase masterpiece); his interest in the creative act
seemed to wane until the job was nearing completion, and "then I
can't hardly quit till I find the balance on a chair;" he would spend
hours looking at the completed object, touching the slats and arms and
stroking the finials and stretchers to feel the smoothness of the wood
beneath his hands, and sitting in the chair before the splints dried so
the seat would have proper "swag," as he called it, and thus would be
comfortable.

During the latter part of the 1950s and at times in the 1960s
Charley produced many other settin' and rocking chairs as well as
counter stools which visually exhibited this same strength of character,
clarity, and economy of line, but he tried other designs and techniques
of production, too, gaining somewhat different effects. I never liked
Charley greatly, perhaps because certain aspects of his behavior reminded me of some traits in myself that I prefer to ignore, and I was
disturbed by some things that occurred during my research and by the
relationship between us. I was, however, strongly impressed by Charley's
artistry. What fascinated me most, I suppose, was that for Charley the

manufacture of each chair posed problems whose solution completely absorbed his attention; this quality, rather than periodicity, is essential to an understanding of the things he made.

Often the dilemmas were self-generated. It was not enough for Charley to find a pleasing design for the feet of his chairs and employ it regularly (figure 21). No, he made the feet large so they would not poke holes in linoleum rugs, but then he thought he should spend a lot of time shaping them by hand so as to reduce their visual bulk; this self-imposed task required more labor than desirable, given the lack of adequate financial reward. Then he made the feet even more pointed than previously, which involved more work than simply leaving them straight; the pointed feet did produce a strong visual impact but also took a toll on linoleum floors. The same observation could be made with regard to the finials on rocking chairs. "I turned 'em on a turnin' lay all kinda differ'nt shapes, an' after I've turned 'em on the turnin' lay I have done some carvin' on them to make 'em look more like an <u>antique</u> or someun or other on the ends of 'em — do a little hand carvin' up on 'em."

A settin' chair Charley made about 1960 with wide feet is unusual in that he incised the front posts with cross-hatching, using a saw. The back posts are plain. Why? Charley just wanted to decorate the chair, justifying the decision to himself by saying that he might be able to get more money for it, but after two days' effort incising the front posts he quit; he did not receive a higher price anyway.

Another settin' chair made about 1961, to which Charley referred several times as "one of my most interestin' chairs," had square posts, very wide slats, thick feet, and diamond-shaped pegs prominently displayed. I never saw the chair because the man who had bought it sold it to a tourist several years before I came to the area.

"I b'lieve that settin' chair is the most beautiful settin' chair I ever made," Charley said.

"Why did you make it?" I asked him.

"I jest took a notion to make the pegs like that to see what it'd look like."

Figure 67. Swamp "willer" rocker (c. 1960) Charley made in emulation of factory-made chairs. It squeaks during the winter when it is dry, so in the spring the owner hoses it down with water and lets it soak overnight.

Other chairs, too can be appreciated as the result of Charley's having taken a notion to make them in a certain way just to see what they would look like. During the early 1960s Charley cleared some "swamp willers" from the creek near his home, thinking he might be able to make a chair from them based on the design of a factory-made chair he had seen earlier in the home of a customer (figure 67). The form is different from that of other chairs Charley made at the time, evidence that periodicity is not a very useful construct for categorizing his chairs, although the chair does exhibit the unmistakable essence of Charley's works. He is not entirely pleased with the product owing to the technique of construction; Charley dislikes chairs that are loose at the joints and squeak, which distracts the sitter, chairs that "have what I call the rickets, and cry." Because the willows were nailed in place, and because the owner keeps the chair in his living room near a large floor vent, the chair dries out during the winter; each spring, however, the owner sets the chair on his lawn, hoses it down with water, and lets it soak overnight so that it does not squeak until the following winter.

Of all the chairmakers I met Charley had the greatest respect for his raw materials: they are not alien objects to be gouged and chiseled until "by God" they looked like pieces of a chair. Charley carefully shaped the posts and rounds with his drawing knife, removing tissue-thin strips as he followed the grain of the wood and working around the knots in order to preserve the integrity of the material. This procedure is particularly apparent in a sassafras "high chair" used as a counter stool in a tavern, which Charley made about 1961; there are slight irregularities in the surface of component elements, such as the lowest stretcher in front (figure 68). This chair is also the earliest one I know of whose front posts as well as back legs are flared outward, which was done for two reasons: to improve the chair's appearance and to facilitate access. Sometimes Charley flared the front posts at the bottom, as well, in order to "make your espensive chair look a leetle bit better." On other chairs made earlier, later, and at the same time Charley inserted the arms below the stiles, but on this stool the armrests are affixed to the stiles. There is no evidence of steady progression and development, for the placement of the arms depends on the nature of the chair and the height of the back. The back of the counter stool is low, but the arms must be rather high if they are to function properly; Charley liked the stiles which are attractive and also add to the comfort of certain kinds of chairs, but if the stiles

Figure 68. One of Charley's sassafras "high chairs" (c. 1961), used as a barstool in a tavern. The posts are flared outward for ease of access and for appearance's sake.

started between the top slat and
the middle slat above the arm they
would have looked absurd.

"Boy, that's a nice chair there,"
said Beechum in reference to the
second "California rocker," which
Charley made in 1967 (figure 69).
"I don't see how the ole man
done it. He just must a took a
lot a time with it."

"He's that way with ever'thing
he does," Rose told me. "He wants
to be sure it's perfect before he
puts it together. He figgers it
all out in his mind b'fore he makes
a chair, I know he does." Two
days earlier, when angry at Charley
for not helping her care for the
children, Rose had used this same
trait of perfectionism in chairmaking against him. "I swear, I
could do as much in half an hour
as he does all day!"

Because craftwork is Charley's
life and love he completely immerses
himself in the task of making
things, whether chairs, cupboards,
chests of drawers, hampers, beds,
bookcases, or banjos. Because he

Figure 69. Charley's second California rocker
was made of red oak in the late spring of 1967.
Charley prefers this chair to the one shown in
figure 42 because the slat and stretcher designs
are better integrated, and because the back no
longer hovers above the chair but is an integral
part of it.

is a perfectionist secure in the knowledge that he has the ability to make
anything, Charley continually challenges himself in production but remains
sufficiently flexible to accommodate to any change in the chair; indeed,

once a new element has been introduced by himself or by a customer, some of the subsequent chairs reveal other alterations that Charley felt necessary to make in order to synthesize most effectively the initial modification.

Take the armrests as an example. Most of Charley's chairs have rather thin arms, sometimes because the materials at hand were inadequate to make thick arms, or because Charley was attempting to economize, or because the other elements of the chair were also rather thin owing to the fact that they were hickory or sassafras or

Figure 70. This ten-slat rocker of sassafras (c. 1961) Charley sold for $40. It has small double pegs, a feature that is found often in other chairs from this time on.

ash, which is strong and need not be thick to serve its purpose. Because the arms were thin it was necessary to drive a large peg through the front end of the arm into the top of the post in order to hold the armrest securely in place (e.g., figure 70). Charley discovered, however, that sometimes the peg would loosen because both it and the armrest were well seasoned, so he put a smaller peg on the side of the front post to hold the bigger peg through the arm. It would have been easier to make the armrests thicker, as in fact he did in the mid-1960s when he made other component elements larger; the heavier construction satisfied his need to express a sense of personal security through solidarity in his chairs, and also satisfied consumer demands for chairs made entirely of walnut, a more fragile wood that requires larger cross sections for strength.

No understanding of the things an individual makes is complete without examination of the interrelationships of such factors as the intended use of the object, the tools and techniques of construction, the materials, consumer influence, and the needs and values of the creator.[7] Furthermore, style (consisting of an object's qualities and traits) is fluid; it is an ongoing process in which these factors, as they affect production, play a part. A counter stool made in the middle 1950s has small pegs at the ends of each slat (figure 71), although Charley did not develop the peg as a decorative feature until the early 1960s, when he made a concerted effort to attract a wealthier clientele and when he began to associate pegs with antiquity. In early 1966 he received written requests by outsiders for illustrations of his chairs; since Charley had no recent works on hand but would have to photograph earlier chairs exhibiting traits he no longer wished to duplicate, he altered the counter stool before taking a picture of it so as to make it resemble more closely what he wanted to produce in the mid-1960's. A peculiar mixing of design elements in four chairs made in the early spring of 1967 is the result of direct, rather than indirect, customer influence (figure 72). A man in North Carolina wanted dining chairs with feet and finials as Charley was then making them, but the customer was also attracted to an earlier chair (figure 21, center chair) of Charley's — a redbud settin' chair with stiles and double pegs — and so demanded that his four chairs also have stiles. The resulting chairs simply

Figure 71. A counter stool Charley made of sassafras wood in 1955; ten years later he revised the design by adding double pegs at the ends of each slat. For easy access there are no arms.

Figure 72. Four black walnut chairs (and table) made by Charley in the spring of 1967 (photo by Charley). The mixture of design elements from several earlier chairs was demanded by the customer, especially the use of stiles which Charley was not then emphasizing on dining chairs.

Figure 73. Mulberry rocker Charley made (c. 1960) for his own use; he revised the design twice. It was originally a six-slat rocker, but Charley "dehorned" it later, and in 1966 he fashioned seat, slats, pegs, and arms in a more contemporary design.

do not fit into a period of production; nor do they represent a transition (and therefore evolution) from one period of settin' chairs with stiles but no finials to a later period of dining chairs with finials but without stiles. A rocking chair of mulberry and hickory which Charley made about 1960 (figure 73) and kept for his own use originally had thin arms pegged from the top, back posts bent high near the top of the chair, no "notchin'," and single pegs at the ends of each slat. Charley "dehorned" the chair a year later by sawing off the top section and the sixth slat because he did not think it was as good looking as other chairs made at the same time which had only five slats. (One of his customers had also "dehorned" a chair of similar construction, which Charley learned before he, too, cut the top off his chair.) In 1966 he revised the chair again by putting on thicker arms pegged from the side of the arm rather than from the top, adding much wider slats which he said provide greater comfort and "improve the looks," weaving a new seat of the more attractive narrow bark, replacing the old rockers with larger ones, and adding decorated pegs. He also shortened all the rounds. The smaller size of the chair, the wider slats, and the thicker arms made the chair more compact, more secure, more protective; the large decorated pegs rendered the chair more "antique."

It is time to consider in more detail this old-fashioned quality in Charley's works. In midsummer of 1965, shortly after he composed "My Old Kentucky Mountain Home" and a few months before he built the bookcase masterpiece, Charley made a rocking chair of maple which, allegedly because of insufficient materials, had very thin posts a little more than an inch in diameter; in order to maximize the strength of the chair Charley added a brace in back (reminiscent of Windsor chairs which he claimed never to have seen), and, more important, the slats and rounds go entirely through the posts projecting half an inch beyond (similar to the chair shown in figure 56).

"Some people called it the 'Washington chair,'" said Charley, "'cause it looked like somethin' George Washington might a set in. But I call it my 'Abner chair;' called it that b'fore I ever made hit."

Why call it an Abner chair and what was the source of the design?

"Oh, I got that outa the Abner comic strip an' comic books an' these here newspaper comic strips. I made it like Abner furniture I seen in pictures in the comic strip."

"How long ago did you see these pictures?"

"Well, it's been about twelve years ago since I saw that picture in the paper, I guess. Li'l Abner settin' in this chair, way it was made and ever'thing. If you notice the furniture an' ever'thing they have is, have all these pieces stickin' all the way through. The furniture in the homes, you know, is thataway—picture frames."

Charley's characterization was not true. The furniture he alluded to, pictured in the Sunday editions of the Louisville Courier-Journal in the years 1952-1954, did not have the slats and rounds extending through the posts; rather the pieces projected beyond the posts because they had been haphazardly nailed to the backs of the legs, and the picture frames had been slapped together at odd angles with ends overlapping.

"This chair I made, I called it an 'Abner chair.' Ever' piece about it went all the way through—back slats went all the way through the postees, the pegs all the way through, the rounds all the way through—they went all the way through the postees an' stick out on the other side. And, uh, it had postees that come through the rockers, come all the way up through the armrests. That's where I thought that Abner chair up."

Charley's chair was made differently from Al Capp's drawings, of course, because Charley would never crudely construct an object without joints. What is of more interest, however, is that a dozen years before Charley made the Abner chair his wife left him in an effort to force him to live near the highway; at that time he began growing a beard, gave up using a turning lathe, and made his first eight-legged settin' chair. In the early to mid-1960s the same events transpired once more, but with greater intensity as his wife had left for a longer time and they lived on the highway for more years than previously.

Charley had a beard and long hair after 1963, when he and Rose moved to their house on a major highway, but other men in the area were clean shaven and wore their hair short. By 1965 Charley was dressing in overalls, as farmers had done earlier and as a few of the older mountain men still did, whereas most men his age and younger wore belted trousers; he also went barefoot most of the year, although other men wore shoes or boots. Charley cultivated a hillbilly image in the 1960s ostensibly to sell his chairs, or to hide a skin ailment allegedly contracted during World War II and aggravated by shaving, but the idea of a beard and long hair had occurred to him a decade earlier when the Abner comic strip first attracted his attention and captured his imagination. Charley wanted to look like the stereotypical mountain man who does old-timey things like making chairs by hand.

"The long hair's one thing that draws their attention more'n anything," he said. "Now you take some kids, they ain't never seen a beard. There's a whole lot a people over in London thinks I b'long to some kind a church organization or club or somethin'. I've had a lot a people ask me what religion I had; I don't b'long to any church organization."

He hid behind a beard for a year or so in the mid-1950s when he moved near the open highway, but for much longer in the 1960s.

"I kept on a-wearin' hit this time on account a hit helped my business," he explained.

"I think hit looks plumb awful," complained his wife Rose.

"I betcha a dollar I'd cut my hair and shave hit off an' I'd lose what orders I got," countered Charley. "Somehow I think that. I might be wrong. Ever'body says, 'No, man, don't you shave that off.' They kin buy furniture off most anybody. There's a lot a people that'd buy the furniture off me jest to get a picture of me. Like the artist in Washington, D.C. I think they bought a chair (figure 38) jest so's they could take some pictures of me," though in fact the customer made only a small deposit on a chair which she never picked up or paid for. Charley eventually altered it to a seven-slat rocking chair, a process that gave him the technique necessary to create his new design.

"If I shave an' the furniture warn't pegged," he concluded, "people wouldn't buy the chairs off me."

Figure 74. A portrait of Charley's maternal grandfather Hat, from whom he learned chairmaking and with whom he now sometimes identifies, and Hat's wife. Said Hat's son Oaklie about his chairmaking, "Buddy, when he threw one together, hit was together."

Economic motivation is surely important in accounting for Charley's appearance, but so is identification with the past. Charley had a framed portrait of his maternal grandfather and grandmother on the wall of his living room (figure 74); like Charley, Hat had long hair and a beard, and I have seen another small, torn photograph of the grandmother with a pipe in her hand and her feet bare. One of Charley's neighbors mistook the portrait of Hat for Charley, or so Charley told me several times. In addition, Charley asked two writers in early August, 1965, to take him back to Pine Mountain to find his grandfather's grave, and at his insistence I took him there in both 1966 and 1967. Regardless of the financial rewards that might have accrued from Charley's behavior and dress, he had adopted the life-style of the mountaineer at a time when he was most remote from a mountain hollow; he had found spiritual kinship with the Yokums and with other stereotyped hillbillies of Capp's and had based his behavior and some of his chairs on the comic strip. At the time Charley was an anachronism in the modern world, purposively, in order to promote his art and to help him adjust to his losses; his problems, ironically, were exaggerated as a result of the additional attention he attracted to himself.

Other ironies and seeming paradoxes are evident in Charley's chairs and in his comments on them.

"People like the pegs the best," said Charley. "They want the purtiest and espensivist stuff they can git." Yet he also admitted that many people did not know what the pegs were but thought they might be large nails or bolts or perhaps bits of wood glued onto the chair. As Charley had noted, "There's a whole lot a people that never even seen a rail fence; they don't understand this handmade stuff." For example, in 1965 Charley told me, "A fella stopped the other day while I was a-gettin' ready to cook some wood and he asked me if I was a-gonna eat it." But Charley also contended that if the chairs were not pegged they would not sell, as "people like it and it makes the chair look better; holds the slats, too." Only two pegs, one at each end of the top slat, are necessary if the chair is made in accordance with the principle of differential seasoning of the parts. Forty to two hundred pegs are a bit excessive structurally, although some of the chairs Charley made in 1967 of wood purchased at a lumber company required the use of several pegs because there was not enough difference in the degree of seasoning of component elements. The pegs on older furniture are hidden from view, rather like the "pins" in Aaron's chairs, but pegs in most of Charley's chairs since the mid-1950s have not only been visible but also are exaggerated in shape and size. By the early 1960s there were two small pegs at the end of each slat, and from about 1964 on Charley made the pegs of a wood that contrasted in color with the wood of the chair, except in cheap chairs made with nails or in chairs the customers specified were to be "solid walnut," a demand that Charley took literally. If Charley had really wanted the pegs to be antique they should have been limited to two per chair, and hidden.

Charley also thinks the tall rocking chairs, which he has occasionally made since about 1962 or 1963, are old-fashioned in appearance. Again they are unique, not antique, for the mountain-style rocking chairs are less than four feet high, whereas some of Charley's chairs are six feet or taller. No one made such tall chairs in the past, for, in Charley's words, "A rockin' chair in the house, if you ain't got much room, is right in the way; you can't hardly get around 'em."

Two other traits that Charley considered to be antique are the octagon-shaped posts and rounds which are common in his chairs, rather than the turned pieces, and the notches or incised lines that correspond with turnings. Neither quality is old-fashioned in the form manifested on Charley's chairs. On the legs of some chairs by other craftsmen in the past one finds a few incised lines, but they were put there not solely for decorative effect or because of nostalgia for the past.

"Well, they do that so the mark will stay stationary there," explained Charley. "Don't matter whether they would sand it or whatever, the mark wouldn't disappear so they could see hit right off. An' hit really looks nice on a chair — pencil mark or a mark caused by a chisel or a knife. You kin see hit right on hit. Those marks is put on there while hit's still in the turnin' lay. But I put my marks on there — used to — with a pocket knife. I jest marked an' rolled the post around on my legs."

Chairs that Charley made in 1966 and 1967, especially, had pencil marks all the way around each post at the places where holes were to be drilled, and Charley left them there. "Looks more handmade thataway," he said. Other chairmakers like Aaron erased or sanded off the pencil marks, but Charley has emphasized a trait he considered old-timey to such an extent that in its exaggerated state it is unique to him.

The eight-sided posts are not reminiscent of antique chairs, either, but are peculiar to Charley's works from the mid-1950s through the 1960s. Charley's grandfathers and great-uncles and other "ole-time chairmakers," however, made posts eight sided with an axe before turning them on the foot-powered turning lathe.

"You can't turn a square piece on a foot-powered turnin' lay," said Charley. The chairmaker would have to "split 'em out, then hew 'em out—you'd have to straighten 'em out with an axe—into eight-square finish with an ax, an then you'd center that with a compass to find the center." At that point the post was turned on the lathe and chiseled into a cylindrical form.

Charley's first chairs were neither eight sided nor turned.

"When I started makin' chairs I made 'em foursquare on account a I wasn't strong enough to turn that turnin' lay myself. And the turnin' lay b'longed to my grandfather an' he, uh, he didn't like for the boys to prank with it, he was afraid they'd tear it up."

Charley made and occasionally used his own lathe, but it was cumbersome to handle, difficult to repair, and tiring to use; it was virtually impossible for one man to wield a lathe effectively while turning posts and rounds. "It kinda gives your leg out an' makes it ache. You run it maybe four or five hours a day, if you've got a whole bunch of stuff to turn, it really gets you. It takes two big men to pedal one of them things all day."

"The last turnin' lay I made," said Charley in the mid-1960s, "hit's been about fifteen years ago." The power wheel broke and he could find nobody to weld it properly, he claimed, "an' it jest kept givin' me trouble, an' I jest quit plumb foolin' with a turnin' lay of any kind."

So how did he make chairs?

"I just turned loose an' started makin' it nothin' but handmade—ever'thing by hand." That was about 1953, when Rose left.

During the years that followed Charley developed in his own mind a distinction between handmade chairs with octagon-shaped pieces made with a drawing knife and homemade chairs produced by hand on a turning lathe; both of them are different from factory-made chairs, whose pieces are sawed by machinery in a factory, then glued, nailed, and screwed together.

"That ole man's a genius considerin' what he has to work with," said Hascal. "A man needs planers, jointers, and everything else to make chairs." Not Charley. All he needs, and all he ever really wanted, is a sharp instrument in his hands so that he can shape his raw materials as directly as possible. Perhaps that is the most interesting contradiction of all: a man who tastes, smells, and feels the wood he works with, and who wants to be in contact with his materials, in 1967 bought himself planers, jointers, and everything else needed to make chairs. He not only made several chairs with the equipment — he used the planer to shape eight-sided pieces of wood so the chairs would still be recognizable as his — but he also used a router on the drill press to make notches on the posts and rounds corresponding to the ornamentation he had previously cut by hand with a pocket knife (figures 13, 75-77). These uneven and irregular incisions with the router somewhat reduced the time and perhaps the labor of chairmaking, which Charley claimed was the reason for doing it this way, and, if rubbed with oil, the darkened notches were supposed to give the chair more of an antique appearance which would make them "better lookin'" than those whose notches were made with a pocket knife.

Figure 75. Charley, using his router on the drill press to make the "notchin'," says this process makes the chair look more "antique." More than once Charley got his beard caught in the drill.

Figure 76. Detail of chair shown in fig. 77, showing rough notchin' made with router.

The electrical equipment gave Charley the opportunity to produce tables and cabinets which had been ordered by outsiders but which he could not make with simple hand tools, and he would be able to achieve a degree of standardization necessary when orders were too numerous to fill by hand production alone as well as, he hoped, to reduce the hours of work. "Now it's a lot easier," he claimed. "That's what I always told ever'body anyhow . . . On that machinery I wanna find out whether I can make a chair faster thataway or whether I can't. That's one thing I wanna find out. I still don't know. Hit's been thirty years since I used that machinery."

The equipment would, he felt, also make possible the fullest expression of his art. "Them shapers with bits can make all kinds a cuts and moldings and sash work and doormakin' and table shapin'," he said; "they's a wonderful thing, the shaper is." Unfortunately, Charley became increasingly irascible and could not control the machines at all.

Figure 77. Charley made this black walnut rocker in July, 1967, using both hand-hewed wood and sawed lumber from a lumber yard. In making the chair he used electrical machinery for the first time since the early 1940s; also, in order to get the job done more quickly and to create an antique effect, he used "rough notchin'," corresponding to turnings on posts and rounds, for the first time.

The earlier clarity of line resulting in a sense of continuity in his work was no longer apparent in 1967, when he tried to use machinery. Discontinu-

the Best I Can figere   CHEST   OF   DRAWERS

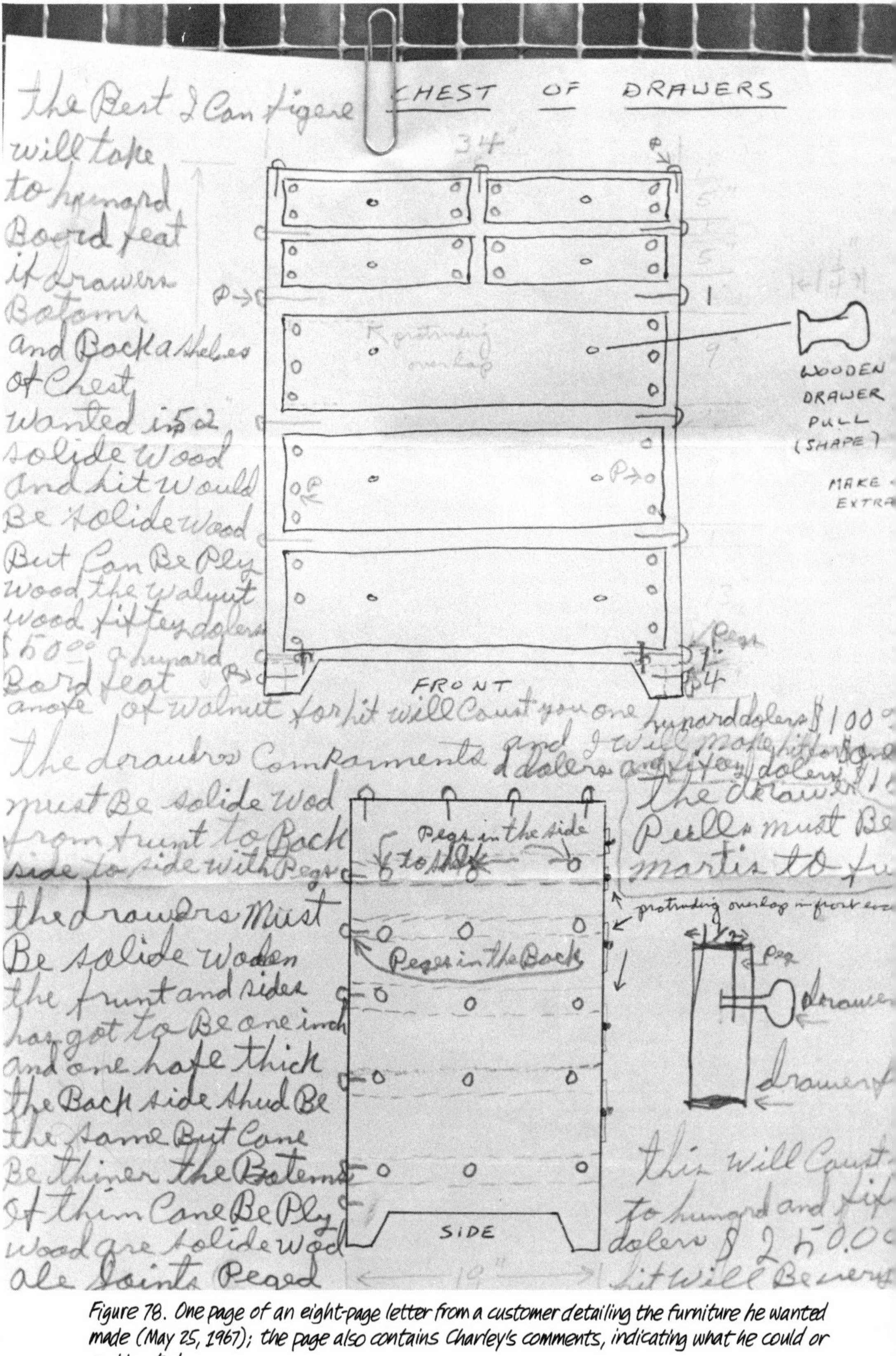

will take
to hinard
Board feat
it drawers
Batom
and Back a shelve
of Chest
wanted in 52
solide wood
And hit would
Be solide wood
But Can Be Ply
wood, the walnut
wood fiften dolers
$50.00 a hinard
Bord feat
a more of walnut for hit will caust you one hinard dolers $100.00

WOODEN
DRAWER
PULL
(SHAPE)

MAKE
EXTRA

the drawrs Compartments and I will make fiften dolers
must Be solide Wod
from frunt to Back
side to side with Pegs
the drawers Must
Be solide Woden
the frunt and sides
has got to Be one inch
and one hafe thick
the Back side shud Be
the same But Cane
Be thiner the Botems
of thim Cane Be Ply
wood are solide wod
ale Joints Peged

Pegs in the side

Pegs in the Back

SIDE

and fifty dolers $150
the drawer
Pell must Be
mortis to fu

protruding overlap in front eae

peg

drawer

drawer f

this will Caust
to hinard and fif
dolers $ 250.00
hit will Be eas

FRONT

34

SIDE

19"

Figure 78. One page of an eight-page letter from a customer detailing the furniture he wanted made (May 25, 1967); the page also contains Charley's comments, indicating what he could or could not do.

ity characterized the chairs. In contrast with the quieting stasis of his earlier
ornamentation, or the swiftly flowing lines of chairs with no "notchin'" at all,
the irregularity of ornamentation on later chairs epitomized by the new design
produced a feeling of nervous movement and visual excitation rather like
Charley's own inner turmoil at the time; this feeling was balanced by
heavier chairs that stood tall and, perhaps, defensive.

   If Charley's chairs were really antique they would be about forty-two
inches high, not six feet; they would have three or four slats, not seven or
nine or ten slats that touch one another; they would not have pegs clearly
in evidence; and they would certainly not consist of four rockers and
eight legs. In other words, the truly antique qualities would not afford
a sense of power and enclosure. Many of Charley's chairs in the mid-1960s
had to provide security and seclusion for his own protection from other
people and from forces he could scarcely control, but they also had to be
antique because of his nostalgia for the past. It matters not that such
chairs are unique rather than antique, for sometimes in Charley's mind
they must be old-timers with walls, high seats that "made you set away
up high like a king or some'un," and deeply curved slats that "hug you."
Let us examine, then, this other quality in some of Charley's chairs, the
quality of enclosure.

CHAPTER FIVE

Like Somebody Hugging You

"I was real sick that winter," said Charley. "I guess if a man gets to where he needs the money real bad, he has to give in to 'em."

Charley was referring to the sale of a black walnut two-in-one rocking chair (figure 27) and a walnut sewing rocker, both made late in 1963 or early in 1964 and sold for $30 and $15, respectively; that sum of money was just enough to pay Charley's rent and his electric bill. Charley spent six weeks making the chairs. It was a cold winter day when he trudged through the snow on his way to town, eight miles and two hills from home, in hopes of selling the chairs to the owner of a department store. The two chairs were strapped to his back. Halfway to town Charley stopped at a roadside tavern to rest and warm himself, and he met a man who lived nearby who offered to buy the chairs for $45. Since Charley needed the money and was not sure he could make it to town in bad weather and poor health, he sold them on the spot, reluctantly agreeing to buy the customer a beer to bind the sale.

The man gave both chairs to his daughter, but she does not like the two-in-one rocker because the front rockers in the middle catch her heels when she rocks and the tops of the center posts in front get in the way of her legs. Also disturbing to father and daughter was the large number of pegs on the rockers, the reason for which neither could divine.

"That two-in-one is a beautiful chair," commented Charley. "It's got quar rockers on hit down here. The rockers has got big pegs plumb all the way through 'em. On the top side of 'em. I think they're spaced about two inches apart. They look like big beads or buttons or some'un."

"Why did you make it that way?" I asked him.

"I don't know, I just thought I'd . . . ," he began to say, and probably would have attributed this unusual quality of the chair to his
tendency to experiment with design elements just to see what they
would look like. But he stopped in midsentence, for there was another reason.
". . . well, one reason I made 'em was I made a mistake borin' the hole.
And, uh, I decided: Now, I can make a peg to fit that with a big round
head on it. I went all through that on all four of them rockers with them
things fixed like that. Boy, it made it a beauty. An' ever' round in it all
the way around is pegged just like that big bookcase rocker you got. Ever'
round is pegged with them big ole pegs."

Other customers have complained that the two-in-one chairs are
not very comfortable because the extra legs and rockers are placed in
the center of the front part of the chair. Besides, it is not easy to make
such chairs. Bottoming an octagon-shaped seat is no simple task: placing
the numerous legs properly on rockers requires much patience and skill,
but drilling the many stretcher holes at the correct angle is perhaps
the toughest problem. Furthermore, the slats for an ordinary rocking
chair are "quarter bent," according to Charley, but those for his two-in-
one chairs are "half bent" and demand additional time and effort; half-
bent slats must have blocks inserted behind them in the slat press in
order to provide the necessary curvature. The effect of these half-bent
slats in a chair is, however, in Charley's words, "just like somebody
huggin' you."

"It's regular difficult to get one 'em right," complained Charley after
he summarized the problems arising in the manufacture of a two-in-one
chair.

Why make such chairs at all, given the many difficulties in production and the criticisms made by users?

"I couldn't sell the cheap chair," he said, "so I just thought up that
kinda chair."

The "cheap chair" was the five-slat rocker priced at about $25, or
the settin' chair selling for about $12, neither boasting much ornamen-
tation but both durable and comfortable and pleasing in appearance.

Although Charley managed to sell the odd and fancy chairs to wealthier customers, the price was not really any more commensurate with the work required than the income from the cheap chairs had been. Besides, he continued to make cheap chairs on occasion. Charley always had mixed feelings about his two-in-one rocking chairs, too. Sometimes he admitted they were attractive and appealing to him, but at other times he said he did not like them or they were too fancy for him. He may indeed have constructed the odd chairs to attract attention to himself in order to sell more chairs at higher prices, but he was also manipulat-

Figure 79. One of Charley's settin' chairs in use. There is no ornamentation that would weaken the chair and there are no finials that would hinder its use.

ing form for its own sake and experimenting with designs. In addition, the half-bent slats were "like somebody hugging you"—just what Charley need-ed when his world opened onto the busy highway. I have already discussed Charley's commitment to and absorption in chairmaking and have provided a few examples of his unique solutions to self-generated problems. It is the two motives alluded to above—economic well-being and emotional security—which I plan to examine and illustrate in this chapter. The meaning of the bookcase masterpiece and several other chairs is also consid-ered more fully, though admittedly my discussion is somewhat speculative.

In 1953, when Charley began making chairs exclusively with a drawing knife instead of turning them on a lathe, he created his first eight-legged side chair and then a seven-legged armchair (figures 39, 40). Charley had been experimenting with the chair parts and discovered that, since each piece he made had eight facets, each facet would accommodate a round with little difficulty; in fact, he could make an octagon-shaped

seat if he used eight posts which would result in an interesting design,
the octagonal seat repeating the octagonal shape of each post and
stretcher. The next step, of course, was to add rockers and more slats
to make a rocking chair, but he did not do that until his wife left him
for the second time, a decade later. In all, he made about ten eight-
legged chairs and five seven-legged armchairs in 1953 and 1954, and one
seven-legged upholstered armchair in 1953 (figure 80) which the owner
later painted black; as far as I know, all of these ten chairs except
the upholstered one were made of black walnut, a fact worth noting in
itself, for few craftsmen work in this expensive and fragile wood which
has become an index of social and economic status for the customer and
has a special meaning when utilized in a chair for the producer's own use.

"That's the first 'n I ever made," said Charley in reference to the
eight-legged chair illustrated in figure 39. "And, uh, I had it settin' over

there on the highway when we
lived in that big log house. I
was over there on the highway
settin' on a stump with some
more chairs. An' Bill Harley come
along an' he seen me with that
chair an' he talked me out of it,
wanted to buy it. I forgit what
he paid me for it; wasn't much."
A year earlier Charley told me he
had received $2 for this chair
and $5 for the seven-legged one.

"An' then he, uh, got a seven-
legged chair," continued Charley.

Figure 80. One of Charley's few upholstered chairs (c. 1953). The barrel arm
design is unusual in Charley's work, he
claimed, and similar to chair arms made
by other craftsmen.

"And the reason he bought it, now, he really didn't need 'em I don't guess; he just bought 'em 'cause they was odd. I don't guess the man really needed 'em. He just bought 'em 'cause they was different."

"That's the first 'n I ever made," concluded Charley. "Bet a feller couldn't buy that off'n him for $60, I bet."

Harley refused to sell either chair to me, though he kept them in his basement most of the time and did not use them. His comment on his purchase of the chairs reaffirmed what Charley had suggested about his motivation.

"It was pretty crude," said Harley of the eight-legged chair. "I mean, he hadn't used sandpaper on it. It was so odd and everything; I could see the sturdiness of it, the oddity, and that's why I wanted it. I believe I gave him $3 for it," although Charley had told me $2.

The chairmaker Hascal said he did not like the chair at all even though it was the most unusual settin' chair he had ever seen. "That back'll bump things when you turn the chair around," he complained. A few minutes later he added: "The design is all right. It's pretty. But that's a useless thing to have on a chair," meaning the two legs sticking out in back; "it could be dangerous."

Beechum remarked, "That I don't like. It should have only four posts. It'd be all right jest to set back an' look at." He said he did not like this "design of a chair for a chair to be set on," argued that "a feller could hurt hisself on them things," meaning the legs in back, and finally concluded that it was one of the ugliest chairs he had ever seen.

Harley claimed credit for the seven-legged chair, which the other chairmakers thought was more appealing, but some of Harley's remarks are dubious, for two reasons: first, he considered Charley mentally disturbed because the latter would not accept most of Harley's suggestions about making chairs; second, Harley was annoyed because Charley would not reveal his "secret of chairmaking." Nevertheless, Harley contended that he had suggested this chair design to Charley after he bought the eight-legged chair.

"I told him about what I'd like to have: 'Instead of getting your legs

in so close,' I said, 'don't bunch 'em up so much.' I drew him out a little
sketch on a piece of paper, you know. I guess that's the first one he ever
put arms on. I guess I was the first man to ever get him started
sandin' 'em."

Charley seldom sands a chair, however, because the process takes too
much time, he does not enjoy that kind of work, and his chairs do not
really need sanding. Harley varnished the chairs himself so he could
"leave 'em out in all types of weather," which he never did and which Charley
cautions against doing as the seat will disintegrate. Harley's comments
evinced amazement at Charley's skill with a "few crude tools," and, he concluded, "Charley doesn't have a worry in the world; he raises a garden in
the summer and just loves to make chairs in the winter."

A chair suggesting that Charley does indeed love the creative task,
and also indicating that he
might have some worries,
is a black walnut dining
chair made about 1961
(figure 81), a year or so
before Rose left him. The
chair is "special" in several
respects. First, the use of
black walnut is rare for a
chair that the craftsman

Figure 81. About 1961 Charley made
a chair for his daughter, vowing never
to sell it; after all, the hearts were an
expression of his love for Bonnie.
Two years later, however, Charley
sold the chair in order to buy the
girl a pair of shoes because winter
was setting in. The brother of the
purchaser said he "wouldn't give
fifteen cents for that chair." But it
is Bonnie's favorite chair, although
she has not seen it since she was
about three.

intended for use in his own home. Second, it is the only true dining chair of all the objects to which Charley assigned this designation: it has five slats instead of three, and it is virtually overwhelmed with ornamentation. Third, Charley hand-rubbed the chair with oil and then finished it with varnish, refinements he infrequently bestowed upon any chair, regardless of the price offered.

I asked Charley what his favorite chair was, excluding rockers.

"You mean the one I like best? The favorite chair in a settin' chair," he said, "I sold it to Miss Smith, works at the employment office — black walnut." At the time of its manufacture the fancy walnut chair shown in figure 81 was in fact a settin' chair, despite its dining chair qualities, because Charley had not yet made a clear distinction between the two kinds of chairs and he did not make such a distinction until five or six years later, about the time I met him, when he was trying to appeal to the values of a wealthier clientele.

Charley admitted that it is an "expensive" chair. "But if I ever make a complete dining room outfit for myself," which he never did, "I'm gonna make it on that design only with a wooden seat in it. I like the backs the way they is made; they's real close together and the backrest is good in 'em." Originally the chair had had a solid wood seat, which Charley replaced with a bottom of white oak splints before he sold the chair.

"My brother said he wouldn't give me fifteen cents for that chair, but I like it," said the woman who owns it. "I was going to have Charley make me a table and chairs till I got this other table."

Perhaps the most unusual feature of the chair is that in the center of each slat Charley carved a heart. And why not? He made the chair specifically for his daughter Bonnie and vowed never to sell it. About five years after its manufacture Bonnie told me it was her favorite of all the chairs her father had built, but of course she no longer had it. Charley sold it to Miss Smith because winter was setting in and young Bonnie needed a pair of shoes.

Several other chairs made in the 1960s have the back slats "real close together," too, among them a sassafras rocking chair with black walnut pegs made about 1961 (figure 70), which Charley finally managed to sell for $40 (after knocking on the doors of many businesses in town hoping to find a buyer). The chair has ten slats nearly touching each other. It marks an early use of small double pegs at the end of each slat and a late tendency to flare the back posts outward and back at a point rather high on the chair, which mitigates against proper balance in so tall a chair. It is one of Charley's last rocking chairs (at least for several years) made without ornamentation, except for cheap chairs made with nails which Charley continued to produce.

There is another trait I have not mentioned before, namely, the seat round is straight in back, which is the way other craftsmen made their chairs; by about 1965 Charley had begun to bend this stretcher for the sake of visual appearance and to increase the comfort and, hopefully, to attract interest in his chairs.

"Hit makes it comf'tabler an' also makes hit look better, an' people got kinda tired of the reg'lar-lookin' things an' I had a change it around a little bit to get more sales," explained Charley.

"Did it help?"

"Hit didn't improve much. Hit didn't improve wouldn't say but a little bit. Specially on the rockin' chair. I guess hit'd be 'bout, uh, 'bout twelve rockin' chairs that I done like this. An' a mighty few settin' chairs."

The earliest chair I know of with a rounded seat in the back is the settin' chair Charley made in 1965 (figure 23), which was special because it was to go to a museum; that is also why it has double pegs of con-trasting color. The idea for bending the seat stretcher may have been stimulated by Charley's manufacture of two-in-one chairs with octagonal seats, and Charley may have included some of them in his count of a dozen chairs, but he was not specific about the source of this design element.

"I just thought that up myself," he said. "Not many people notices that. No there ain't, there shore ain't. Ain't many people notices that that buy a chair — a rockin' chair or a settin' chair, either one. I've had two or three to notice hit," which may well include Charley, my wife, and me. "'Bout two or three is all."

Such a remark makes one doubt that changing the appearance of a chair for the sake of increased sales is the most significant motive. Yet that was the reason given for making his two-in-one rocking chairs, beginning in late 1961 or early 1962 and ending in early 1967. (As nearly as I can determine, he never made any others after he went into hiding in the Midwest.)

"If you make a simple thing you gotta sell it at a simple price," Hascal said, "and Charley's tryin' to make a livin' at it."[1]

"These are just a marvel to look at as art," said Hascal of Charley's two-in-one rocking chairs. "I respect any man that's got the patience. He oughta get five thousand dollars for that chair," meaning the mayor's rocking chair (figure 26) for which Charley received a one-hundred-dollar bill. "Must a taken a month and a half of solid work to make that."

In reference to the mayor's chair Charley said, "If that bark was laid together it'd run plumb acrost the United States," which is why he made only one other chair of this type, in the winter of 1966 at the special request of a woman in the area who then moved to the Midwest; the duplicate is taller but narrower and has slender, elongated finials instead of mushroom-shaped ones.

Charley told me in 1965 that the mayor's chair was the prettiest chair he had made because it required the most work, he received the best price for it, and it attracted the greatest amount of attention.

"A hunnert people saw that chair when the mayor first bought it," said Alvin Hampton who owns the swamp willow chair that Charley made earlier and who thinks Charley is "the best chairmaker I've ever known; he's always been a chairmaker; he takes the time an' he's got the patience." Some people, he said, thought $100 was too much money for the mayor's chair, "but there's a lot a work in it."

Everywhere I asked about Charley's chairs people enthusiastically directed me to the mayor's chair, which is also referred to by the mayor's name, that is, "Dolph's chair" or the "Dolph rocker." As it is now in the basement of the mayor's department store probably everyone in town has seen it; at the time the mayor bought it there was an illustrated article in the local newspaper calling attention to the chair, the mayor, and Charley.

"The only reason I make a chair like that," explained Charley, "is you find people that's interested in somethin' differ'nt, you know; they want somethin' that nobody else's got."

According to rumor the mayor bought the chair with the intent of giving it to President Kennedy, ostensibly in gratitude for his program of economic assistance to Appalachia but really for the purpose of promoting himself politically. Only a few months earlier the dean of an educational institution nearby, and several state politicians, had presented Kennedy with a rocking chair of spotted walnut and a checkerboard seat made by Hascal and his father Verge and another man named Aaron; they had made it in the school's chair shop, so perhaps the mayor was inspired by their example.

At any rate, there were mixed motives for making the two-in-one rockers and for buying them, too. The mayor's rocking chair was the third one Charley built, though many people consider it the most attractive and most comfortable of all eight of them.

The first two-in-one rocking chair is of white walnut with black walnut double pegs (figure 24). To my knowledge it is the earliest example of Charley's using two pegs at the end of each slat; the chair also has extensive "notchin's," which was unusual in late 1961 when this chair was made. Charley said several times that the rocker required 356 hours to make, and he asked $300 for it, but no one wanted it at any price regardless of how many hours of work had been put into it.

Ed. Nunn, who owns one of the automobile franchises in town, did not want the chair either, but Charley stopped by the shop and his home so many times trying to sell it to him that "finally I asked him what the lowest price was he would take for it," said Nunn, "and Charley said $50 so I said I'd take it." It was the first and only piece of furniture that Nunn bought for his overly furnished house, as he always left such duties to his wife. After he bought the chair Nunn sent it to Lexington to be sanded and varnished. When he showed it to me in his bedroom he made two comments about it: first, he remarked upon the beauty of the chair's finish, which had cost him an additional fifty dollars; second, he expressed puzzlement as to the reason for the four rockers.

Charley created his second two-in-one rocker a few months later, in 1962 (figure 25). This redbud chair, purchased by Phil Banks who also owns an automobile franchise in town, is one of the few with spokes under the arms as in Charley's early square-post, panel-back chair. It is the first chair that has so many pegs — eighty or ninety of them — all of which have been carved with a pocket knife in a pattern of alternating ridges and depressed areas. Charley does not know where he got the idea for the peg heads but the motif is fairly common, as on the glass or plastic decorative pieces used to hold mirrors to walls in public rest rooms in service stations in the area, although he may have conceived of it independently; he used decorated pegs on only two other chairs, the bookcase masterpiece and the rocking chair he owned, which he revised in 1967.

"I don't like that there design on a rockin' chair for myself a-tall," said Charley. "Lot a people does." He claimed that the decorated pegs especially are "too fancy for me," but that was a year before he had made them for himself.

The second two-in-one rocker and the Dolph rocker were manufactured only for "rich people wantin' somethin' differ'nt," Charley contended.

"That chair's too fancy for a poor man," he said in reference to Banks's rocker. "Takes a rich man to buy stuff like that. Hit's really beautiful, hit really looks handmade, but it's too espensive for me. If I was wantin' one fer myself I'd like that one Tackett has."

Banks paid Charley $75 for the chair, which Charley said took him about three months to make. Coated with paste wax for protection, the rocker sits in the corner of Banks's office.

"Charley's quite a character, isn't he?" asked Banks, trying to make small talk as I examined the chair. "He doesn't have a worry in the world; he loves to sit out there and make chairs." Banks was sitting at his desk piled high with bills and receipts and other important documents, and, with a far-off look in his eyes, he contemplated for a moment Charley's life. "He doesn't have a thing to worry about. Or at least if he has, he doesn't worry about it. I wish I were as lucky. What do you think of that old man? Yes sir, he's quite a character," repeated Banks, shaking his head and shuffling the papers on his desk.

It was in 1963 that Charley "took a notion" to build his first book-case rocker, which he considered a masterpiece at the time because of its uniqueness; but then he made his real masterpiece two years later. The first bookcase rocker was also the third two-in-one rocker, the mayor's chair (figure 26). In addition to eight legs and four rockers, it has three panels for the back made of woven hickory bark, baskets that serve as armrests and may be used to hold books or knitting equipment, and a footrest that extends in front. The chair's uniqueness attracted the attention of many people, a few of whom seemed to derive visual pleasure from the chair, especially the juxta-position of colors and textures. Bill Sexton, who owns a used furniture store in town and frequently drives a pickup truck into the mountain hollows to peddle junk to isolated mountaineers, asked me one day: "You seen that chair that Dolph's got? That's the prettiest chair I ever seen." And Alvin Hampton several times called the mayor's rocker the "prettiest chair Charley ever made." He remarked upon the uniqueness of the chair as well, noting that the extra rockers in front "are pretty" and comment-ing favorably on the contrast of bark against wood. He explained that the chair is "a sewing rocker for an old woman to put her sewing stuff in the basket arms," but Charley called it a "bookcase rocker."

In the winter of 1964-65 Charley made yet another two-in-one rocker of black walnut (figure 28). He sold it to a man from Tennessee who returned with it in 1966 to have Charley replace the rockers (which he never did) because they were too small for the chair; Charley had used the small rockers because his supply of walnut was limited. Somewhat more interesting, given the circumstances of manufacture and use, is a sassafras two-in-one rocking chair (figure 82) Charley made in the late spring of 1967 for Melvin Begley, who owns a funeral home situated across from Phil Banks's car franchise.

"They varnished it," Charley told me, "and said hit's the prettiest thing

Figure 82. This sassafras two-in-one rocker was made by Charley in the late spring of 1967 to pay a debt to a funeral home for ambulance service for his crippled son. The chair was supposed to be a copy of the one shown in figure 25, but obviously it is not.

ever was," though Charley did not seem particularly attracted to the chair.

Begley had provided the ambulance service to transport Charley's son to the hospital after Lester slipped on the ice and broke his hip. Begley asked Charley to repay him not with money but with a chair, specifically a chair exactly like the one owned by Banks.

"That am'blance is chargin' me $45 to take Lester down there an' back. First three trips I made 'im a rockin' chair to pay for the trips. He allowed me three — b'lieve it was three trips — or was it four? Had to pay 'im $25. An' I still owe 'im $25. That's the way hit was; he allowed me four trips."

The chair Charley made for Begley was placed in the reception room of the funeral home, but later Begley moved it to small living quarters on the second floor rear of the building. It is not in fact an exact replica of Banks's chair but differs in several ways. Because many people had complained about the front rockers of this kind of chair "bitin' their heels,"

Charley varied the angle of the rounds so that the two center posts in front would not project so far forward; "that's the reason on the last chair I drawed them posts in a lot," said Charley. As Beechum remarked when looking at photographs of some of Charley's earlier two-in-one chairs, "I like ever'thing about that chair 'cept it oughta had two rockers left out a hit. Fella could hurt hisself on them posts in front." He added, however, "Them walnut pegs really make them chairs show up; I really like 'em."

Begley's chair, while somewhat more comfortable than earlier two-in-one rockers, lacks the complexity of design found in Banks's chair. Charley had no intention of duplicating the earlier rocker for Begley's benefit. The chair that he ultimately sold to Banks was a tour de force, a chair that required months to construct, and, as apparent in the careful attention to detail and the meticulous rendering and synthesizing of complex elements, it was an act of total involvement on Charley's part. The chair was made not as a result of someone else's specifications but in accordance with Charley's own predilections at the time. In contrast, Begley's chair was constructed under extenuating circumstances by a man who simply did not want to make it at that time and who felt imposed upon because of Lester's accident. When Charley initially told me about having had to make the rocker for Begley his tone was bitter; no doubt it was a disconcerting interruption in his work at a time when he had pressing commitments to other people for many chairs, and the value of the ambulance service was equal only to what Charley was then getting for one ordinary seven-slat rocking chair of black walnut. Charley made the rocking chair rather grudgingly and with little interest, as evident in the absence of "notchin,'" the presence of six rather than seven slats, the use of very wide bark which can be woven rather quickly, and the simplicity of design.

The implications of these modifications are important for analyses of making things, including the present one. The expressive quality of the object includes the values associated with the finished product but it also results from the embodiment of certain values achieved during manufacture of the object. As such, this quality includes the values of both the maker and the user of the product. [2] On the basis of the object alone, however, it is impossible to determine whose values are expressed— those of the producer or those of the consumer— and to what extent, a point that must be recognized in attempts to ascertain the factors responsible for the features of a particular object. Furthermore, visual pleasure is only one of many purposes served by the object; others include prestige enhancement, economic gain, political advancement, greed and status (which Charley sometimes appealed to), and even philanthropic satisfaction. (For example, one man bought several chairs, stools, and benches because he knew Charley needed the money, though he had no interest in or use for the furniture and stored it in his basement.) Thus, neither the chair in emulation of Dolph's rocker nor the one patterned after Banks's two-in-one was invested by the maker with much emotional significance or personal interest, as were several other strange chairs, for both resulted from consumer demand.

Another example of the impact of consumer influence is a series of chairs (for an example, see figure 56) Charley made late in 1965 and early in 1966, right after he built the bookcase masterpiece. The form and the design, in an attenuated state, are derived from the Abner chair of a year and a half before, but they resulted more from the desire to take shortcuts in production in order to fill the demand than from Charley's wanting to make chairs with an old-timey quality. It takes much less time to drill holes through the posts, then insert the slats and saw them off to the right length, than to measure slats precisely to fit into the mortised holes. In addition, Charley did not cook or bend the posts or the slats, although he set the back legs at a slight angle for greater comfort and tipped the front legs slightly outward as well; he made the slats wavy (they are somewhat reminiscent of Calvin Manning's chair in figure 66) to give the chairs some visual interest. Furthermore, Charley used a large single peg in most of these chairs, instead of the small double pegs he had been using at this time, again to decrease his hours of work. "I jest don't like the looks of it, the design of it," admitted

Charley; he prefers slats that are straight along the bottom edge.

One chair, by way of illustrating customer influence, is the "California rocker" which owes many of its qualities to the man who ordered it. Two of these chairs were made (figures 42, 69). On November 18, 1965, Charley wrote to Don Ford in California, "What a surprise to here from you all and to get a sail to Boot . . . Well I shere wold like to Bild the Rocker that you desined your self Hit will be a Butfule Creaton I ame shere."

"I Reley wanted to make somtin in a new Fashon and this one is hit," Charley wrote in mid-January, 1966, to the same man. "I ame shere this Rocker is going to Be a Butey in Every Way are is one my mind." Because of the difficulties that arose, which reveal much about producer-consumer relationships and about Charley's personal problems, the first California rocker was not completed until late December, 1966.

Actually Charley feels that the second version of the chair, made in late spring of 1967, is better than the first. "I like the way that one's balanced," he said. Despite his preference for rounded slats, he thinks the straight slats in the second chair look better, which in fact they do; indeed, the customer had indicated his preference for straight slats, but Charley was unwilling to relinquish the use of shaped slats when he made the first chair. The customer had also requested rectangular arms, but Charley refused to make them because "they wouldn't look good; only them curved arms look right." When the second chair is examined from above, the curvilinear lines of the arms certainly do break up the straight lines, adding exciting contrast. The first chair was not an integrated whole nor was it visually successful. The back seems to rest tenuously as a separate entity on the bottom section of the rocker, which serves as a separate platform owing to the very long points on the bottom ends of the back posts, the excessive width between the front posts under the arms, and the rounded slats whose form is not repeated beneath the seat. The seat itself is strange; it is Charley's interpretation of the rush seat that Ford had roughly sketched in the drawing he sent to Charley; in Charley's version, planks pegged together form an empty space in the center, with the bark woven around the planks and over the hole.

Although Charley was not quite satisfied with his own version of the chair, the customer seemed happy. "As I _recall_," the latter wrote me, "we sketched a plain ladder-back rocker. Charley's rocker has curved back rests much fancier than we requested. However, we _like_ Charley's design better than our own and we're delighted that he made it as he did!"

It is unfortunate that Hattie Tuggle did not live long enough to say the same thing about the chair Charley made for her, which she never saw and had not even ordered (figure 55). This was Charley's "old-timer." He made it, as nearly as I can determine, in early 1963, only a few months before moving to the house on a major highway where I met him two years later. The character of the chair may be the result to some extent of indirect customer influence, as we shall see in a moment, but, like some of the other works mentioned above, the chair is an expression of Charley's needs at the time; in addition, the old-timer and the bookcase masterpiece epitomize both the antiquity and the sense of enclosure apparent in several chairs Charley made in the 1960s.[3]

Late in 1963 or early in 1964 Charley sold the chair made for Hattie Tuggle to an unidentified tourist from Lexington, receiving half the $127 he was asking for it. Before he sold the chair, Charley took two photographs of it with a box camera. The chair has nine slats which are so wide they nearly touch each other, and the slats have double pegs at each end; the posts are thick and are capped with mushroom-shaped finials rather than the more slender and elongated finials on Banks's two-in-one rocking chair of an earlier date or on the ornamented seven-slat rockers made somewhat later; the posts are bent backward and outward near the top rather than from below the seat in back; the seat is about two feet from the floor, a quite extraordinary height in a rocking chair; and there is a woven basket beneath the seat into which a footrest slides when not in use, much like the mayor's rocker.

"That was the most beautiest chair, I mean for a reg'lar rockin' chair, I ever made," Charley told me in June, 1967.

He had built half a dozen black walnut high chairs a few months before he made the "old timer" for the arthritic Mrs. Tuggle, for which he received $10 each. These chairs have roomy seats which are closer to the floor than is usual in high chairs or counter stools so that Mrs. Tuggle could climb in and out of them more easily. Charley "took a notion" to make a rocking chair for her, too, he said, and that is why the seat in the old-timer is so much higher than is usual in a rocking chair; ordinarily the distance from seat to floor is about fourteen inches for a rocking chair. The height of the seats in these counter stools and in the rocking chair, therefore, is about the same.

"You got to make a chair to rest in comfortable, you got to make 'em pretty low," he said, but the seat in this rocking chair was pretty high.

In November, 1965, Charley and I discussed the old-timer. "How many big chairs have you made?" I asked him.

"Well, last winter I made the two-in-one, and, uh, winter before that I made an 'old-timer' — I call it that. It's, uh, a big chair with a real high back and a real high seat an' it had a footrest that would fold up in front, and when you set down you could reach that footrest an' it made you set away up high like a king or some'un."

At that point Charley laughed nervously. It was the same peculiar twitter or giggle that followed his remark that the half-bent slats are "like somebody huggin' you" as well as other serious comments, thus indicating that what he had just said was not funny at all but of special significance.

"I called it an 'old-timer,'" he repeated. "I sold it to a man down in Lexington, Kentucky. I don't remember his name. I just only made one of 'em. If they wasn't so much work an' so much expense — I couldn't get more'n half of what I asked for it an' so I never did try no more of 'em — like the mayor's bookcase rocker, I never did try no more of 'em (though he did make another bookcase rocker the following year on special demand).

"Why did you make this old-timer?"

"Well, there was an old lady in London, I don't recall her name [he did a

a few days later], but she's passed along now — she was gettin' well up
in the years an' she couldn't hardly set down or get up — an' she got me
to make her six big high-back armchairs that she could set down in. An'
I took a notion to make this rockin' chair an' make it in that design an'
ever'thing so she could set down in hit an' get up easy. Made a footrest
that folds up here in front for her to rest her feet in so her feet
wouldn't have to be on the floor. Make a chair real high like that so she
could set — that's really what caused me to make a chair like that. She
passed on b'fore I got the chair done. I b'lieve I could a sold it to her
if I could a got it done."

"How tall was the chair?"

"I don't recall how tall the chair was, but the seat was 'bout twenty-
four inches from the floor up to the seat," so the chair must have been
between six and seven feet tall.

"Is that the usual height?"

"I usually make a chair, from the floor up to the seat, 'bout fourteen
or fifteen inches to rest in. Now to make a chair to rest in you got to make
'em pretty low. Like a davenneck chair— these here upholstered chairs?—
they're mightly low chairs to set down in. If you wanna rest comf'tably in a
chair you gotta make it so you kin stretch your legs out an' rest. If you
make any kinda chair an' you're gonna set in it, you gotta make it kinda
low to rest in. Like these dinin' room chairs like I made for you—they're
made with extry high seats, you see," which is why dining chairs are for some
people in the area an index of social and economic status: they are made
with much ornamentation which increases the price; they are made of expensive and fragile wood; they are to be used only for brief periods of
time; and they are not the only chairs in the house, in contrast with the
homes of poorer people in which there are few settin' chairs. [4]

The old-timer was "the most beautiest chair" and the first and third
bookcase rockers were "masterpieces." Again Charley had created a chair
that to him epitomizes the kind of chair made in the past—an old-timer
— but it is actually unique to him. Many of his chairs, including especially
the old-timer, generate a feeling of power and control for the occupant and

also create a sense of protectively enclosed space secluding the occupant from the external environment. The two factors are closely related— one has power and control in the world that he himself creates —and both qualities are expressions of Charley's desire to isolate himself from others and to control what goes on around him; as Jung has suggested, "A lonely island where only what is permitted to move moves, becomes the ideal." [5] The chairs offer Charley control and protection, security and power, because they are very large, they elevate the individual above others, and they surround the person who sits in them. But Charley also at times has a marked nostalgia for the past, and would like to live in the past, or live as in the past, and Pine Mountain is Charley's ideal of a "lonely island" where he is in control of events. That is why this chair is an old timer.

Consider this theme of power. The old-timer is certainly not the kind of chair one could rest in, for "if you wanna rest comf'table in a chair, you gotta make it so you can stretch your legs out an' rest." Charley is too small a man — only about five feet eight inches tall— to rest in this chair. What else would one use a rocking chair for, then, if not to rest in? Well, as a starter, the high seat in this chair "made you set away up high like a king or some'un." The contradiction between making a rocking chair to rest in and then not being able to rest in it because the seat is too high, and Charley's having drawn an analogy between the chair and a throne, suggest that the chair might serve as a symbol for the owner (and the maker). If Charley owned the chair now, could he perhaps feel like a king in, and exercise control over, the fantasy world he sometimes created in the things he built?

His bookcase masterpiece is relevant at this point. Although Charley never overtly likened it to a throne, most other people who have seen it have called it that, probably because of its gothic qualities, including the spires. "At first I liked it real good, uh, but I'm kinda like other people, I —it don't look right some way," said Charley, and then he giggled, indicating that what he had said was not funny but serious and, because it was serious, he tried to make it sound funny.

"You don't think it looks right?"

"No, it don't. It don't look like it b'longs here." Again the nervous laugh.

"It doesn't look like what?"

"I said, I believe, uh, it don't look like it b'longs here yet. I b'lieve it come here too early, or some'un or other, or too late, one."

After a moment he said, "Uh, it's so odd that, uh, bet it come too late or too quick, one; I don't know which." He twittered again.

If Charley has any basis in fact for considering these chairs antiques and old-timers, perhaps it is because they resemble thrones; thus, indeed, they came too early or too late, but either way they symbolize to Charley power and control and rulership which he has sought in his own life and affairs but perhaps not always achieved, although he has proven by the kinds of problems he set for himself and solved (epitomized by these chairs) that he is a king among craftsmen. Charley certainly conceives of himself as a master craftsman, though each weird chair was at first a a statement of doubt and then, when completed, a reaffirmation of this identity and a source of strength for the man and the artist. Journalists who have published regional and national articles about Charley have portrayed him as a superior artist without equal, and many people have written the same sentiments to Charley in letters or suggested them in person; in a recent popular article the author wrote that Charley "is possessed of an inborn knack and inventiveness that in another time and setting might have made him an official cabinetmaker to a king." What better way to inform the world that one is without equals, or that one's furniture is fit for royalty, than to build a throne and carve one's name and address on it? That is precisely what Charley did with his bookcase masterpiece.

It will also be recalled that shortly after he began work on a special chair for my wife and me Charley suddenly received nationwide attention and was inundated with letters: "then Lettres Went to Comin in froum East South North West Wantin to no if they Culd Buy a laddre Back Rockker and they said they Engoid Redid Abut me in the . . . news papre." But Charley had "never herd of this news papre." To him, "Ever'thing is so strang,"

just as he described the chair on which he was working during this unexpected incursion into his privacy. Did this chair, then, offer him protection,
with its massive barriers, against the superciliousness of others who had
suddenly invaded his world? Had he built for himself a domicile, with
storage space for the necessary condiments, to insulate him against this
new onslaught for which he was unprepared and which he could not fully
comprehend? Or was the strange emotion that was driving him on simply
conceit, reaffirmed by the many letters, that he was king of the chairmakers? Did he build a throne to demonstrate it?

The feeling of enclosure was most pronounced in his eight-legged
chairs of the early 1950s and in the six rocking chairs, made between
1961 and 1965, with eight legs, four rockers, and many slats close together or with solid bark or wood backs and sides. Even the "ordinary"
seven-slat rocking chairs are very tall and have many wide slats.
These characteristics were most apparent at the time of Charley's
emotional and economic problems, of his moving to the highway, of his
change in body image to that of the stereotypical hillbilly, and of the
composition of his song about his old Kentucky mountain home.

All the two-in-one chairs, whether slat back or bark back or wood
back, "hug" the occupant. One might make something of the generic name
for these chairs: "two-in-one." Relevant to what I am now implying is
Charley's reference in his song to "the place where I was born," his desire
to return there, and his knowledge that he cannot, combined with his
wanting to find the graves of both his grandfather, with whom he identified, and his mother, with whom he had lived and for whom he had
built a cabin; also relevant is Charley's propensity to make chairs with a
sense of "completeness," as well as of enclosure, as in the masterpiece.

Somewhat more speculatively and spectacularly, did Charley build not
a house or a throne or a womb, but a coffin? As noted earlier, Charley's
song, which was composed a few months before the masterpiece was built,
gives no indication of the particular war that the narrator was fighting in;
perhaps Charley, from his point of view, has had many battles to struggle
through which, in his mind, derived ultimately from his experiences in World

War II. I also pointed out that Charley had not in fact returned to his old Kentucky mountain home, and I suggested that neither had he found victory. The solution to his battle may well be, or have been, death.

Charley told me something interesting about the bookcase master-piece. After he said that the chair "don't look like it b'longs here," I asked him, "Is there anything in particular you don't like about it?"

"Well, uh, the particular thing I don't like about it is, uh, fella have to have, uh, footrest to go with it, stool to lay your legs upon to make it more comfy and, uh, it'd have to have, uh, to make it look just right, it'd have to have a genuine leather upholstery cushions for the back, seat, an' arms, and, uh, I found out what'd cost to get the leather to make the cushions," at which point he twittered nervously.

"Quite a bit, is it?"

"Oh, boy! It'd cost two-three hunnert to get enough leather to make cushion upholstery. Out a genuine leather. I didn't know who else to see about it but the shoe shop over there; he said genuine leather, enough to cover that'd cost two-three hunnert dollars." To be "more comfy" it needed a leg rest and "genuine leather upholstery cushions."

About seventy years ago in Chenango County, New York, one Henry Caulkin, a skilled craftsman specializing in wagons and furniture, report-edly made his own coffin in his spare time. He built for himself "a roomy, high-backed chair, complete with arm and foot rests. It was well-padded and covered with the traditional funereal cloth. Now to complete this strange coffin he built a box in the shape of the chair, but without a back and deep enough so that it could be placed over the chair and its occupant and fastened tightly to it. This, too, was lined with tufted cloth, and the upper part of it was glass."[6] It is an intriguing coinci-dence: Charley's bookcase masterpiece is remarkably like Caulkin's chair-coffin. Interesting, too, in this respect, is the old-timer, with its high back and its footrest, which Charley made for an old crippled woman without her knowledge who "passed on b'fore I got the chair done." Would the old-timer have been a throne for the aged woman who Charley knew was ill, a chair in which she could "set away up high like a king or some'un," or would it have been her coffin (or Charley's)?

For several years I considered the two-in-one bookcase rocker, masterpiece of furniture, out of place in Charley's productive career, as it does not fit well into an evolutionary scheme; it really should have been, I thought, the last chair made before committing suicide. Not only is Charley still alive, but he also continued to make more chairs; many of them are towering forms and massive structures in between which were squeezed small, unimposing works to be sold cheaply, and also other chairs of clean, swiftly flowing lines, all produced within the same few years of work. If the chair symbolized death to Charley then it came too early; there is no need for a tomb or for a heavenly throne, either (disregarding Charley's temporary identification with the tormented Christ). If the chair meant life or rebirth, it came too late, I reasoned, because Charley's world, or at least the world of men, collapsed within the next three or four years; no wish to return to the womb and try life once more would have helped him. If the chair was intended as an earthly throne, it still was not of this place and time, I thought, because Charley never, in my opinion, mastered the outer world, and even as a king of chairmakers he ruled few subjects and had no heirs apparent.

Nevertheless, one has the feeling that these themes are related in some way, and that in them we have identified several strands in the tangled skein formed by this man's behavior, the beliefs expressed, and the experiences described. There are the female and male elements: the womb and the tomb = enclosure = security, plus the source of creativity; and the throne, Pine Mountain, and the huge chairs of powerful form = virility and self-assurance as a man and a master crafts-man. Together in the bookcase masterpiece, in which these elements are balanced, they produce and reveal the whole man; this chair is not out of place at all but is necessary in the life and art of Charley. "Such a consciousness would see the becoming and the passing of things beside their momentary existence, and not only that, but at the same time it would also see the Other, which was before their becoming and will be after their passing hence," wrote Jung about individuals such as Charley.[7]

Perhaps this unusual craftsman, with his strange visions and his unique subjective perceptions, can indeed see the becoming and the passing of things. But of one thing I am now certain, that the process of grieving over a loss, resulting in the nostalgia for the past and the withdrawal from others expressed in Charley's chairs by old-timey traits and a sense of enclosure, is related to the creative process as well. And in this relationship lie the significance of the two-in-one bookcase rocker for understanding certain aspects of human behavior generally and the chair's meaning to Charley as a masterpiece.

The subject of bereavement has intrigued me for several years, since a series of illnesses and a recent death in my family, especially the way in which grief is related to personal expression and the making and doing of things. There is no question but that bereavement affects the works of an individual already making and doing things expressive of himself, as we have seen in the nostalgia and the withdrawal apparent in Charley's chairs; among the many personal experiences upon which an artist draws or which make themselves felt in his works, it is an especially poignant one. More interesting is the way in which grief can precipitate the process of personal expression, resulting in the production of a few objects, stories, or songs during a brief period of time, or, more rarely, causing recurrent expressive activity from that moment on. "Many times out of sickness, disappointment or sorrow, there will be some good come out of it," wrote an elderly farmer in Kansas who had composed a "sacred song" some years before while recuperating from a serious accident; "had those mules not run away with me I would never have written these inspiring words."[8] Seldom does intense involvement in production and performance endure after precipitation by grief, though occasionally it does; some for whom it did continue are Tab Ward, Olla Bell Reed, Gib Morgan, Anthony Piotrowski, Theora Hamblett, Larry Gorman,[9] and Sarah Ogan Gunning, whose "Girl of Constant Sorrow" was composed "about 1936 in New York, where her first husband, Andrew Ogan, was fatally ill. The text was descriptive of loneliness away from home and anticipated her bereavement." Sarah, two of whose four children died in the depression years and who was frequently ill, "worked out some of her sense of geographical separation and personal loss in song composition." [10]

There certainly are happy poets and playful painters, Charley's rocker is a masterpiece just because of the skill apparent in its manufacture which is unrelated to grieving, and on a smaller scale the motives for making or doing things, associated with grief, are common to many people during such daily experience as cleaning or ordering the house, cooking "creatively," mowing the yard or polishing the car and then taking pleasure in the results; these activities sometimes are engaged in when one is unable to solve some other, vexing problem. But many individuals who only rarely in their lives produce songs and stories or make things do so while grieving over a loss. Public expression relieves the burden of possible guilt for having caused the loss, generates sympathy for one's plight, and projects the problems outward away from oneself where they can be dealt with more easily. For some people, a song or a story expresses the anxiety or frustration of a life filled with personal failures; the expression perhaps exonerates the individual who finds the cause of his problems in the machinations of others, but also helps him find and express order and meaning in his life. Incapacitation, incarceration, or the loss of a friend or a relative or of one's own health fosters introspection which in turn may promote the production of a song or a story or of another work expressing one's feelings; such expressive activity helps the individual to regain part of what has been lost or to compensate for that loss in an attempt to readjust to life and its vicissitudes. The individual who has suffered loss is charged with nervous energy, sensitive to the human condition, and most aware of himself and his own frailty.

Part of the grieving process itself for any individual, metaphorically speaking, is the death of oneself or a part of oneself, and rebirth as a different individual. The grieving process and the creative process have much in common and sometimes are almost one: the search for structure and order, and the reaffirmation of self. In grief there is loss, followed by a feeling that the world is empty and poor; in communicating through expressive structures such as stories and songs there is filling the void caused by the loss, first a state of doubt and then order and belief and wholeness once more. The intensity of mourning and the introspection discharge the emotions of loss, hostility, and guilt and, ultimately, provide a reintegration of the self. "Now the war is over," sang Charley hopefully but perhaps prematurely in 1965, "so I thank God in heaven that I'm on my way back to my ole Kentucky mount'n home." His "ole Kentucky mount'n home" is less a place than a state of mind, a state of mind at peace, attainable only through creative activities such as chairmaking.

When his self-assurance as a man and as a craftsman faltered on the threshold of the outside world, when the severity of his problems increased and he lost the security and strength allowed him within his hollow in the mountains, Charley attempted to adjust to his losses and thus to reaffirm his identity by building chairs that gave him his cherished protection; in the process he was reborn, his strength was renewed, so that once again he could stand proud as man and artist and produce any kind of chair. Dreaming of a return to Pine Mountain was escape and perhaps death, but building chairs was adjustment and regeneration. Chairs like the old-timer and the bookcase masterpiece are testaments to both the creative and the grieving processes as they coalesce; in constructing these chairs, Charley began with doubt, but ended with certainty. (The human problems were real enough; the artistic ones, precipitated by the others, were self-generated as a test of strength and identity and, because successfully solved, served to rebuild the man.) The two-in-one bookcase masterpiece, more than any other chair, epitomized both processes, demonstrated Charley's enormous skill, and afforded Charley the opportunity to reconstruct himself, his life, and his world — a process of rebuilding that was not complete until he was finally alone with his inner reality and thus safe from other people and from forces in the outside world. Now that he is alone Charley is making chairs as he did in the early years, with a wholeness and strength of character and a clarity and economy of line which bespeak once more an aggressive self-certainty as an artist. [11]

Not everyone who makes things does so with the skill of Charley or with his commitment to the creative act, and therefore not every object commands attention the way some of Charley's chairs do. Furthermore, the making or doing of things requiring order and resulting in a sense of accomplishment and pleasure in the outcome is common in daily activities, but seldom does it attain the significance for others that it has had for Charley. But other craftsmen are worthy of study if for no other reason than to heighten one's appreciation of Charley and his works. As we will see in chapter 6, however, some of the others often say much about themselves, and sometimes something about life, through their chairs.

CHAPTER SIX

It Takes
Half a Fool to
Make Chairs

"I always liked repair work," said Verge, who since 1915 has occasionally made chairs. "I'd rather repair 'em than make 'em new. You can make good money 'cause the owner thinks it's a good chair and there's not too much work in it."

Verge is, as well as a craftsman, a retired musician who put down his banjo when he took up fundamentalism. Tight-lipped and stern, he is not a man to joke about either religion or chairmaking. But his son Hascal, another man named Beechum, and the craftsman Aaron, all of whom have worked in the same shop as Verge and whose chairs exhibit many qualities in common, enjoy repeating one of Verge's favorite sayings. "It takes half a fool to make chairs," Verge often remarked, "and a whole fool to make baskets."

Most men seem to feel the same way, which partly explains why there are few chairmakers and fewer basketmakers in this section of southeastern Kentucky. Even Verge, who "makes 'em for the money" and not for the "sake of makin' a good chair," as one of his relatives charged, would rather repair than create chairs because the financial rewards are higher.

Many times when I asked if there were any chairmakers around I was told that none remained: "You should have been here a decade ago in the 1950s; there were a dozen of them then." In point of fact, however, in the mid-1960s I met or learned about more than a dozen chair-makers.[1] Few of them engaged in craftwork with much enthusiasm or superior skill, but there is no reason to suppose the situation in the past had been radically different. The basic techniques of construction are rather easily learned by men who need to fashion make-dos for their homes, or by those who must find an immediate source of income to help them through financial crises, or by those who simply want to keep busy during the winter and decide to make a few chairs. All are called "chairmakers" by someone else, even though these men do not "do it for a livin'" and are not "old-time chairmakers."

As a lifetime occupation, chairmaking is bound to attract few individuals, because, like any process of making things, it requires considerable interest in and commitment to the creative act.

"Do you think it takes a special talent to be a chairmaker?" I asked Charley.

"I don't b'lieve so," he said.

"You think anybody could be a chairmaker?"

"No, I don't b'lieve just anybody could—too hard a work."

"Does it take some special skill?"

"Yes sir, it does. It takes a skill specially for, uh, you got to learn how to use that drawin' knife — use it just right to take off hick'ry bark with or whatever you're making," though other chairmakers use a drawing knife much less frequently and for fewer tasks than Charley does.

"Can anyone learn how to use a drawing knife?"

"I'd say so, exceptin', uh, you got to learn to get interested in anything to learn it— you have to learn to get interested in a thing like that before you could learn it. And anyway, I b'lieve anyone could learn how to use a drawin' knife and do that work."

"Anybody could learn how to be a chairmaker, then?"

"Well, yes, they could, but they'd have to learn to be interested in that first."

"Do you think you have a special talent for making chairs? Something you're born with, an ability to work with wood?"

"No, I don't think so. I think, uh, what you grow up with is one reason that you do that."

We have already considered what Charley did and why he did it, but what about other men who grew up with chairmaking? What happened to them? How much interest did they have and what did they learn? Who were the dozen chairmakers in the 1960s, why and how did they make chairs, and what has happened to them in the past few years? Let us begin with Verge and the individuals who were influenced by him.

When Verge found religion he lost all interest in fancy things. His chair style is so plain it would make a devout Shaker, with his own gift to be simple, think he had backslidden (figures 83, 84). "For myself, I like a decent, plain-made chair," declared Verge, who objected to turnings and other ornamentation used by Charley, Aaron, and his son Hascal.

A "decent" chair, as Verge's works indicate, would be made of a material better known for its structural soundness than for its appearance, such as ash: "Now it makes a good chair—solid and heavy." Verge has also sampled hard and soft maple because "that makes a good

Figure 83. Armchair with bark back and seat made by Verge (1934). Another chair-maker, though deeming the chair "fairly comfortable," complained that it was "not as pretty as ladder-back chairs" and that "it takes too much bark to make."

Figure 84. Bench and rockers made by Verge (c. 1935-1940). The tapered arms, said Verge, are "pretty;" there are no "knobs" or "nubs" because "I like a decent, plain-made chair."

chair;" white poplar; walnut which is "pretty but not too strong" and therefore unsuitable; oak; sassafras which is "easy timber worked, and light, but awful easy burst;" and white "linn" which is "pretty soft and easy worked but not too stout." Verge finally settled on plain ash.

"I don't like the nubs on the posts," he said, referring to all chairs made with finials. For Verge, the most offensive chairs are many of Charley's works. "Some of them rockers are the ugliest chairs I've ever seen." After viewing each photograph of a chair made by Charley or by Aaron he repeated, "I don't like all them rings and nubs." He was also displeased by the height of their rocking and dining chairs. "I don't like a low seat with a real high back. I always made my own front posts nineteen inches and the back posts forty-one and a half inches."

Verge claims never to have altered those dimensions in half a century, although he did change designs with a view toward greater simplicity. Born in 1895, Verge began helping his father at the age of eleven, learning first to turn the chair "spokes" or stretchers on a foot-powered lathe and then to make the posts; finally he learned the most difficult task of all, bottoming a chair. He is still critical of other men who do not know how to make chairs but who offer to bottom them. "Most don't know how to do it. They don't weave the bark underneath — just let it hang — so the seat sags." His father, said Verge, "would brag on my work, of course, if I got it right." And Verge is pretty certain his way is right. His earliest chairs, he said, had flat, wide arms, but eventually he tapered them so they would be "good lookin';" a chair without tapered arms, he says now, is "ugly." The taper of arms varies considerably on his chairs, but one feature is constant: the absence of turnings. His brother Everett, who flirted with the useless, chiseled two circles into the back posts of his chairs, but Verge could not quite accept that much ornamentation.

In his own defense, Verge contends that most of the "people around here say I make the best chair of any one fella that's made 'em around here. They don't say I make the best-lookin' chair—just the best one." A vociferous minority, however, refuted Verge, claiming that he was more interested in making money than in "makin' a good chair." He implied as much in his remarks about preferring repair work. In addition, his notion of an ideal business is that of quantity production with modern machinery on a contract basis, "so you know you have a sale for a certain design." He said, "the better the machinery, the more you can make," meaning both chairs and money. Like many men, Verge was especially concerned with the rapid production of huge quantities of chairs, even suggesting that there was a diminished number of chairmakers, owing to the absence of adequate remuneration: "Not many chairmakers around now 'cause they can't make chairs fast enough to make any money." Yet when I asked Verge for his definition of a good chairmaker, he said, "He'd have to work slow enough to do perfect work." Verge claimed that he always boiled the slats of a chair and pressed them, unless of course he was rushed and had to put the slats in the chair green, which seems to have been often, and he said he seldom marked the back posts but mortised them by sight so that he could make chairs faster. When Verge stopped helping his father and started his own chair shop at the age of thirty, squeezing in chairmaking between farming and delivering mail, he sold most of his settin' chairs on contract for sixty cents each to a settlement school, which in turn resold them; he also peddled a few for fifty cents apiece to local people, usually coal miners, "'cause that's about the only money there was in this part of the country then." By the mid-1930s a settin' chair sold for a dollar and a rocker for three; thirty years later the price was five times as much.

Verge was vague about the sources of his designs, but he did mention that some came from mail-order catalogues and some from his father and brother; others "we'd just figger up ourself to see which different designs would sell better." After all, the "more designs a chairmaker'd know to do, the more sales he could get." But Verge's designs were not numerous. A chair of white ash and hickory bark splints, which he made in 1934 and still owns, is typical of his work (figure 83). Most of Verge's armchairs, rocking chairs, and benches have been bark back rather than slat back or panel back. The design is not unique to him, but he has used it the most. Aaron said that the bark-back chair is "fairly comfortable, but not as pretty as ladder-back chairs. And it takes too much bark to make." Aaron objected to the design because he hates to skin bark, prepare it for weaving, and bottom the chairs; when Verge, Hascal, and Aaron worked together it was Verge who bottomed all the chairs, a task that, like repair work, he seemed to enjoy. On each arm of the chair shown in figure 83 there is a flat surface at the end, underneath, to which a small projection of the post is affixed with a nail; whether the arm is flat on top (as Aaron makes them), or flat underneath like this one, or entirely round depends on the customer's request, although Verge prefers the particular design he used. More recent chairs made in the early 1960s have no flat surfaces on the arms at all; the chairs look somewhat more squarish; and the bark panels in the backs are narrower.

The times of Verge's greatest productivity were the early 1930s and the 1960s; in both periods of time he worked in a chair shop at a local school founded by a woman from the East, ascetic to an extreme, who shared the fundamentalist values of Verge and other "creek people" in his area. "She didn't want no finish work," said Verge; "she just wanted what you done with the chisel," which suited him. Although bark three-quarters of an inch wide looks the best in chair bottoms, "she wanted inch-and-a-half bark 'cause she said the wider bark lasts longer." In essence, "she didn't care for the looks. The same way with buildings. Put 'em rough 'cause that was the cheapest. She said she'd rather have more rough buildings for more scholars to get an education instead of just a few pretty buildings for just a few scholars." Verge's chairs and his remarks evince much the same attitude that this woman had, and he continues to speak of her with reverence.

The years of least productivity for Verge's son Hascal, however, were the mid-1960s in the same shop. During my eight visits to the shop only Beechum was working, not Hascal; Hascal managed to explain away his inactivity by saying that he could get into more trouble with the school by doing the wrong kind of work than by not working at all. He also contended that the administrators would like him to work all the time, though slowly, but they wanted so many chairs that if he worked he would have to work rapidly. If he had his own shop at home, he said, he could take his time and make chairs slowly and properly, but then he said he was too nervous and wanted to finish a job as soon as possible after starting it, although in the chair shop it was Beechum and other men before him who finished the projects suggested by Hascal. Hascal claimed he did not like to work in the shop because he had to produce to order and could not experiment, yet if he had his own business he would prefer mass production of standard items to ensure large sales; and he said that during slack times, as in the summer of 1967 when I was in the shop, the school in fact permitted him to make sample items following his own design. He was not doing so because, he said, he was not supposed to set up the equipment to make certain kinds of chairs as it might be the wrong setup for what the administrators wanted next. Hascal wanted to make chairs, he said, but he was really not able to because he needed electrical equipment to render the task easier; nevertheless, the shop was well equipped with drill presses, jigsaws, and an expensive lathe — more and better machinery than other chairmakers had — which Beechum used but Hascal never touched. Finally, he said that he was supposed to train others to make chairs, not produce them himself.

Hascal, who was thirty-two years old when I met him, was the only one of Verge's three sons to identify himself as a chairmaker. Asked why he made chairs, Hascal replied, "I saw everyone else was doin' it an' it looked like good money," but then he complained about his low income. The job was a form of relief work for which the men were paid $40 a week plus food stamps in exchange for making chairs to be used at the school or to be given as gifts to outsiders who provided donations supporting the institution. Hascal had considered a job offer from a furniture factory in Berea at thrice his wage but turned it down because, he said, it was not as much money as he needed or thought he was worth. Although he had tried several jobs — "I get tired of doing the same thing after four or five years and change"— he said he would never stop making chairs; in August, 1967, he quit the chair shop and assumed janitorial duties at another school because, he said, "there isn't much work to it" and "I wanna work as little as possible."

Chairmaking, however, was the only job he had tried which did not make him nervous, he said, spilling tobacco on the floor as he attempted to roll a cigarette. He has a "sick stomach" so he cannot eat greasy foods but must drink "sweet milk" and cream; chairmaking, though, did not "bother" him. Perhaps that was because he did not work at it.

As Hascal was not making chairs at the time (and according to Aaron, who worked in the same shop earlier, Hascal never made many chairs), it was impossible to note in detail his work procedures, but he posed for pictures and summarized his production techniques, which are common among other chairmakers. As he hopped from one piece of equipment to another, it was apparent that when and if Hascal ever made chairs he did so rapidly, not steaming and pressing slats but putting them in green and refusing to bend walnut posts or slats at all because of the patience required to do the job properly; and, as Aaron's brother said, Hascal "was so nervous he nearly cut himself with the chisel while mortisin' chair backs; his hands really shook."

Hascal claimed to have originated many chair designs himself, but he was embarrassed when we looked around the shop and could not find any; he said that a person could not make anything good in the shop, that the administrators who did not even know what a round was tried to tell him how to make a chair, and that he would prefer working at home where he was free to innovate and where, "if I wanted to spend two weeks on one thing I was really interested in working on, I could." Later he asked me for some photographs of chairs so he could "get some ideas" for designs if he ever started his own shop.

Hascal said he was the designer of, among other chairs in the shop which I photographed, an unfinished maple rocker made about 1963 or 1964 (figure 86), which looks rather like an early chair of Aaron's. This and other works also exhibit similarities to Verge's chairs, such as the tendency toward simplicity of design and execution and the tapering of the arm at the end that enters the back post. A layman in the area who looked at the photo of the maple rocker said he did not like it because it was too simple and without turnings at all (in fact it does have turnings on the posts beneath the seat).

"The seat's too little in hit and the rounds are too close to the bottom," said Charley, assuming it was an armchair and not suspecting that it was an unfinished rocking chair. "Look a whole lot better if the rounds was at least six inches or better from the bottom. Hit wouldn't make it no

Figure 85. Maple armchair made by Hascal (1963 or 1964) at the request of a woman who never picked it up.

Figure 86. This unfinished rocking chair, allegedly made by Hascal (c. 1963 or 1964), is remarkably similar to Aaron's early chairs. The type of rocker that should be on the chair, said Hascal, "scoots worser on a rug or where you've waxed the floor."

solider but you take a chair now, in a few years it'll wear plumb off to the rounds.

"It looks like it's got a comf'table back on hit," continued Charley. "The only fault I see with that chair is the bottom of hit, the way it's fixed.

Hit's too 'dubby' I call it. If you wanted to get a rubber gasket to put on it to keep from damagin' the 'noleum rug, you couldn't find one to fit."

Charley made the same criticism about another of Hascal's works, a maple barstool made about 1964 (figure 87), which Hascal said he had designed himself; it was one of more than a hundred he had made. Charley proclaimed it "a very nice-lookin' stool, but they fixed the points on the bottom so peaked you can't put any rubber things on it." He also said he would have added another round so the stool could be used as a stepladder and he would have carved out the seat "to make it comf'tabler."

Figure 87: Barstool made by Verge's son Hascal (c. 1964). "That's a very nice-lookin' stool," said Charley, "but they fixed the points on the bottom so peaked you can't put any rubber things on it."

Another of Hascal's productions I photographed is a maple footstool dating from about 1965 (figure 88). In Charley's opinion, "Hit's too open. It'd look a lot better if the rounds hadn't been so close to the floor. An' if it wasn't square it'd looked a lot better. It's interestin' to know that some people don't try to change their patterns none."

Yet that is precisely what Hascal said he was doing. How was it possible that this man could claim originality of vision in a mode of production in which he seldom engaged and in products that seemed rather conventional? He had learned the techniques of chairmaking from his grandfather, his uncle, and especially his father, so why could he or would he not build chairs, and what was he doing in a chair shop?

Most of the time Hascal talked, expounding to everyone his religious views, his drinking excesses, and his extramarital sexual exploits, subjects that constitute the kind of personal information men in this area keep to themselves. Not Hascal. Although he was born and raised in this small community, and his father and his kin were still there, Hascal considered himself an outsider who did not share the fundamentalist religious beliefs, the asceticism, and the puritanical attitudes of the "creek people," including his father, just as he challenged (in his mind anyway) the conventional chairs made by his father and by other men. To his own regret Hascal never finished high school, but guided by correspondence with a Seventh Day Adventist preacher, he studied the Bible thirty minutes a day for a couple of years: "It didn't cost me anything as long as I got a C in the course," said Hascal. "That was the only thing I ever got free from church." He also taught Sunday school for a year and a half, but complained later that he never got paid for it although he "managed to get a suit out of it." He claimed to be religious, but of course in an unconventional way; he summed up his attitude with the following anecdote: "A man told me he might get me a job as pastor of a church and another guy standin'

Figure 88. Maple stool made by Hascal (c.1965). "It's interestin' to know that some people don't try to change their patterns none," said Charley. "Hit's too open," he continued. "It'd look a lot better if the rounds hadn't been so close to the floor."

there interrupted an' said he thought pastors ought to be religious or at least believe in God. And the first man said, 'To hell with God, this man needs the damned money!'"

Hascal had no compunction about expressing his attitudes toward sex as well as religion, and sometimes he mixed the two topics. For example, there was a story he told twice with great relish, repeating the punch line several times, concerning a preacher with "a fourteen-inch tool" who had "ruined" several women — "killed one or two by rupturing their wombs" — and who wanted to seduce a married woman in church. Hascal also reminisced about his own mostly extramarital sexual activities, particularly to the other men in the chair shop. Several of them later told me that at least some of the exploits were probably true.

Without question Hascal relishes the attention of others; for this reason he once worked as a disc jockey on a local radio station and also performed with a band called the Floyd County Sweethearts. Nothing pleased him more than an audience held at rapt attention by his unceasing flow of words. What Hascal had to talk about in the chair shop, however, was of interest only because it titillated. He held attention by degrading himself and offending other people, an act that tended to deny him acceptance by many people in the local community; at the same time he achieved notoriety, which brought many men to his shop to listen to his "wicked" ideas and hear about his activities; and by denouncing local customs and beliefs he proved the originality of his ideas and attempted to endear himself to outsiders, to whom he felt spiritually akin in some of his values and with whom he sought friendship. In making his sins public and in reveling in them before an audience of local people, however, Hascal seemed also to be punishing himself by exposing his excesses to the very people who would indeed be most shocked and most inclined to censure him.

Hascal is an intelligent man with some skill as a musician and as a woodworker; he has the potential for contributing significantly to several traditions; and he sincerely wanted to develop his unique insights and discoveries. But he seemed to be paralyzed. In the chair shop he did not work but merely talked about what he would do, or would like to do, or could do, or allegedly had done. His ideas for new chair designs were never executed; he wanted to work slowly but lacked the patience; he hoped to make chairs, as his father did, but could not. Always when he started a job there was enthusiasm initially, but tasks were left unfinished and aspirations went unfulfilled: his hands shook and his tongue rattled. Hascal's "nervousness" was like the classical example of an experienced singer who suddenly cannot reach the high notes because of an inhibition verging on hysteria. Hascal no longer knew what he wanted, or he wanted impossible things, and he could do nothing at all. The bravado of his demeanor before an audience in the chair shop belied the existence of problems that he was at the time unable to solve; that is why he quit the shop altogether and picked up a broom, mechanically swinging it back and forth across the floor as he pondered the glorious things he might have done.

Hascal had become obsessed with needs and drives that he claimed had been repressed by other creek people, including his own father, and by himself in the past. He tried to release them. His joyful description of his indulgences to others, however, was probably not always simply a rejection of conventional values, as he claimed, but sometimes an obsession with the gratification of the self. Combine a propensity toward unconventionalism with a selfish or even brutal expression of desires, stir in a large quantity of extroversion, add a dash of imagination, season heavily with guilt, and let simmer for several years under the lid of paternal control, repression of certain desires, and an unhappy marriage which interrupted a high school education, and one has a volatile mixture indeed. It may have exploded by now.

Aaron, who also worked in the chair shop in the early 1960s, is, in contrast, a quiet, even-tempered, retiring man who does not say much to anyone about anything but devotes most of his attention to shaping, sanding, and shellacking chairs with a finesse not characteristic of other craftsmen in the area. Aaron is careful — no, meticulous — and patient. He is also of good humor and is generally satisfied with

Figure 89. Maple settin' chair (painted green) made (c. 1960) by Harry, a neighbor (now dead) of Aaron's. Aaron learned to make settin' chairs by copying this one.

Figure 90. Aaron's first copy (1962) of Harry's chair (fig. 89), but there are differences: Aaron's chair lacks the pegs; the back posts are not flared out so far; the slats are more nearly equal in length.

himself, his work, and the things he makes.

Scrutinizing a rocking chair he had just constructed, Aaron said, "The way it is now looks balanced to me. Now I don't know how the general public would feel about it." He cares about the feelings of others, and he is responsive to consumer demands if they are reasonable. Sometimes they are not. The "ugliest" chair Aaron ever saw was one he himself had made on demand for an arthritic woman who wanted it built with a high seat, a tall back with four slats, and one armrest so she could crawl in and out of it more easily. He also has been asked to make chairs with posts "as thin as a broomstick," but he feels that the legs now "don't look so chubby," and posts smaller in diameter would make the chair "too frail lookin.'"

Despite his general satisfaction with the things he makes, Aaron is not pleased with all his works. Earlier rockers had too many "spools" that were not well made, he said, and while present chairs are "kinda pretty," they don't set too good, 'specially the dining chairs." He and his brother Myron joked that a dining chair should not be too comfortable anyway, as a person might sit at the table too long and eat too much. In order to increase the comfort of the dining chair, Aaron made the back posts half an inch shorter than the front legs. Nevertheless, "Nothing 'cept upholstered chairs set as good as settin' chairs."

But Aaron does not make many settin' chairs, first because this kind chair must be made of a strong wood like ash or hickory and he prefers to work with walnut, which "makes a pretty chair but it's easy broke;" second, because the five or six dollars he usually gets for a settin' chair is scarcely worth the effort to make one; third, because its design is too simple to appeal to him; and fourth, because he just does not like to make settin' chairs and has had little practice.

Actually he started making chairs in 1962 by patterning a settin' chair after one made by a neighboring chairmaker who was no longer alive. Aaron measured Harry's work exactly and duplicated as closely as he could the chair's features and dimensions, and, on the basis of a smattering of knowledge gained from his father and other men, he built his own settin' chair of maple and ash (figures 89, 90). The two chairs are not quite the same. Harry put a large peg in each end of the top slat, whereas Aaron used small pins of wood which blend with the chair; the posts of Harry's chairs are flared backward in a fashion that would never appeal to Aaron, who is soft spoken and tends to be personally undemonstrative; and the distance between the top of the back posts and the bottom of the legs is more nearly equal in Aaron's chair, again suggesting greater containment in expressive quality. All these elements indicate that every handmade chair, even a copy by a neophyte, is in fact a unique product, exhibiting characteristics peculiar to the individual who made it.

From settin' chairs Aaron graduated to rockers and stools and dining chairs, but he does not remember how many of each he has made. "Never thought I'd make enough to fool with keepin' track of 'em."

Why fool with making chairs now? "I swore I'd get a job two years ago, then last winter, but I never did," he told me in the summer of 1967. In fact, Aaron held several jobs before he began to make chairs. Born in 1926 and never married, he lives at home with his father, an unmarried brother, and a married brother and his family. After Aaron returned from service in the Pacific at the end of World War II he attended the local academy where a decade and a half later he would make chairs for a couple of years. He taught in elementary schools in the area for three years, but despised the work so much that he allowed his certificate to lapse to force himself to find some other kind of employment. Then for several years, he wandered from one northern city to another, working at various semiskilled jobs such as operating a drill press and making television cabinets and stands. Disillusioned and unhappy, he finally headed back to the hills of Kentucky, where he started doing what many southern mountaineers are infamous for, drinking.

One day in mid-1962, while recovering from a weeklong bout with the bottle, he heard that the school would soon reactivate the chair shop and needed craftsmen. Several men had already signed up to work under Verge's supervision, and one of the teachers who had befriended Aaron encouraged him to accept the job, which he did. It was a half-hearted response, because the shop reminded Aaron of the factories where he had given up his freedom to work under someone else's direction. Verge and Hascal were amazed at Aaron's skill and knowledge when he joined them, and they remarked upon his diligence and his talent as a craftsman—when he worked. Often he drank, taking a nip on the job in defiance of the academy rule forbidding faculty and staff to smoke or drink at all. It was not the first time Aaron had broken the rules, for when he was a student at the school in the late 1940s he was the only one who lived at home rather than in a dormitory and the only one who had a car and roamed about at will. But Aaron the chairmaker went a little bit too far when he ventured onto the post office lawn one day, lay down, and drank his bourbon lunch.

In early 1964 he was again without a job. He began to make chairs at home once more, at first to support his drinking habit but later to help overcome it. By the time I met him he was firmly on the wagon, with a tight rein on his problems, and the empty half-pints lining the walk to his house were like ruts in a road, covered with more than a year's accumulation of dust.

It also took awhile for Aaron to shake himself loose from Verge's and Hascal's influence. The form of a black walnut rocker made about 1962 and owned by Aaron (figure 48) is typical of works produced at the inception of his career. It is a panel-back or vertical-back chair with indistinctly defined turnings. The back posts have stiles because the post on the right had a structural fault, which Aaron cut out with a drawing knife, and because Aaron happened to like stiles at that time. Another black walnut rocking chair, made in 1963 or 1964 (figure 49), has more distinctly developed turnings and a more sharply defined form, suggesting greater self-certainty in its maker. The rockers are still rounded on the top edge, a design element that Hascal claimed to have developed; the academy dean who "wanted something a bit different" suggested the idea, and Hascal said he "figgered out the best way to make 'em was to hew 'em out and take the corners off" on the drawing horse, but "this type scoots worser than others on a rug or where you've waxed."

Both these chairs resemble those I found in the chair shop made by Hascal or his father, but they differ somewhat in that they have less taper to the posts; they are of a more fragile, expensive, and "pretty" wood — walnut; they reveal a definite interest in ornamentation; and they exhibit the unusual trait of a hole in the top slat which Aaron admitted was his trademark. Some customers would like all the slats in a chair to have a notch in the center, but, Aaron said, the notch weakens the slat or panel and should not be there at all. Why make the notch then? He said he made some chairs with it and others without, and potential customers always chose the chairs with the notch so he began making all chairs with a notch in the center of the top edge of the slat; but he was also seeking to develop his own distinctive kind of chair.

"I like that chair," remarked Verge about Aaron's earlier work reminiscent of chairs produced in the shop under Verge's supervision; "but for myself I wouldn't have them rings and nubs. But you gotta make it how the customers want," he said, not realizing that Aaron was making the chair as he finally wanted to. "I like the round arms," concluded Verge; the rounded arm was the only major element of Verge's and Hascal's chairs which Aaron maintained in his later works, though he wanted to depart from it.

Charley was more explicit than Verge in his assessment of Aaron's early chairs. Of the rocker shown in figure 48 he said, "That's a good-lookin' chair if they was a few improvements in it." He listed nine.

First, he would have bent the crest "to fit the head better." Also "the top slat [the crest] oughta been wider where it goes into the postees." Furthermore, "you need the panels nar'er than that to make it comf'tabler." Fourth, "I'd a put more rounds in hit, put in at least two rounds b'low the seat." In addition, "Hit shoulda had more designs [turnings] b'low the arms kinda like the decoratin' b'low the seat." Sixth, "I never did like this type of arm," by which he meant the barrel design, the only element in the chair of which Verge approved because it was similar to his; Charley, however, usually makes flat arms, although he has used barrel arms on quite a few chairs. "Now that decoratin'," Charley noted, "hit's unusual an' a little bit differ'nt. I've never seen decoratin' like that b'fore. That's what people are lookin' for." Charley agreed that "the number of panels is right for the chair. But if he'd made a real crook in the backs like I made 'em he'd a had to a made the panels nar'er an' he'd have to have more of 'em." Finally, "the chair needs patchin'—you need to patch the gaps in 'twixt the bark."

Actually the gaps in the seat were formed when the splints drew away from each other as they dried. To my knowledge only Charley uses winter bark (skinned in early fall) taken directly from the tree. Aaron and other men in his area use summer bark, which has more sap and consequently shrivels up more when it seasons. In addition, Aaron and others strip off and discard the top half of the inner bark; thus the splints are only half as thick as Charley's and the edges turn down as they dry, leaving holes which Charley finds objectionable.

Charley was more impressed with Aaron's recent works, as was Aaron himself. "That's a new design on me," Charley said about a chair made in 1967 (figure 50). "I've never seen that decoratin' before on a chair. Whoever made this chair's interested in makin' somethin' differ'nt." Charley had never met Aaron or seen his chairs; rather, he selected these works for special comment from a stack of photographs of chairs I had given him. "The wood in them backs has been sawed," he continued; "it's not been riven out 'cause the grain in each slat's differ'nt; can't can't tell 'bout the postees. I'd a put that bottom round closer to the seat—that big hole don't look good. Hit's a well-built chair like the other'n; there's nothin' out a line. That's the reason I'm sure he's an old-time chairmaker."

That remark would have pleased Aaron, who was generally content with his recent works which he thought were "kinda pretty" in form and design. Aaron's brother said that the dining and rocking chairs were pretty because "they got all them knobs on 'em." Referring to a black walnut rocker he made in late July, 1967, however, Aaron muttered to himself that "it ain't the prettiest one I ever made." He said that the wood showed knots and whitewood and that the grain was not straight on all the pieces; to Aaron the perfectionist, the component elements should have matched in all respects.

For the most part, however, Aaron felt that his chairs were attractive in their harmony of design and form: the spools were of the proper shape and number and location on the chair; the wood was inherently pretty; the chairs were of good proportions with design elements unified. By the time I met Aaron in 1967 he was making rocking chairs on which the turnings had become quite clearly delineated, the rockers and slats were sharply defined, the form—slat back rather than panel back—no longer resembled factory-made chairs, which looked "cheap" according to him, and the back posts had been made smaller in diameter, increasing the elegance of the chair. In other words, Aaron was executing works

Figure 91. An unnamed piece of
furniture Aaron made in August,
1967, for a customer who wanted
an end table; Aaron makes chairs
and stools only, not tables, but
he was loath to call this table
a stool.

Figure 92. Black walnut dining
chair with arms made by Aaron
in August, 1967, for a customer
who did not want the typical
barrel arms. Aaron borrowed the
design, not wholly successfully,
from Charley's recent chairs.
Said Aaron, "They can be
improved on."

that were distinctly his own with only a nod of recognition to his predecessors, chairs in which, from his point of view, all the elements were
perfectly integrated.

If that was so, then why did he make a dining chair in August,
1967, with flat arms that were obviously not in harmony with the rest
of the chair (figure 92)? There are two important reasons. The barrel
arms still disturbed Aaron because they were like Verge's; he had wanted
to employ some other design but had no idea what. In mid-July I had
shown Aaron photographs of some of Charley's works, a few of which he
examined closely, but he remarked only on the arms of two of the
chairs (figures 47, 69), saying, "Both of 'em's pretty. That armrest's
pretty and it'd be easy to make." I did not realize at the time why
he had singled out the armrests for comment, or suspect what he had
in mind. In late August a niece of Aaron's asked him to make eight
dining chairs, one of which should have arms although Aaron usually made
such chairs without arms. His niece thought that the surface area of the
arms should be larger than that of the barrel arms, and Aaron agreed, so
he tried to make them like the armrests on Charley's chairs. The results
disappointed and embarrassed Aaron, who became apologetic. Although
his niece seemed satisfied, Aaron said the arms were too thin, the small
ends of the arms which fitted into the posts were not small enough, and
the inside of the curve was too deep. In essence, the chairs "can be
improved on."

Aaron felt the design had possibilities and might be attractively
realized, but it was a problem he would have to work on in the future.
That he has the patience for such a task was obvious. As I watched him
make chairs, he measured each post with a handmade micrometer in order
to get every two exactly alike: "Get 'em all alike and you don't have to worry
about whether they'll set right or not." Aaron sanded each piece while it
was on the turning lathe, using fine sandpaper and emory cloth, despite
his contention that "I dislike this job worse'n any job of chairmaking —
too dusty." Meticulously he measured the angle of every hole he drilled in
the posts, carefully he tested the smoothness of each slat he sawed to

Figure 93. Beechum in the shop where several craftsmen learned from one another; his miniature corn sleds seem to epitomize what is taken locally to be "art."

shape and sanded, and conscientiously he turned the rounds twice a day as they seasoned above the wood-burning stove in the kitchen: "If you don't turn 'em like an ole hen turns her eggs," he warned, "they get a crook in 'em."

"He's experienced as a chairmaker," said Charley as he examined photos of Aaron's chairs. "He must be a slow worker an' a sure worker." Aaron, in fact, is second only to Charley in his willingness to "fool" with chairmaking, that is, to take it seriously.

Many other men were making chairs in the 1960s, but not necessarily with pronounced skill or real interest. Two men who helped Verge build chairs in the early sixties both switched to tuning up cars at a service station. Beechum, who was born in 1940, worked in the chair shop with

Hascal for a few months because "they was about to close me out" of carpentry work. In July, 1967, he said he would not make chairs if he could find other work because "the money's too slow. I just can't make much money at it." A month later he quit the shop and headed north to find money to support his wife and three children whom he had left behind in a mountain hollow; he tried four different jobs in a week and that was the last I heard of him.

What about Charley's relatives? His sons of course could not learn chairmaking from him. Two cousins and a nephew who helped Charley make chairs in the early 1940s never became chairmakers because the financial rewards were inadequate and the work was uninspiring. Charley's uncle Oaklie spends more time repairing seats than making chairs. He was once known for the speed with which he produced chairs, turning them on a foot-powered lathe; he never made octagon-shaped chair parts, as Charley does, although he admires his nephew's work: "Never had enough patience to shape 'em out . . . Man, they're pretty the way he makes 'em." Charley said his uncle "was a fast worker, but I've had people tell me they [Oaklie's chairs] weren't no account. He put 'em together too green or somethin.'" Oaklie does not put them together at all now because "I'm too nervous," that is, he is an alcoholic.

Charley's brother Steton could never make chairs properly either, and he, too, spends most of his time drinking. "I think he makes one ever' now an' then, but he's not able to do much work," said Charley, rather charitably. On another occasion Charley told me that his brother "couldn't put 'em together, no sir; he put 'em together lopsided and every which way," as apparent in a chair on Steton's front porch (figure 94). The posts were turned on a makeshift lathe Steton keeps in a shed behind the house, but the rounds were roughly hewed with an ax, the arms are ill fitting, the panels in the back were chopped from boards, and the chair as a whole is poorly constructed. Steton told me that he had not made chairs for several years because he could find no customers to buy them. That seems not to have bothered his wife Emmafair, who, according to other members of the family, "doped" Steton into marrying her, that is,

Figure 94. Rocking chair made by Charley's brother Steton (c. 1955). The posts were turned on a lathe; the rounds were hewed out roughly with an ax. The chair is barely usable.

"charmed" him with affection and with her skills as a housewife. Deformed from birth, she is a jealous wife who used to follow Steton wherever he went for fear he would desert her. A few years before I met her, when Steton was getting bark in the woods to bottom a chair, she fell and broke her hip and now cannot walk at all. "Lord have mercy, ain't that awful?" exclaimed Oaklie. "Poor ole Stet. Boy, I wouldn't have that on my hands, would you? Lordy!" I am told, however, that Emmafair is an excellent cook.

　　Living near Cumberland were three other men who, I was informed, were chairmakers. Courtney, however, is a farmer who made two rocking chairs during the winter of 1964-65, turning them on a neighbor's lathe (figure 95). Charley thought the chair in the photo I showed him looked like a factory-made chair. Hascal remarked, "I just don't like them kinda chairs; they're just an ordinary chair built on rockers." And Aaron concurred: "I don't like it. It's nothin' but a settin' chair on rockers." To pass the time Courtney also whittled a few chairs with a pocket knife, like the small cedar chair in figure 96. Courtney claimed that a man from Harlan wanted him to make eight settin' chairs at eight dollars each, but he had not done it by the time I left in 1967, and there is no reason to think he ever did.

Hugh, a coal miner who wants to work with wood when he retires, was not a specialist either (see figure 20). Said a neighbor, "He ain't no chair-maker; he jest pranks around with it."

One might reach the same conclusion about Morris, a farmer at Highsplint. Morris, who is in his early thirties, has made a bed frame, a table, a dulcimer, some baskets, a picture frame, two banjos, and a couple of chairs, but he does not want to be a full-time craftsman because "I can't make no money at it. I'd always be a poor man." Morris could not tolerate poverty, for then he would be unable to maintain his home and grounds which were the neatest and cleanest in the hollow, a point made by a neighbor from whom I asked directions to Morris's home; Morris is a

Figure 95. Rocking chair made by Courtney in the winter of 1964-65. Hascal said, "I just don't like them kinda chairs; they're just an ordinary chair built on rockers." Nor did Aaron like it: "It's nothin' but a settin' chair on rockers."

Figure 96. Cedar settin' chair made by Courtney in 1964; he whittled it with a pocket knife.

fastidious man who refused to be photographed with his chairs because he feared the soil on his work clothes might show up.

In use in Morris's home are two chairs with square posts which he made about 1958 (figures 97, 98); the electric lathe he then owned was of no use to him because he had no electricity. He had a drawing knife, too, but no drawing horse, so he hewed out the pieces with an ax and tried to smooth them on a bench using a hand plane. The slats were hewed out also and were not cooked or pressed, and the bark for the seats was thin, poorly cut, and full of knots and weak places, but Morris seemed not to notice. One chair originally had arms but he cut them off because anyone larger than himself (he is five feet, five inches, and weighs one hundred twenty pounds) could not sit in it.

"Morris can make chairs so good you couldn't tell 'em from those you buy in the store," one woman told me. Not everyone agreed with her. Another layman said that

Figure 97. Rocking chair Morris made (c. 1958) with an ax. Charley's judgment was: "Whoever made that chair's not a chairmaker. . . . Hit's not true; it's a little bit sygoglin, I calls it. I'd say it's got the rickets; ever'thing was made green."

the chairs were too simple, heavy, and plain, and "the rockers are tapered too thin in back and won't hold up." Hascal remarked simply, "I don't like all that flatness." And Charley also disapproved of Morris's work, commenting

on the rocker: "Hit's not true; it's a little bit sygoglin, I calls it. I'd say it's got the rickets: ever'thing was made green. Hit's not a good-lookin' chair a-tall. Looks too much like a factory-made chair. Hit's got too low a back. A body couldn't rest in that chair, less'n he was gonna use the banister for a footrest — the seat's too high.

"That rockin' chair's made for an old lady — real high up 'un," he continued. "Hit's hand-made — ever' bit of it," though that was a fact, not praise. "They ain't 'nough rounds in 'em — they'd oughta had another round in back like I make 'em. Don't see why them postees is square and the rounds is round. Hit don't look right thataway."

Figure 98. Morris made this chair (c. 1958) using only an ax; it was supposed to have been an armchair, but nobody except Morris could get in and out of the chair so he had to cut off the arms.

Charley was certainly correct in observing, "Whoever made that chair's not a chairmaker. He don't do it for a livin'. Looks like he made it for his own use."

Morris would like to pick up a few dollars making baskets or musical instruments, but he has an inflated notion of the value of his products. A heavy, poorly constructed, improperly made banjo, he felt, was worth a lot of money because his father, who once was a pretty good banjo picker, told him that "it rings like a five-hundred-dollar banjer." According to a recent article in a popular magazine about craftsmen in Appalachia, Morris "produces handsome furniture, looms, and musical instruments for family and friends." Admittedly Morris's baskets are fairly good, and he makes a few things for his family, but the "handsome," as applied to his banjo and his furniture, is patently an overstatement.

Two other men should be mentioned. Coy, who was born in 1894 in North Carolina, has lived in a mountain hollow near Harlan for more than forty years. He claimed to have been called to the area by the founders of a nursing service to make chairs, a craft he learned from his stepmother who showed him pictures of chairs. In the sixties he was still occasionally making chairs, which he said he sent to an outlet in Massachusetts, but the only customers I know about were tourists who stopped in front of the town courthouse where Coy was peddling his stools. Of Coy's chairs (figure 99) Charley remarked, "Them look jest like factory-made chairs. He's copied them off a factory-made chair shore 'nough." Hascal even suggested that one of the chairs was not handmade at all but rather was a factory-made chair which Coy was falsely claiming as his own. Coy was old and in poor health when I met him; since his sons refused to make chairs or to help him make chairs (one is a farmer, the other a coal miner), Coy was then producing only a few stools and rolling pins.

The other man is O. P. at Wayland. Born in 1891, he had had, he proudly repeated several times, only five months of formal schooling. His son, who lives close by, makes beds, chests, and tables in cherry and black walnut in direct emulation of the imitation early American highstyle furniture produced in the furniture factories in Berea. "I never liked to make chairs and still don't; you can't make no money at it," said O. P.'s son, who claimed to have taught his father how to use a lathe and how to make chairs. Until 1930 O. P. whittled chairs with a pocket knife; together father and son "packed 'em" five miles to Wayland to sell, receiving one dollar for a settin' chair and five dollars for a rocking chair. "Boy a dollar them days looked big as a bedspread," said the son; "we thought that was a lotta money." Thirty years later they had increased the price of a rocking chair

Figure 99. Two settin' chairs allegedly made by Coy in 1937 (left) and in the early 1950s (right), but the later one may not be handmade at all. "Them look jest like factory-made chairs," Charley said. "He's copied them off a factory-made chair shore 'nough."

ninefold, but wanted still more.

O. P. contended that the box-bottom chairs (figure 100) and stools he once made were based on his own ideas. "I don't have no education, never been to school more'n five months in my life, but you know there's gotta be new designs once in a while. You can't keep goin' with only one design. I just started makin' chairs with box bottoms an' everyone liked 'em so I kept makin' 'em." Coy, who also claimed to have originated the double- or box-bottom chair, said that somebody in the Wayland area got the idea from

Figure 100. My photograph of a photograph by O.P. of two box-bottom or double-bottom chairs he made about 1960. He claims they were original with him, but Coy says O.P. stole the idea from him. Why did O.P. make them? "I don't have no education, never been to school more'n five months in my life, but you know, there's gotta be new designs once in a while."

him about 1960, and that is indeed the time O.P. said he began to make that kind of chair. O.P.'s works over a quarter century exhibit a great deal of eclecticism (figures 100-102); it would therefore not be surprising to discover that he had in fact borrowed the box-bottom design from Coy, although I do not know when or from whom Coy got the idea. Box-bottom chairs are also found in western Kentucky, although Coy may have developed the idea independently.

By the mid-1960s O.P. was no longer using bark for the bottoms of chairs or stools because he could not skin it himself in the hills or pay anyone else enough money to do it for him; instead he used "reeds" (white oak splints) bought from a furniture store in Wayland. He did not cook or press the slats or posts, and for the preceding six or eight years he had not made slat-back chairs but plaited-back ones. By the time I met him he was making no chairs at all, only stools.

Like Coy, O.P. was too old to spend much time working in his shop. Nor could he find anyone to assist him in producing chairs, although he complained that a young man nearby had borrowed the idea of the box-bottom chair from him and was competing with him by

Figure 101. Plaited-back rocker made by O.P. (c. 1940).

charging only half as much for dining and rocking chairs of this design.

What is the future of the tradition of making chairs? In 1965 Charley believed that "in a few years chairmakin', it's gonna fade plumb away."

Anyone who asks whether or not there are any chairmakers around today will probably be told that none remain, that he should have been in southeastern Kentucky a decade ago when there were a dozen of them. Some of the men who made chairs in the 1960s have died; a few lacked the interest to develop their skills further; others have been crippled with arthritis or debilitated by alcoholism. Beechum and several others just "pranked around" with making chairs until they found more lucrative employment. Hascal became paralyzed emotionally, although he may have solved that problem by now. Charley's sons were too "nervous" to learn chairmaking; his nephews and cousins who know how to make chairs prefer singing and storytelling as modes of expressive behavior and load-

ing coal and pumping gas as vocations; and Charley himself, who has gone into hiding until the world prepares for his return, now makes few chairs. Ironically, of the dozen men mentioned in these pages, only Aaron is actively engaged in chairmaking in the 1970s — Aaron, who never learned the craft in his youth, who did not grow up with chairmaking, and

Figure 102. Dining chair made (c. 1940) by O.P., who used a stencil for the slats. O.P.'s son claims to have taught O.P. how to make chairs.

who backed into the occupation at forty years of age while trying to keep
other problems at bay. But anyone can learn the craft and someone else
will, as Aaron's career reveals.

Later Charley corrected himself, saying, "People'll always have to
set, an' my opinion, there'll be a need for chairs as long as time lasts."

There will also be people who need to make chairs or pots or
purses or quilts or rugs or tie-dyed shirts. Charley's bookcase masterpiece as an example of handicraft is not out of place in the modern
world. Technology may be changing rapidly in some areas of life, but
the social order and people's values are more enduring. Many individuals buy the latest gadgets on the market, yes, but they also seek continuity between the past and the future in order to maintain stability
in the present. No matter how many consumer goods are available,
there are people who prefer to purchase a handmade article. There is
still a need, too, to manufacture for one's own use practical objects
serving utilitarian purposes, to express oneself and deal with personal
problems by making things, and to satisfy a creative urge by producing
something that is pleasing to look at and use. Only a few individuals
now or in the past have engaged in such behavior occupationally,
however, because the vocation of making things by hand, which is also a
mode of expressive behavior, requires commitment to and involvement in
the creative act.

Many people in both rural and urban areas sample alternative life-
styles in search of an identity; they initiate or perpetuate family traditions
in order to communicate their love for spouse and children or to establish
their position within the flow of life and communicate to their offspring
values they consider important; and they participate in some kind of
creative behavior — whether dancing, singing, storytelling, or making things
— as a vehicle of social interaction, a mode of personal expression, or
a way of solving practical problems. A few people even become specialists
in these activities. More often the needs and the activities are sporadic:
the satisfaction derived from ordering what is random or scattered or
seemingly chaotic, the pleasure resulting from shaping things into balanced

and harmonious and appealing forms, are achieved by engaging in many kinds of behavior, without necessarily conceiving of the activity as either an occupation or as art. As long as individuals continue to form primary networks of communication and interaction in daily life, and as long as expressive structures, designs, and techniques are learned and employed mainly in face-to-face interchange, what many researchers have called folklore and folk art will be characteristic of much individual behavior.

In fact, as I write these words I have in front of me two recent newspaper clippings, one from a large metropolitan paper claiming that the present "quilt craze" is a "reaction against the computers in our lives." As a result (there are other motivating factors, of course), "quilt stores have sprung up in many cities, housewives are busily stitching for fun and profit in suburbia, and farm women have formed cooperatives to market their patchwork products." The second item, from a small paper in southeastern Kentucky, advertises hand-fashioned chairs made by a man whose works exhibit some features in common with Charley's chairs (shape of armrests and slats) and with Aaron's chairs (turnings and seat); I have just been informed, too, by a young museologist preparing a survey of contemporary craftsmen, that at least half a dozen other chairmakers are at work in southeastern Kentucky today, none of whom I knew about in the 1960s. Aaron was certainly not the first craftsman, he is not the only one today, and he will not be the last, so the student of art will continue to have subject matter for study.[2] The only problem that remains for consideration (in my final chapter) is how to examine the material.

CHAPTER SEVEN

The Beauty Part and the Lasting Part

"Buddy, when he threw one together, hit was together," said Charley's uncle Oaklie about his father Hat. Charley agreed, though complaining that the chairs made by Hat and other kin "weren't comfortable, but one thing about it, my grandfather's chairs — if you could see one today — it'd be good an' stout. They didn't make for the beauty part, they made for the lastin' part, he did." Charley said he himself made "an awful good easy chair, restin' chair an' ever'thing, but I still say, I'm not as good as my grandfather in makin' a chair that'll last." Hat's chairs, he said, "don't set good but they last good." Charley also felt that Hat and Oaklie, as well as his paternal grandfather Pike and Pike's brother Hiram, did not have so wide a variety of designs for feet or finials or use so many different patterns and splint sizes for the seats of chairs as he himself does. But imagination in chair designing is not an important criterion for Identifying a "good" chairmaker; at best it merely increases the possibilities of sales.

The chair seats or bottoms made by Charley's kin were all of one standardized width of hickory bark, about an inch, whereas Charley uses several different widths, depending on what he thinks he can charge for the chair. To get the narrow strips of bark, Charley has to cut and strip hickory poles only two or three inches in diameter. His kin, he said, "would never fool with makin' a little bitty nar' chair. The wider you make it [meaning the strips of bark in a chair bottom], the longer it'll last is the way I look at it. 'Course, the nar' looks better and sets more comf'table. But I doubt it'll last as long as that big, wide, ugly stuff would."

"If I had two chairs settin' out there, one of 'em with wide weave an' t'other with the nar,'" said Charley in reference to customer preference, "they'll pick the nar' ever' time. So they pick for the looks, not the lastin' part."

Appearance and durability: both are requirements of useful design, and it is important to note that distinctions are made between craftsmen who emphasize one and those who emphasize the other. First, this differentiation offers the researcher insights into the motivations, technical skills, and commitment of the producers as interpreted by the people most directly concerned with making and using the objects. Investigators have tended to employ their own typologies without recognizing meaningful local distinctions, as between chairmakers in southeastern Kentucky who "make 'em to sell" and those who "jest prank around with it," those who "make 'em for the money" and those who "make 'em for the sake of makin' a good chair," and those who "make for the beauty part" and those who stress the "lastin' part." Such dichotomies as "artist" versus "artisan," or "true artist" versus "clever craftsman," are value judgments generated by the investigator to help him describe which producer he personally thinks is more imaginative or innovative than another; they are often based on the premise that "art" is confined to a particular medium (e.g., painting and sculpture), serves exclusively aesthetic ends, or is external to an object and may be added or deleted at will.[1] Second, Charley's distinction between the beauty part and the lasting part is important because it underscores one of the points of this book: that much of what has been called art is both a tool and an end in itself. This is not to suggest that what has been called folk art is uniquely or exclusively utilitarian; most art serves a multiplicity of purposes, although this fact is sometimes neglected in the study of what have been called primitive art and the fine arts. "In the twentieth-century Western world," observes Roy Sieber, "we tend to ignore the ultimate persuasiveness of art; we have tried to destroy its utility and remove it from the realms of propaganda and moral discourse . . . . As a result we tend to oversimplify the role of art in other cultures."[2]

Many problems have been generated by researchers who fail to recognize the dual nature of the useful and the useless in what they claim to be art, who restrict art to objects, and who think that what they label folk and primitive art can then be compared with what they refer to as the fine arts, which are usually assumed to be great monuments that elevate the mind and produce exclusively aesthetic responses. I have already (in chapter 1) dealt with the relationship between what has been designated folk and primitive art, noted the similarity in circumstances of firsthand interaction in which the behavior so labeled is learned and manifested, and explained that the fine arts as commonly conceived cannot be compared, on a qualitative basis alone, with these other skills and activities that have been isolated for study, because the sources of information, the relations between participants in the events, and the motivations of the producers or performers are usually rather different (as implied by the researchers themselves when proposing the dichotomy between folk and fine art).

Each type of production should be examined on its own grounds, although, owing to bias, this principle is not always followed. In large measure snobbishness is responsible for the relegation of folk art to "child art on the adult level" or the contention that behavior outside a limited elite tradition is "a copy of a copy of something professional," which "suffered" the "degradation that each copyist with the originality of incompetence introduced, until it reached the puerile, the infantile expression of the mass soul." And an overaction to such elitism helps explain why some defenders of folk art maintain that it is characterized by sincerity, unselfconsciousness, spontaneity, and democracy.[3]

Even the study of so-called primitive art has suffered from the excesses of the fine art tradition of scholarship. Many researchers, preoccupied with masks as sculpture, or with shelters as architecture, or with clay vessels as ceramics, disregard the utilitarian qualities of these objects; the separation of figural representations as "art" from the rest of a drum or a canoe or a pot, which is conceived of as "craft" and then

ignored, betrays the bias of Western elite art training. Many recent works
on primitive art and aesthetics are marred in this way, and thus their
usefulness for others is diminished. Decorated pottery is not simply utilized
in dance and religious ceremonies at an altar within a building, for
that would suggest a utilitarian purpose which art is not supposed to
serve; rather, such pottery has its "architectural and choreographic set-
tings" or "coordinates." Or artists are not simply conservative, relying upon
rather common patterns learned from others (a tendency that is apparent
in most things that are made and done); no, producers are described
as exhibiting "tactful creativity," of making innovations that are "perforce
discreet," of not disturbing the "necessary illusion of the continuity of
ethical truths in their abstract purity."[4] These circulocutionary exalta-
tions leave the reader bewildered and ill informed. Too often every
indication of likes and dislikes expressed by the native is taken to be
evidence of an "aesthetic attitude," when most of these reactions are
more generally examples of excellence and preference, based on association and personal predilection, having little to do with the compositional traits of the object or the expressive qualities of the behavior (which
in no way makes such reactions any less significant for study).

Methodological problems abound, but many difficulties can be avoided
if we do not limit ourselves to a concept of art as merely objects (or
perhaps not even use that term at all when studying the making and
doing of things), if we understand that modes of behavior may be learned
and utilized in different situations, and if we consider the proposition
that products of human manufacture and modes of expressive behavior
evincing qualities of harmony, symmetry, balance, and centrality serve
many purposes, including practical ones. In the remainder of this
chapter I set forth a number of interpretations of useful design, including furniture production in southeastern Kentucky, which grew out of my
observations of people making objects that other individuals bought and
used. These interpretations suggest that several assumptions in past
research are untenable and that certain concepts are not very useful. I
have organized my remarks in such a way as to suggest some of the

ramifications of admitting that objects are made for both the beauty part and the lasting part, and to reveal some of the implications of examining the making of things as well as the things themselves.

Because what one perceives and reports is necessarily guided by one's presuppositions, it may be useful to indicate some of the notions that have given shape to this work, and some of the influences that other people's ideas have had in the formation of my own. It was David Pye's work on the nature of design which led me to recognize the importance of useful design in the manufacture and use of objects in daily life, and to reconsider the meaning of the word "art." Thomas C. Munro's examination of the many nonaesthetic functions of art and his survey of art, broadly defined to include skill and the production of utilitarian objects (rather than narrowly defined as the expression of emotion in the creation of art for art's sake), seemed to justify a treatment of furniture making in terms of the decorative, as well as the practical, and the contemplative or evaluative dimensions. D. W. Gotschalk's explication of the formal, expressive, functional, and material qualities of the product, his discussion of the "material principle" and the "quasi-creative fecundity" of the raw materials, and his reference to the "artistic transaction" initially helped open up other avenues for investigation. From R. M. MacIver's criticisms of the more popular models employed in the study of social phenomena I learned some of the pitfalls in the analysis of art. And from MacIver's remarks on social causation and his emphasis on process, combined with some ideas from Gotschalk, Alan P. Merriam, and George C. Mills, I developed a model of my own of designing for use as a system of processes and events which I thought would help me discover a broader range of factors influencing the nature of the product and assist me in organizing my interpretations.[5] The model I considered presenting to the reader is that of art as a system within a social and physical environment consisting of the process of production and consumption (the objectification of ideas on the one hand, and the distribution, utilization, and evaluation of products on the other) unified by the "artistic transaction" and manifested by unique events precipitated by a social demand or emotional need at a conjuncture of

multiple technical, emotional, cultural, and social forces which results in
the manufacture of objects serving both as tools and as things for contemplation; the development, continuity, and change of individual, social, and
epochal style in art result from the interrelationships of factors in the
system of production and consumption, as those factors remain relatively stable or are altered by a precipitant. Subsequently I abandoned
that model, and most of the constructs incorporated in it, as I have
several other models.

The test of a model is whether or not the analogy postulated has
some semblance to the real world and leads to new avenues for research,
although we seem also to want models and theories that are not only
concise and viable but also "beautiful." Too often models that generate
major conceptual problems are still lauded because of the ease with which
they can be employed to provide facile answers to complex problems, and
the simplicity and grace that recommend them to others for use; having
long ago been proven useless, many models are still accepted because of
their elegance (or more complicated models may be subscribed to because
their obscurity makes it difficult to perceive their limitations). It must
not be forgotten, however, that no matter how elegant the models might
be, and thus pleasurable to work with, analogies are not the reality to
which they are addressed, and they have been developed as working hypotheses which further research may (and probably will) disconfirm. Metaphors
can make abstractions concrete and thus easier to understand, but the
images we use should not cause others to misunderstand the phenomena we
describe. Furthermore, while it is apparent that model building is fundamental
in science, and that models must be reviewed frequently to test their viability,
it is also clear that model building is a practical endeavor, which means that
elegance, supposing it is present, is not enough; the models must also be
useful.

Studies of human behavior, as of other activities and outputs, might be
considered a tradition in which there are many conventions. Most of these
studies, though unique in important respects, represent generally some
perspectives in analysis or schools of thought because of the concepts and

models employed; broadly speaking, they seem to incorporate not only a number of similar practices and rules that earlier researchers have developed, but also several terms, some of the most common being "culture," "group," "society," "personality," "style," "folk," "art," "taste," and "aesthetics," as well as "tradition" and "convention." Reliance on many of these constructs and concepts, especially the first six and last two, encourages the researcher to assume homogeneity and universality in behavior and to utilize static models in analysis. Words such as "convention" and "tradition," for example, usually establish a frame of reference emphasizing the conservatism and uniformities in the behavior of many people (as in the phrase "tradition and creativity"), even when the commentator takes great pains to employ qualifying phrases. The use of these and other words tends to systematize, standardize, and fix limits on the behavior under scrutiny. Human behavior is individualistic and dynamic, however, as noted by many human beings.

How can we solve the problem of not misrepresenting the reality that we know obtains, of actually allowing for diversity and fluidity in behavior, and of describing in a meaningful way what we observe? A popular solution is to say that one is speaking "figuratively" only, as when it is admitted that culture is not superorganic and does not determine a person's behavior, but the researcher writes "as if" culture does this, saying that culture "changes and evolves," that it is "embodied in its carriers' personalities," and that it "deeply and conclusively etches its mark on persons." It is also common to say "for heuristic purposes only," implying that what is about to be proposed is really not true but a "useful fiction." A third procedure is to conclude a classificatory system of some aspects of human behavior with a category called "miscellaneous" or "unclassified." Another technique is to use a general word such as "personality" for "the sake of convenience," without specifying that in one situation it is an individual's beliefs being referred to, in another, his aspirations, and in a third, his values. A fifth solution is to try to give an old word a new meaning, as I was tempted to do with "art" (following Munro) and with "folklore" (because often I identify myself as a folklorist), and as others have done

with the terms mentioned above. The inevitable conclusion in regard to
the study of human behavior, however, is that one cannot "put new wine
in old bottles," for the taste of the earlier vintage remains. There is no
unique mode of behavior which can be readily isolated from the rest of
behavior and labeled folklore or art, despite many attempts to do so (which
is why there is no concensus of opinion as to what art or folklore is), and
there is no type of response, usually called the aesthetic, that exists
independently from all other reactions to activities and objects. Words
such as "personality," "group," "culture," and "style," no matter how defined,
are collective terms requiring attention to the "thin strands of uniformities" each researcher thinks he has abstracted from the complex and
unique activities he observes, and demanding the freezing of a momentary action which is in fact always changing. Furthermore, the referents
of these terms (the terms themselves are constructs and theoretical
concepts) do not exist but must be shaped by the researcher as he interacts with other people. One does not have a personality; rather, one
expresses one's thoughts and one acts in some fashion in the presence of,
and partly because of, another individual who then interprets that behavior
on the basis of his own beliefs and experiences. Culture, group, and style
(as well as world view, health system, and belief network) are arrived at
in the same manner. That is to say, the researcher generates a system of
ideas and behavior on the basis of his conception of significant similarities
among the unique acts he observes; sometimes he then says the system
or culture or tradition "allows for variability in behavior," even though it
was the researcher himself who restricted individuality and disregarded
the uniqueness of activities when he generated his systematic view of events.

    The foregoing remarks seem to indicate that not only have I avoided
answering my question, but I have also painted myself into a corner because
I have given my own interpretations of the behavior, beliefs, aspirations,
and sentiments of Charley and other chairmakers with whom I interacted.
What I am quite willing to admit, however is that research is biased. The most
we can hope for, I suppose, is to be more or less objective about our sub-
jectivity, and through the process of introspection, dialogue, and self-criticism,

to come a step or two closer to understanding what is actually happening in the activities we claim to examine. But we must examine those activities, on their own grounds for what they are, and maximize the potential for multiple interpretations of events; both similarities and differences can be dealt with, and given proper perspective, by following this procedure. More often a researcher throws up his hands in despair at the complexity of events he witnesses and participates in and reduces the causes of human action to a single factor, operative in perpetuity, by appealing to a theoretical construct for its alleged explanatory power, thus begging the very questions to which others have addressed themselves in research: "Whatever and wherever the origins," too many investigators conclude about some aspect of human behavior, "it is now a cultural tradition," as if that really explained anything. Sometimes no solution at all is offered, because it is not realized that there is a conceptual problem: "What do you mean, rural communities historically in America were not small homogeneous societies in which certain modes of behavior were universal and nonchanging until the forces of urbanization and industrialization disrupted the equilibrium of established institutions causing cultural disintegration, anomie, dietary deficiencies and rotten teeth, not to mention the death of folk art?"

The procedure of focusing on the activities themselves, and of submitting one's thoughts and acts to critical assessment, is needed especially when a researcher is part of the data base, as I was in southeastern Kentucky and as many others have been elsewhere in the world. For instance, one often encounters studies in which the investigator disparages major changes in the things produced by natives resulting in contact with outsiders, but not all researchers admit the extent to which they may have been responsible for the condition; frequently the researcher has brought the more highly prized manifestations of Western life to the natives by bartering for local objects with things such as tobacco and metal goods, especially knives, which sometimes affect the natives' behavior and the things they make, as well as the quality of those things. (Understandably, craftsmen may put down stone implements and take up metal

ones, and some natives offer to the stray visitor objects hastily and poorly
made.) My presence in Charley's home, and my attention to his work, probably increased the tension between his wife and him; my questions about
personal matters were an intrusion, and they opened old wounds; my
praise of Charley's work and my search for examples of his earliest chairs,
some of which I wanted to buy for a museum, certainly played a part in
his expressing concern for the fate of these objects and his purchase of
several chairs for donation to a museum. Without photographs of some
of Charley's chairs which I showed him, Aaron might not have found a
model for the new type of arms on the dining chairs he made in August,
1967; in me Hascal found an audience and what he hoped would be an
outsider sympathetic to him and his plight; my inquiries to some people
about the handmade chairs they owned seemed to precipitate a change
in attitude toward those objects. In other words, many things that
happened might not have occurred had I not been present, and my interpretations of the events derive from who I am and what I have
experienced.

There is an answer to my question about reporting events. Objectivity
may be unobtainable to the degree that we desire, but actually examining
the activities that interest us is certainly feasible; sometimes only from
such close scrutiny can we be made to realize many of our biases and our
influences on the activities of which we were a part. Appealing to culture,
personality, group identity, or tradition as an explanation of human behavior limits research to a realm external to that behavior and inhibits
recognizing as well as understanding the internal dynamics of unique events.
Explanations of expressive qualities in objects and activities that invoke
evolutionism, diffusionism, and functionalism obviously betray researchers'
biases, at the same time—and this is what is most important—that the
behavior under study is often ignored. It is unlikely that someone bent on
proving an a priori assumption about the equilibrious nature of culture in
folk or primitive society by reviewing the functions of some things such as
masks, for example, will devote much attention to the actual making and
using of those objects. (Why should he? He is interested less in the masks

than in the culture construct.) This is not to say that such works are without value; fortunately, biases often can be inferred and then taken into account, and scattered throughout these studies are many perceptive observations, which, if they are brought together, can suggest important hypotheses about behavior, although the hypotheses have not been tested because of the other preoccupations of researchers. The method of analysis needed is not one that encourages superimposing one's theory of culture or society on the data, but one that directs attention to the behavior and what is revealed by it; not a method that reduces the causes of actions to one permanent determinant, but a method that allows for multiple interpretations of what at most seem to be influences. When answering my question why he had put so many pegs in the rockers of a chair Charley said, "One reason I made 'em was . . . ;" he did not say, "_The_ reason was . . ."

The model I described earlier was developed to take into account many factors, posited in several fields of study, claimed to influence an object's form and design. A major weakness of the model, as with many other models some of which are less ambitious than this one, is that it ignores the actual activities of people making, buying, and using things. A simple example of ignoring what transpires is that of ownership: sometimes there are no customers at all so there is no transfer of ownership, although the unifying theme in the model is the "artistic transaction," and often the transference is among customers rather than between producer and consumer. The factors allegedly determining the nature of the object — cultural, social, psychical, technical, and stylistic — are promoted by researchers in different disciplines for whom culture, society, personality, and style are central to their notions of these fields of study; citing such factors, then, brings together the theoretical terms of several disciplines but does not give us an understanding of how or why the two-in-one bookcase rocker, masterpiece of furniture, was made, of why Charley revised some of his chairs a decade after they were built, of why Hascal wanted to make chairs but could not, or of why Aaron made flat arms on a dining chair. The eclecticism of the model is troublesome largely because the factors referred to as causes of design

selection are best general and diffuse conditions whose impact is minimal in
any particular circumstance of making and using an object. Terms like
"culture" and "style" get in the way, as the extra legs on some of Charley's
chairs circumscribe the use of those objects. Interpreting form and discovering why it is so can be achieved most fully by investigating what was happening during the manufacture of an object. This understanding cannot be
attained by positing style periods and supposing that one object's features
account for the traits of another object; it does not result from preparing a life history of an inanimate object and tracing the object's presumed
genealogy to a progenitor in some other place in the remote past; and it
cannot be attained by assuming that people constitute a homogeneous
group living in a state of equilibrium and producing objects according to a
cultural norm promoting social cohesion. Furthermore, the model set forth
earlier, as well as others mentioned above, suffers from the tendency to
reify human thought and expression, to make static that which is dynamic,
to assume perpetuity rather than to admit temporality, to render uniform
what is individualistic, and to systematize and order in an artificial and
simplistic fashion that which is extremely complex, sometimes contradictory,
and maybe even chaotic.

  At different times when I talked to Charley he claimed preferences in
different chairs, which is hardly surprising as he was subject to many experiences and emotions before and during that time. Neither Charley's
thoughts nor his chairmaking can be said, even for heuristic purposes or to
speak figuratively, to constitute a system, that is, an assemblage of objects
united by some type of regular interaction or interdependence. The reasons
for features in an object escape understanding if they are said to be the
result of a conjuncture of multiple technical, emotional, cultural, and social
forces. In Charley's chairs a quality such as the back posts bent outward
and backward can be interpreted as a metaphor of organic growth (for
whatever purpose that might serve), as visually desirable, as structurally
useful in balancing the chair so that only minimal pressure is necessary to
tip it back against the wall which is often the way a settin' chair is used, as
a way of increasing the comfort to one's back when sitting in a chair for a

long time, as a statement of aggressiveness and self-certainty as a man and a craftsman, as an indication of concern for people who might use one of his chairs, as a result of a customer's request for that feature, or of Charley's inference that customers would prefer this trait and therefore buy his chairs; and as none or all of these things, and others besides.

If the researcher considers the things he himself makes and does, and why he makes and does these things, and if his perspective emphasizes his subject as a fellow human being, then the subject is no longer an alien or his behavior strange, the motivations of his acts need not be given fanciful interpretations or ignored by appealing to one or another construct, and the explanations of his behavior will not be restricted by systematic reduction to a single causal factor; this would be so because the researcher would be evaluating his interpretation of his subject's behavior on the basis of his own behavior, and therefore he would know what was meaningful and what was not. Unfortunately, however, use of the equilibrium model, in combination with the assumption about the homogeneity of folk and primitive society and the supposition that one's subjects (from an "alien culture") think differently from oneself because some aspects of their behavior are different from the researcher's own, has led to comparisons between "them," our subjects whom we do not know, and "us," whom we know all too well and whose behavior disconfirms the equilibrium model and many of the other interpretations that have been made. Many researchers maintain, for example, apparently as a matter of faith, that there is a marked contrast between folk art and elite art, contending that the folk artist supports the normative values of his culture, neither castigating nor condemning it as the modern elite artist does; in contrast with the folk artist, we are experiencing the fragmentation of our value system and the disintegration of coherence and symbolic unity in our art. Such claims result to some extent at least from continuing to use a model in a situation involving the researcher's subjects, when the researcher senses that it does not apply in another circumstance — his own — but the equilibrium model is itself not tested as a hypothesis in either situation. Probably in part the model is not tested because it has

been assumed generally that there is a significant difference between researchers and their subjects (hence, such labels as "folk" and "primitive"), and the
maintenance of the equilibrium model in regard to the subjects is a means
of reinforcing this belief.

Why have many researchers made a distinction between themselves
and their subjects? The study of behavior of people in southeastern
Kentucky who make and use things in daily life seems to indicate that
they are not fundamentally different from researchers who study their
behavior; the major distinction between the subject whose behavior is
studied, and a researcher who distinguishes himself from his subject,
appears to be that the researcher makes such a distinction. Why has the
label "folk" or "primitive" been meaningful to some researchers studying
what people make and do in interaction with other people? Labeling in
general provides a means by which many phenomena can be treated as
one, and at once, in a rather easy fashion for the goal of simplication,
although, as indicated in chapter 1 in regard to definitions of folk and
primitive art, "Too many different kinds of art produced in too many different circumstances are involved." Sometimes, perhaps, use of such labels is
thought to delimit a disciplinary field of study; consider the number of
scholars whose earliest works set forth the characterizations of subject
matter claimed to be peculiar to their field, the degree of debating
about how one discipline differs from another, the kinds of questions most
frequently asked by students new to the field. Precedent is important, too, for one
learns from one's mentors with whom one may sometimes disagree but for
whom one usually has some respect; several investigators have sought
substitute labels for folk and primitive, such as "popular" and "ethnological,"
or they have tried to give new meanings to the older words, objecting to the
connotations of the earlier terms but seeming not to question the assumption that the referent is a distinctive phenomenon with unique qualities
characteristic of the behavior of beings who are fundamentally different;
essentially then, what was once a vice is now, allegedly, only a habit. Occasionally the labels serve to reinforce a belief in differences which seems to be
desirable for many reasons, whether to suggest one's own superiority, or to

show how far science and the arts have advanced man from the murky depths of an uncultivated intellectual state, or to demonstrate the extent to which civilization has polluted the minds and hearts of men who once lived in the unsullied backwaters of natural innocence. Often minor differences in some aspect of behavior, usually dress or language or physical traits, lead the researcher to assume differences in thought processes; the task then becomes one of characterizing the process in thinking alien to one's own intelligence, and of seeking other manifestations of the differences more significant than the obvious, superficial ones. In this regard, Charley's behavior admittedly posed a problem.

Careful examination of Charley's works, his actions, and his ideas as expressed verbally by him indicated that although his phraseology might be unfamiliar to the researcher, or some of his chairs rather striking, or his commitment to chairmaking unusually acute, or the extent of his problems uncommon, the man himself was not significantly different from any other man. Indeed, it was surprising sometimes to discover how similar the subject and the researcher are, contrary to expectations engendered by the scholarly literature. Because of my growing conviction about the fundamental similarities between researchers and their subjects, quoting Charley's remarks in this book generated mixed feelings, as did describing his dress and including photographs of him and of his chairs. I was taught to characterize in print as accurately as possible the speech of one's subject, but everyday speech is certainly not the same as the mode of expression used in written discourse; thus Charley's speech contrasts with my writing, probably to his detriment because of what seems to be his use of nonstandard English which too frequently is thought to be substandard English (and we know how often language usage is taken to be indicative of one's background, experiences, and education — in a word, one's worth as a person). Furthermore, Charley has encouraged others to think of him as being different in order to promote the sale of his chairs. Wearing overalls and long hair, making things without the use of modern machinery, and even employing certain words such as "postees" (and a couple of times "arm restees") seemed to be calculated to make him stand out from others; some of his chairs and his song he called strange or queer. Weird, odd, striking, peculiar, and different are qualifiers that float through the air, and visions of misfit, deviant, and abnormal take shape in the mind. To quote Charley's phraseology, then, and to describe him and depict his chairs, which he himself encouraged, is to put one's nose in the trap and sniff the bait. The bait is certainly enticing; many researchers have been snared with less.

To summarize the discussion thus far, this book has not been about art and artists in their sociocultural context, about aesthetics, about the relationship between personality and style, and about folklore or folk art. I have been concerned with individuals who make and do things, and those who buy and use things, in interaction with other people; I have called attention to some experiences and ideas (sometimes seemingly contradictory and always momentary and elusive) of individuals which are related to, and expressed by means of, the things they make; and I have focused upon everyday things which are appreciated for the skill required to produce them. There is a world of difference between these two perspectives: the first, rooted in the use of common theoretical terms the very sight of which delights many researchers, stands at a distance from the subject matter for investigation; the second seeks solutions to questions about activities within those activities themselves.

What else can be learned, especially in regard to the evaluation of basic concepts and models in several fields of study, by reviewing the making and using of chairs? Consider again Charley's distinction between the beauty part and the lasting part and some of the ramifications of this and the two other dichotomies. What is suggested by these three distinctions taken together is that there are specialists as well as amateurs, that some individuals are motivated by economic considerations and others by the pleasure of making things to the best of their ability, and that the objects produced are things to look at as well as to use but some producers are concerned more with one purpose than with another. The meanings of these distinctions are simply stated, but exploring their significance is more difficult.

To begin with, these distinctions call attention not to objects alone but to skill in the making or doing of that which functions as (among other things) a stimulus to the appreciation of an individual's mastery of tools and materials, the outputs of that skill, and the activity of using the skill. What is produced, as well as the production or performance, may serve purposes in addition to that of generating a contemplative and appreciative attitude in someone, such as utility, prestige enhancement, political advancement, economic gain, spiritual elevation, personal commemoration, and so on. Furthermore, the activity of production need not be a separate or special pursuit divorced from daily life, although what has been called art, in the Western elite tradition and in academic study, tends to be conceived of in just that way. Many students of art demarcate between what sometimes have been referred to as the technological and cultural orders of reality; the major influences on the nature of an industrial object are claimed to be tools, techniques of construction, and usefulness, whereas the primary influences on art are generally thought to be the creative personality, the stylistic tradition, and the values and sentiments of patrons. When it is recognized that most handmade objects are instrumental in achieving some practical results as well as engendering a contemplative and appreciative attitude, however, it must be acknowledged that influences on the nature of the product comprise all six of these factors, in addition to others. [6]

Because much of what people make and do, which may have been called art by someone somewhere at some time, is an integral part of human life in daily experience, objects are produced by many people with no thought to occupational specialism; in chairmaking in southeastern Kentucky, however, there are a few specialists for whom production tends to occupy much of their time, though often subordinated in importance to other economic activities. Regardless of the researcher's attitude toward production, chairmaking is not called an art and only rarely a craft (for example, by Aaron, who had an art appreciation course in school in which he learned that few people in the world, himself included, produce art) by those most directly concerned with making and using the objects; it is simply chairmaking, even though chairmakers produce stools, cabinets, tables, baskets, and musical instruments, and the producer is a chairmaker rather than an artist. Chairmaking serves as a technological means to practical ends, and that is one reason that the production itself was not called a form of art by chairmakers I talked to, though many individuals appreciate the skill exhibited by the finest chairmakers. Some people in the area may "pick a banjo," or "swap lies," or "build chairs," or "prank around with jugs and dishes," but few individuals "create art." No matter what they call themselves and their activities, however, several chairmakers obviously derive pleasure from manipulating the raw materials to create forms that are satisfying both visually and practically.

To the chairmakers and some of their immediate customers with whom I spoke, "art" seemed to be two kinds of phenomena: representational drawing and painting; and ornaments, or objects serving primarily an ornamental purpose, which are responded to as something "special" and not for ordinary use, though these things are seldom called "art." For example, Aaron told me about one man, now dead, who could have been a "real artist" for he made excellent drawings, such as the pencil sketch of a boy beside a lake fishing, which depicted a pole stuck into the bank with the line adrift in the water, the boy asleep with a straw hat tipped forward on his head and a can of worms beside him. Three or four other people also spoke of the paintings of a local woman as if they were art, and several people decorated the walls of their homes with images, especially illustrated calendars and framed photographs of relatives.

There appeared to be four principal realms of art as ornament or as art serving an ornamental purpose. For several people it seemed to be embellishment on utilitarian objects, not usually the objects themselves but the ornamental features or the fact that an object was embellished. Thus, one man, when thumbing through a stack of photographs of chairs, remarked upon only a few of the chairs which struck his fancy because of the ornamentation (this does not mean that he did not appreciate the other chairs, only that he found a few of them sufficiently special to comment upon). Charley's bookcase rocker, admired by several other people as well (though the mayor's rocker is the chair most talked about and also the chair seen by the most people), "is a pretty one," he said; it is also "pretty" because of the decorative elements, especially the phalanges and pegs — "all this little work up here." And of a recent chair by Aaron this person said, "That's another good un, too, buddy — pretty." Half a dozen other people, too, remarked upon the attractiveness of Aaron's recent chairs. Second, when asked what they thought art is, a few individuals cited as examples arrangements of flowers or leaves and cones and the like, or knicknacks having only a decorative purpose; such things were referred to as a "pretty" or as "pretties," but not specifically as "art" by the people I talked with, although Charley did, when pressed by me, call "art" the wooden jewelry that a visitor had made and proudly shown to us. I also heard some young children use the term "a pretty" or "pretties" in reference to a broken toy or a chewing gum wrapper or other object that appealed to them but seemed to have no recognizable utilitarian purpose. Third, what was treated as something special by a few people appeared to be objects whose decorative quality overrides their useful features to such an extent that the intended practical use cannot be served; a chair, for example, whose extensive ornamentation prohibits active use or interferes with comfort becomes something special and may be called "a work of art" or treated as if it were, as in Charley's comments about the stool of northern European design made by a semiretired coal miner, which Charley said was just something to look at and not to use, and in Hascal and Beechum's response to Charley's bookcase masterpiece and a few other chairs, which they said were works of art. Finally, art to most of the chairmakers and to some of their customers, although not specifically called that, seems to embrace small-scale replicas of utilitarian objects which cannot serve the use intended for the full-scale models, such as a miniature corn sled made of expensive wood which is sanded and varnished and placed on a table or mantel and which then serves solely as an object of contemplation and admiration.[7] Had I talked to more people about the nature of art I might have found additional conceptions; those mentioned above are the opinions of a few individuals, expressed by them or more often inferred by me, and they are not the "group attitude" of "southern mountain people," for most of the interviewees did not know one another, much less share a sense of intimacy and community, and those conceptions are not peculiar to them.

Because chairmaking as an activity was not called art by chairmakers or some of their customers (nor is it often called art by other people I know), although some objects were treated as special, it might be appropriate to examine the nature of chairmaking as an industry before exploring other aspects of production and consumption concerning the beauty part. The range of technical procedures, inferred by me from talking with or observing a dozen men, includes selecting and securing raw materials, seasoning, initial preparation (hewing out, cooking or steaming, and bending or pressing), final shaping, assembly, and application of external finishes. According to my inference the instruments relevant to those procedures comprise such items as axes, saws, pocket knives, drawing knives, drawing horses, and workbenches; presses for bending slats, posts, and rockers; tubs for cooking wood; turning lathes; and braces and bits. Specialized knowledge in this occupation consists of criteria for selecting materials, the alleged traits of raw materials, the proper times for executing various procedures, argot, and various prohibitions and restrictions. It cannot be said that these procedures in manufacture are subject to considerable variability by the chairmakers I observed, because the procedures were not set forth by them or others as rules to be abided by; not every craftsman applies an external finish to his chairs, nor need he do so; not everyone steams and presses slats for all chairs; and not every chairmaker uses a lathe.

The same observation obtains regarding the arrangements between producers and consumers. Although it appeared to me that the producer does not have complete control over the processes of production but is restricted by the consumers' implicit expectations of or explicit demands for kind of design, size of object, and materials of construction, it cannot be said that there is confusion as to the respective rights and duties among producers and consumers in the artistic transaction unifying the system of production and consumption. There is confusion, yes, but that is because there is no system of exchange known and agreed upon by all parties, in part because there are too many parties. It cannot be stated categorically that the consumer has the responsibility of paying the amount of money requested according to the terms agreed upon, or that he has the right to specify the exact nature of the object to be made, the right to reject an object not prepared according to specifications, and the right to barter over price before the requested object is made or if the producer is trying to sell a previously manufactured object. Producer and consumer have different roles, and the rights and responsibilities just mentioned, plus others, might or might not be considered by an individual, but each transaction I observed was unique to the occasion manifesting few significant similarities. For example, in some instances local customers expected lower prices and received them, but in other instances they did not receive them; sometimes a craftsman unexpectedly offered a discount to an outsider so as to attract additional or repeat orders, or perhaps to make the transaction appear less impersonal, but other times he did not offer a discount, even when asked, no matter how many chairs were purchased. [8]

The different ways to exchange and distribute the product also promote or circumscribe the freedom of the chairmaker, depending on whether he makes objects the way he wants and then tries to peddle them, or whether the customer specifies what he wants and the objects are produced on a contract basis. Contractual arrangements, while generally preferred by chairmakers, were not common. The researcher might try to organize the transference of ownership as an informal contractual relationship, since a formal one was rare. A multi-interest, dyadic relationship, which may be either vertical or horizontal, for instance, obtains when the product is exchanged for goods or services between two persons of different or the same socioeconomic status, in which event the two participants share more than just an interest in transfer of ownership. [9] In other words, sometimes a chairmaker trades his chairs to someone in the area (who has either the same amount of money or more money than he) for timber, groceries, or rent on his home. More important is the fact that prices, which are not constant, are influenced by precedent, cost of materials, amount of labor required for manufacture, and the values, expectations, and money of consumers, as well as the feelings of a craftsman at a particular moment; the amount of ornamentation and the technical quality of the product tend to vary with price, but not always, as several of Charley's chairs demonstrate. Significant, too, is that chairmaking is usually only one of several major sources of income for an individual; the others are government subsidy and subsistence agriculture, mainly for family consumption. Many chairmakers subordinate chair production to agricultural pursuits; hence they are not free to devote large amounts of time to experimentation or to the development of new traits in the objects they make (but few are interested in doing so anyway). The income from

chairmaking usually is not high enough for the craftsman to have withholding
power in the sale of his products, which tends to make him responsive to market
demands in the production of objects evincing certain material and expressive
qualities congenial to the values of a particular clientele; thus chairmaking,
like the manufacture of other visually appealing objects serving practical uses,
combines decoration and use in a mutually beneficial relationship,[10] in that
ornament and attention to the intrinsic qualities of raw materials promote
economic production, and industry provides an occupational outlet for one's
desire to make appealing but useful things.

    Because chairmaking as an industry results in the manufacture of objects
by hand, the individual producer is the agent responsible for the making of
things (although customer's desires are influential), and his sentiments, values,
experiences, beliefs, and needs often find their expression in what he makes
and the way he makes his products. Chairmaking, therefore, is not anonymous, although authorship may be unknown to the researcher if the unsigned object was made before he arrived in the area; and authorship,
especially of things made in the past, may be unknown because there is no
cult of the artist. The producer is not called an artist, and the primary
concern of users is the object's technical qualities of durability, structural
soundness, and usefulness; since the author of things made long ago is now
dead and cannot produce useful things, there are few reasons to remember
his name, although sometimes one may be curious because knowledge of the
manufacturer adds to appreciation of the object. The products evince individual qualities and unique traits, however, by which others, especially experienced
craftsmen, can distinguish the works of different producers, although the actual
identity of the authors may be unknown. Living producers certainly claim authorship, but their works are usually unsigned, which is not surprising when one
considers the quantity produced and the conception of the manufacturer as
simply a chairmaker.

    Referring to himself simply as a chairmaker does not mean that the
craftsman mechanically produces objects with no thought to their nature and
without revealing in those objects something of himself and his reasons for
engaging in this occupation. In some instances the making or doing of things is

associated with the process of adjustment to serious problems,[11] but in other situations a man makes things because he needs the objects for his own use, or he has learned the techniques from others and has found a way of getting money, or he wants to keep his hands busy, or he takes pleasure in shaping pieces of wood into recognizable and usable forms. This pleasure in making things is often called creativity,[12] and the act of bringing into existence something with a new character is often referred to as innovation.[13] Other researchers have suggested that the creative act depends on certain conditions each associating paradoxical opposites: immersion-detachment, passion-decorum, and mastery-compliance.[14] All three conditions are evident in chairmaking, at least among the most committed craftsmen, but they are to be found in other activities as well, including scholarship. Further, as has been suggested for art forms, there are two major phases of creativity in chairmaking, the objective phase marked by overt manipulation of raw materials, and the subjective phase which does not lend itself readily to observation. The manipulation of different raw materials requires different techniques to translate the vision or idea into tangible form, and, when viewed from a distance, these techniques seem to be fairly standard, at least among chairmakers who learn from one another. This situation might suggest to the researcher the use of the concept of small-group culture to conceptualize about both similarities and differences;[15] but it is necessary only to note that the techniques in fact are not systematic, only appearing to be when individual differences within families or other interactional networks are minimized in order to emphasize the similarities, and in turn to emphasize differences between the interactional networks. In chairmaking there are also apparent extremes in the manipulation of raw materials,[16] but in the process of making something, whether seemingly spontaneous or planful, the producer usually discovers new properties in the materials requiring revision of his ideas as they are objectified.[17] As part of the subjective phase of thought and action in chairmaking — the part that Boas and others have found so difficult to penetrate, which is one reason why many studies of art are simply descriptive of the physical activities themselves — is the assimilation of ideas from several sources into a novel unity for which certain mental skills are requisite.[18] Techniques of composition or the basic ideas for the object are arrived at from several sources. [19] One is supernatural, and another is by means of dreams, but in addition the object may derive some traits from other products the chairmaker has seen, including not only chairs made by other men in the area but also chairs depicted in catalogues or shown to him by customers.

Chairmaking is essentially designing for use, combining the general requirements of useful design with individual principles. Perhaps the most interesting of the major requirements of useful design is the requirement of appearance, but the others are equally important to chairmakers. [20] The criteria of form, not usually articulated by craftsmen but abstracted from the context of construction and inferred from the product and from the chairmakers' behavior and comments, include symmetry, balance, harmony of surface and lines, and proper integration of design elements; but craftsmen vary in the manner in which they achieve these qualities, if they achieve them at all. For example, the criteria of finish, including smooth or rough surface quality, the presence or absence of ornamentation, and the presence or absence of applied finishes, such as varnish, shellac, and paint, are not constant among the chairmakers or even constant within one man's production. The principles of design, which are essentially requirements of appearance, also vary. The emphasis may be on simplicity, with little ornamentation and perhaps a rather rough surface, or on complexity, with a smooth surface and extensive use of decorative elements and motifs in both the primary and secondary layouts. (The back posts, for example, may be the primary field of decoration, which is also subdivided into decorative fields above and below the seat or between the stretchers.) These principles governing the use of different compositional elements in chairmaking, in contrast with the criteria of finish, are often expressed by chairmakers, although some of the chairs do not conform to the principles articulated (perhaps because the craftsmen have changed their principles over time, or because customers request certain features); Charley's remarks quoted in the preface exemplify the articulation of compositional principles, both technical and decorative ones.

One finds, too, varying degrees of originality and conventionalization among men as well as among the objects that each man has produced,[21] even occasionally to the extent of seriation.[22] One reason for the limited number of major innovations is technological. Chairmaking is designing for use, in which several requirements concerning practical use must be satisfied. It is difficult to attend to all requirements of useful design, even for the most experienced and gifted individuals, for few people have sufficient talent;[23] hence, little energy can be expended on originality of vision. It is especially difficult to innovate in form; as a consequence, forms demonstrated by past use to be satisfactory tend to be accepted by craftsmen in the present. Furthermore, the learning process (usually emphasis is placed on technical principles, and one learns mainly through observation rather than by means of direct verbal instruction) and limited experiences and sources of information may reduce the possibility of recombining existing elements into new forms. A second reason is that the chairmaker may lack the necessary skill or imagination to originate in form, or he may possess the skill but not the incentive. A third reason has to do with the consumer's values. Sometimes customers demand a particular form which may have served as a model for the production of many chairs over the years; on the other hand, some individuals are attracted to, and even seek, the unusual and the unexpected in form and design for practical objects. As we have seen, however, many chairmakers, like many painters and architects and sculptors, possess originality of vision, and some chairmakers, like some painters or architects or sculptors, do not.

Evaluations of chairs are made by craftsmen and customers, but the criteria differ considerably among individuals and seldom exhibit attention exclusively to the visual dimension of an object or to the object as a perceptual form which serves as a stimulus generating certain suggested images and meanings of the object. Some generalizations can be proposed if the individuality of responses is not lost sight of. Perhaps the concept of taste, vague as it is and loaded with negative connotations, comes closest as a concept to subsuming the many examples of preference and excellence, including judgments on the basis of association and context, the criterion of fitness for use, and responses having the quality of what has been

called the aesthetic. "Taste" has been employed generally to mean the habitual preference of a person manifested by the selection of objects or by overtly
expressed judgments and evaluations; it has been thought to be conditioned
by one's values as well as by sensibility and skill in apperception.[24] Certainly
standards of excellence or preference are not constant (and they may not be
habitual); they change from one generation to another, or within an individual's own lifetime, or from one moment to another, owing in part to additional
experiences, changes in values, and the impact of other individuals. These
standards are influenced in large measure by past experiences and by
association (often marked by emotional involvement, which is not a criticism
but a fact of life), and they are not universally accepted but sometimes are
conceived of by others as good or bad. An essential factor in evaluation is
sensibility, which results in part from experience, training, and familiarity
with the production of objects being criticized; consequently the quality of
judgments varies from the most naive to the most "disciplined"[25] or
sophisticated. It is therefore not surprising that, in the making and doing
of things in everyday life, individuals engaged in production often seem
more perceptive in their remarks than do other people with little knowledge
of the activities. Instead of trying to organize all responses to an object by
marshaling to the fore the concept of taste, which often has the connotation
of a reaction that is bad or naive, it would be more useful to say simply that
one is interested in reactions or responses, preferences, and evaluations; then
the researcher would be more inclined to examine the expressions and behavior
of people in the situations in which they occurred.

What is important in the evaluation of chairs? Visual appearance comes
to mind immediately, but chairs are not presented to only one sense; rather,
they are often presented to the visual, the tactile, and the kinesthetic senses,
and even sometimes to the aural sense. In regard to the sense of movement,
a chair must have the proper tilt or balance so that at rest the rocking chair
leans backward a bit, though a slight breeze will set it in motion; or a settin'
chair should have such perfect balance that only the least effort is required
to tip it backward against the wall, which is the way it is frequently used.
In other words, the user should not have to strain in order to rock a chair

backward or hold it there, which would mitigate against the comfort it is
supposed to provide. Rocking or sitting should be pleasurable, and if it is,
this quality adds to one's enjoyment of the object produced for this purpose,
as the comments of several chairmakers and customers quoted earlier in
this book indicate. Another sense affected by an object such as a chair is
the tactile, as evident when one watches a chairmaker shape his materials, but it is apparent, too, in the concern for weaving a chair bottom
properly, for choosing the type of bark to be used in a seat, and for
bending the slats and posts. Finally, a chair may be criticized in regard
to the sounds it makes, a fact of considerable importance to Charley
when building each chair; one of Charley's customers watered his chair
every spring so that it would not squeak. Some of these actions or
concerns might at first seem silly, but they are worthy of serious consideration because they indicate important criteria for evaluating
objects; often, they are more important than the criterion of visual
appeal in ascertaining the quality of a product.

   Fitness for use is essential, whether the object serves a practical
purpose such as resting one's body, or whether there is some other
instrumental purpose involved, as in the case of masks and many similar
objects. One of the factors most often cited as part of the concept of the
aesthetic, however, that of psychic distance, is calculated to disregard the
instrumentality of an object and the criterion of fitness for use. Psychic
distance has usually meant the detachment and isolation of the object
from its utilitarian purpose, or from the context in which it was made
and used; one is supposed to maintain "objectivity" and examine the object
critically and exclusively in terms of form and expressive impact apart from
the object's circumstances of creation and use. If we find a frame around
a graphic image, or if bodily movements are performed or sounds produced
on a lighted stage in a large and darkened room, or if a thing is set upon a
pedestal or a museum shelf, we suspect that this object is supposed to be
a work of art which has been set apart from its environment. The percipient has already been given the necessary cue to the appropriate response,
and he has been relieved of some of the responsibility of thinking for himself,

as there has been an initial attempt to detach the object from its context
of production and use and to set it apart as a perceptual thing. But what
if the image is a floral design on a chest of drawers, the sculptural work is
part of a canoe or gravestone, the kinesics is the rhythmic movements of
human beings possessed by the Holy Spirit in church, the songs are sung in
a hearth-warmed kitchen by some fisherman who lubricates his throat
frequently with pulls on a whiskey bottle, or the object is a pot or a chair
in use in someone's home? To many people, it is difficult to conceive of
these ordinary, daily, familiar activities as works of art to which they
should remain emotionally aloof; usually it is not desirable to divorce
the object or mode of expression from its context of use. If the object
was made for practical use, then it is unfair to both the producer and
the object to evaluate the product only from the perspective of psychic
distance, for the object was made not solely for contemplation of its
formal qualities.

When appealing to the concept of the aesthetic it is all too easy to
ignore the actual responses of people (which include associations and
fitness for use), as well as to suppose that only great monuments generate an appreciative, contemplative, detached attitude in the percipient;
but this attitude may occur at any time, instantaneously and usually in
combination with other attitudes and feelings, and seldom if ever is it
manifested either in the pure form or in the language that the student
of art is usually seeking. It is possible for the researcher to discover
that many people during work, relaxation, or reflection direct their attention momentarily toward the object as something to be perceived and something that also represents or suggests different meanings to the individual,
as the expression in the Midwest that "them hills ain't hard to look at" serves
to imply. The actual verbalization of such responses, however, may appear to
some investigators to be naive or clichéd owing to the subject's disinterest
in the object as a work of art, to his lack of training in the verbal expression
of things that move him, to embarrassment at expressing an interest in
emotional reactions, or simply to a difference in his mode of expression;
these qualities cannot gainsay the fact that people may take objects in

their environment and events in everyday affairs as perceptual objects stimulating an appreciation of their forms and an interest in their meanings. For example, according to James West, in the rural Midwest the "people admire a well-kept house, freshly painted, neat indoors, and well-maintained without," the women "sometimes take an aesthetic pleasure in the labeling and arrangement of glass jars of canned fruit," and the "men who farm admire a straight furrow better than anything else in the world."[26] Certainly in the Great Plains where I grew up many farmers admire rows and furrows "straight as a rail," and quite a few were self-critical for making rows "crooked as a dog's hind leg." I remember, for example, that on one occasion my father plowed parallel to the road, though that was more difficult and time consuming than plowing the length of the field, because the farmer across the road, who plowed perpendicular to the highway so his work could be admired by others, always made perfectly straight rows but my father did not; my father was embarrassed at the prospect of passersby comparing the fields and skills of the men who had plowed them. The things that rural people find pleasing to look at, then, are often related to their agricultural experiences. One Kansas farmer, a neighbor of ours, talking about his adolescence when he helped plow virgin land, remarked with awe, nostalgia and pleasure, "You'd go clear around the field sometimes an' that sod wouldn't even break; it'd just turn off and lay just in a string clear across the field." And when he described the use of corn-picking equipment he could not restrain his excitement that on "some clear, frosty morning about daylight you could go out in the yard, and you could hear ears throwed against the bump boards perhaps in three or four different directions: thump, thump, thump. Really, it sounded rather nice."

Although, in the aesthetic experience, attention is supposed to be concentrated on the object, one is also supposed to maintain some detachment from the object and from its context of manufacture and use, so that the response to the object will be "disciplined," thus avoiding the "highbrow's" anathema, sentimentality and naive involvement with "irrelevant" details of context or suggested meanings. Other similar paradoxical elements are responsiveness and reserve toward the object of attention, eager submission and sensitive dis-

crimination, and fusion contrasted with reflection. Nevertheless, it is difficult
in a given situation to determine the degree of involvement with or aloofness
from the object, or to ascertain whether the response has been generated by
the perceptual form of the object, or, more probably most often, by associations engendered by the object.

I am reminded of a photograph I took of my wife with our infant son
in her arms which I showed to a friend of mine, who has advanced degrees
in the study of Eastern and Western art and aesthetics, and also to Charley's
wife Rose, who never went beyond the second grade in school. The photograph had great appeal to my friend who immediately likened it in expression
to Renaissance paintings of "Madonna and Child" because of the angle from
which the picture was taken, the back lighting that softened the features,
and the attitude expressed by the mother; Rose was also attracted to the
photograph and said that "Hit's the purtiest one in the whole bunch" of
photographs that I showed her of us as well as of her own family: "Jane looks
so peaceful." I find it nearly impossible to distinguish between these two
people's internal responses to the same object, although the nature of the
verbalized expressions certainly differed. Both people apparently reacted
to the same thing in much the same way, or so it seemed — the expression
of love and repose — and both were seemingly involved and yet reflective.
My friend's comments, of course, were worded rather carefully to avoid suggesting sentimentality and to stress the formal qualities of the object that generated his submission to the picture, whereas Rose was not so careful in
verbal response but immediately expressed in a straightforward manner her
own involvement in the photograph. Rose's association, however, was particularly
acute, and she could scarcely avoid responding on a very personal, rather than
abstract, level; but that is the way people react much of the time in daily life
to things they make or do or see or use, and there is nothing reprehensible
about it. From verbal expression alone, it is quite difficult to determine
who really responds in what way in a specific situation, and from objects
alone it would be impossible. A well-articulated response evincing the proper
qualities of a disciplined aesthetic may really shield a superficial reaction;
and a seemingly poorly phrased reaction, or one that is expressed in rather

conventional ways, may hide an emotional involvement of great intensity and an aesthetic experience of profound depth.

To upgrade the data base, or to justify studying what other investigators might consider inferior or perhaps unseemly, a researcher may find it helpful to use the aesthetic concept as a way of referring to the responses of his subjects. And it should be possible to abstract the principles underlying such common remarks as "them hills ain't hard to look at," "I don't like all them rings and nubs on that chair," "that picture ain't half bad," he can make a chair so pretty you can see your face shinin' in it," "it's a pretty good likeness," "his rows are straight as a rail," "you couldn't keep from chokin' up to hear him sing it," "a chair made out of walnut is pretty but it's awful easy burst," a figural representation "resembles somebody," and so on. These expressions may suggest to the researcher such heightened qualitative expectations as mimesis at midpoint, or such standards of formal excellence as balance and clarity of form and line, serenity of expression, functional simplicity, perfection of finish, delicacy and regularity of ornament, order, harmony, disdain for vulgar display, aversion to overcrowding, positioning, symmetry, movement and tension, or many other criteria of formal appearance. The researcher may even contend that the principles he has abstracted from the comments of others represent a canon of aesthetic criteria or artistic criticism. If our concern is understanding human behavior, however, we need only examine the response for what it is, not what we think it should be or what we would like it to be.

In people's responses to objects and activities the element of association is as important as attention to formal qualities, probably more so, and, like the criterion of fitness for use, it cannot be ignored if the researcher wants to understand the reactions. Consider, for instance, the comments by Charley concerning his favorite songs.

"I'd rather hear 'Pretty Polly' better'n any song I've ever heard b'fore. Next I like 'John Henry.' But the most touchin' song I've heard is 'Constant Sorrow.' An' the best person I've ever heard sing that song is Harry Fordham who used to live on Kings Creek. You couldn't keep from chokin' up to hear him sing it."

What was the appeal of "Man of Constant Sorrow?" The performance and

perhaps context itself apparently had much to do with the song's attractiveness, for Charley associates it with the singer, but perhaps the primary
appeal is the content and message of the song and its meaningfulness
in respect to Charley's own troubled life and his many unhappy experiences,
because it served as the basis for the composition of his own song "My Old
Kentucky Mountain Home." Whether or not Charley considered "Man of
Constant Sorrow" pretty or good, or the performance beautiful or pleasing,
was not clear when he made his comments; I had just asked him to identify
the "prettiest" song he had heard, and he began his response with "Pretty
Polly," which I have known him to request musicians to play, as well as
"John Henry" and "In the Garden," which seem to be his favorites, but he
ended with "Constant Sorrow" on which his own song was based. Why
Charley preferred Harry Fordham's rendition of the song is unclear, also,
but seemingly it was in part because of the perfection of the performance
or the way in which emotion-laden meanings were presented by the singer;
however, Fordham has always lived in the area where Charley was born and
raised, which is what Charley's own song is about, so there may in fact have
been some connection between Charley's preference for Fordham's rendition
and the actual circumstances of composing his own song.

    This association between the object and some other event in one's life
seems not only to dispose one favorably toward the object, regardless of
whether or not it is supposedly beautiful or its structure can be identified
as producing a certain emotional response, but also to encourage one to acquire
the object or learn a particular mode of expression. I am reminded of Frank
Proffitt's alleged response to the ballad "Lord Lovel" which he occasionally sang
and which he liked especially because of the memories it brought him of his
father from whom he had learned the song. The situation is similar to that of
the singer-musician Fields Ward who learned many of his songs and tunes from
his mother, "and such memories would make for only the best associations
with the family's music. Fields found the music beautiful and meaningful in
its own right, but the strong ties it had with his family and home led him to
take it all the more seriously." The author's remark about the meaning of
the music for the Ward brothers serves to indicate the importance of association

in one's response to objects and activities: "To Wade and Fields this music was an important part of their lives. It was a means of self expression, an outlet for their feelings, and a lasting link with their families, friends, and homes. These personal qualities are the framework for the movingly beautiful music they have performed for so many years."[27] If a man sings a song because he associates it with a loved one, or because it sums up his attitude toward some event in his life, or because it restores his ties with an older way of life, is that not important enough for the satisfaction that is got out of the performance? It is common to imbue an object or an event with a personal significance that it does not inherently possess; for this reason the object is often endeared to one and often generates the emotional involvement one has with the object, rather than because one stands aloof and subjects the song or thing to critical analysis in terms of its formal and structural qualities. To argue that one should do the latter, or to concentrate one's investigation exclusively on the problem of whether or not the object is so analyzed, is to miss the reality and the complexity of the response.

Several factors, then, have been suggested as forming the Western elite concept of the aesthetic, such as the manipulation of form for its own sake, the attribution of emotion-producing qualities to the object, the attribution of beauty to the product, psychic distance, and the presence of a philosophy of the aesthetic, most of which can be found in people's behavior if one searches, but none of which seems very meaningful or useful when one examines reactions to the making and doing of things in daily life. The question has been raised by one researcher as to whether or not, without a verbalized canon of aesthetic principles (which he found to be absent among the people he interviewed), there could be an aesthetic at all: "We may pose the crucial question, then, of whether an aesthetic exists if it is not verbalized; the answer seems to clearly be that it does not."[28] That remark itself should cast doubt on the utility of using the aesthetic concept when studying what we make and do, for use of the concept presupposes many things about objects and activities and about reactions to them. For several reasons there is probably no extensive system of verbalized

aesthetic principles codified into a canon transmitted and guarded by a
group of critics. Nonverbal activities may not be conceptualized in language;
it is difficult for anyone to describe emotional reactions or to ascertain
their underlying principles; some people do not easily express their ideas
and emotions in words; many individuals seldom appreciate objects that
serve useful purposes in any way except in regard to the practical ends
for which they were created, or at least this practical quality is of greatest
concern.[29] Furthermore, a philosophy of aesthetic criticism implies that
the objects or activities are conceived of as the fine arts are supposed to
be conceived of, which is seldom the case, even in regard to the fine arts.
It is not at all surprising that in much of what we make and do in daily
life there is expressed no philosophy of the aesthetic; one need only
reflect on experiences in which songs were sung, jokes were told, or
tools were used to realize that this statement is true and to discover
the reasons that it is true. The lack of a codified critical canon does
not indicate, however, that we do not evaluate a performance or the
production of objects, that we do not have preferences, that we do not
make judgments in regard to excellence, that we are not appreciative
of the skill required in performance or production, that we do not become deeply involved in the formal qualities and their suggested meanings and images, that we do not respond because of associations, or
that we ignore the criterion of fitness for use if it is applicable. An
absence of a verbalized philosophy of the aesthetic simply means an
absence of a philosophy of the aesthetic, expressed in verbal form; it
means nothing more, and nothing less.

   In the analysis of useful design, basic concepts that others have
depended upon include type and style. "Type" seems most often to mean
the basic form and compositional elements of an object, which may be
most directly grasped in attempts at localizing and dating the object; it
has been employed not only to identify the basic form of an object but
also to avoid suggesting that the object is art or is being treated as art,
and sometimes even to justify the disregard of decorative features and
purposes in useful objects. "Style" is employed to mean the recurrent

formal qualities in a work in addition to expressive elements and peculiarities of creation and execution — constancy in the use of certain proportions, shapes, lines; arrangements of masses and interrelationships; treatment of surfaces; conception and rendition of details — as inferred by the researcher who supposes that these constancies reveal personality traits and group values. [30] The concept of style, then, has been used to subsume type, to provide a means by which the artistic and aesthetic aspects of production are emphasized and examined, and to allow for dealing with similarities in the objects produced. I have discussed the concept of style before, particularly in chapter 4, noting some problems in the emphasis on similarity and constancy.

Several general and many limited hypotheses have been advanced to account for the development, continuity, and change of group, epochal, and (rarely) individual styles in art, a few of which have been applied to what has been called folk and primitive art. All the theories generate conceptual problems, and none explains the traits or qualities in any particular object. The lexicon of stylistic analysis tends to reify behavior and to suggest that stasis and constancy characterize folk and primitive art until some major external force, such as a "culture change," precipitates alteration. When focusing on change, group, and style, it is as if the researcher viewed the making and doing of things through the wrong end of a telescope: inconstancies disappear, little moves, and individual qualities and the peculiarities of shapes merge into a single form. Ironically, the overall image appears to be sharper than when things are viewed the other way in order to detect specific details, which may help to account for the appeal of this viewpoint. What is needed ultimately is a critical history of folk and primitive art study that would review research preoccupations and trace the development of individual perspectives, but for present purposes some common analytical approaches may be remarked upon.

The literature on what has been called folk art is still very much informed by images of a life principle involving a model of the closed organic curve. Proponents of the life-principle idea assume the birth, maturation, and eventual death of folk art in a social and economic environment that changes from agricultural and preindustrial to urbanized. During the first one hundred and fifty years of American history, for example, "conditions were unfavorable for the growth of any art" because "the people were too busy settling a continent and building a nation," and because American democracy, which American folk art allegedly epitomizes, had not yet been officially secured; hence, only after the Revolution, when "America came into its own as a nation, with its American independence won in the Revolution," did American folk art, "a free artistic expression of the very spirit of the flowering American democracy," bloom. But the toxic effect of "photography, mass printing, and machine production" was to wither this flowering of American folk art after the mid-nineteenth century.[31] Different modes of human behavior, however, are not aging organisms with a germinal life principle; ways of life are sustained by people's attitudes that remain in operation during the phenomenon; and objects and their production change as attitudes, values, and interests change, rather than because of an investment with a life such as that possessed by the men who make the objects.[32] In addition, the making of things such as chairs has not died but continues to be developed among the more skilled and committed men who need an outlet for their talents as well as a source of income. Industrialism has been attended by a growing dissatisfaction, among many people, with mass-produced objects and by a desire for handmade things, thus stimulating hand production rather than destroying it. The hypothesis that making or doing things in daily life was brought to an end by industrialization or urbanization has little to recommend it.

If we accept the proposition that the making of things by hand continues, and if we examine it in the present, or even if we study it only in the past, how can we explain the nature of the product? Diffusion is one popular explanation. It has been suggested that the general regional style of chairs in Appalachia historically had its antecedents elsewhere, but there are few examples of contemporary works whose features can be traced immediately to some external source.[33] In general, the results of diffusion study merely place the compositional framework of the object in some vague historical period and geographical area, but they do not account for the specific characteristics of a particular object.

Related in many respects to the idea of diffusion is the notion of gesunkenes Kulturgut, involving a devolutionary premise and a model that might be described as a corroded downward spiral, whose proponents assume the debasement of what they conceive to be elite art as it sinks and spreads outward to the lower socioeconomic levels of society, at which time it may be called folk art. As one art historian has written, "the thesis that folk art consists of 'cultural goods that have drifted downward' is a commonplace that hardly anyone now thinks of doubting." [34] One museologist, however, dissatisfied with this thesis, went so far as to say that objects such as salt boxes, tables, or dressers are "no-style" furniture, that is, they are "without style and with little variation." [35] Such a remark was apparently meant to be a way of designating "pieces of furniture which do not exhibit characteristics derived from the various historical styles," that is, epochal styles in an elite tradition of utilitarian art production. [36] Nevertheless, the imagery of "folk debasement of elite art" informs much of the published work on what has been called folk art. One husband-and-wife team, for instance, insists that "if any point is to be made, it might be that the more like the formal furniture, the more able the craftsman." [37] Another writer contends that "most of these country joiners or cabinetmakers seem to have possessed a certain amount of creative ability — or at least a retentive memory for the graceful designs of more accomplished works." [38] Few examples of such copying can be found in the furniture production I witnessed in southeastern Kentucky, although some chairs were inspired by unimaginative and poorly constructed factory-made chairs; the few inferior reproductions of commercial furniture, executed mainly by individuals with minimal interest in chairmaking, were duly criticized by other craftsmen for their deficiencies. Researchers may be correct in claiming that the contemporary slat-back chair in Appalachia is a descendant of the fancy chairs mass produced in the early nineteenth century, [39] though I am suspicious of this interpretation, based as it is on little evidence and coinciding with certain doubtful assumptions about what has been called folk art. Even if it is true, however, it leaves unanswered questions about specific features in chairs made today, features that are marks of individuality, of contemporary customer influence, and of the ideas of many craftsmen

which have developed over a long period of time. This particular form of diffusion-
ist theory does not grant the fact of originality or explain the many instances
of production in which there is no mechanical copying of earlier models. Furthermore, it disregards the role of the consumer in affecting production both directly by means of stipulation and indirectly by the craftsman's attempt to
attract him. Less important perhaps, but of some interest, is an apparent
contradiction: proponents of the hypothesis of the downward diffusion from
culturally higher to culturally inferior strata of society attempt to render
the producer alone the agent responsible for the nature of the product —
for it is he who allegedly debases the art — and yet presume that the
producer was merely a fortuitous inheritor of a cultural legacy; in addition, the producer is condemned for his irresponsible behavior, that is,
inept copying.

 Certainly a common, and perhaps the most persuasive, explanation
of style is evolution, based on the premise of cultural progress graphically
portrayed with an image of the continuous upward spiral,[40] an explanation
that when first used in studies of primitive art consisted of the application
of "biological deductions" to designs. I do not suggest in chapter 4, when
reviewing some of the conceptual problems engendered by this explanation,
that there is no development of ideas out of preceding experiences; but little
is to be gained by implying that the features of a work are preordained and
that unique discoveries and inventions are mutants or misfits in the next and
necessary evolution of a tradition. With hindsight it is now easy to see a
development in some traits in Aaron's chairs between 1963 and 1967. The
earliest works are a bit amateurish, the forms are vaguely defined, and the
lines lack clarity. In the most recent examples the turnings, which certainly
have antecedents in the earliest chairs and which certainly developed from
them, are sharply delineated; the chairs now are more professionally conceived
and constructed; and the recent works exhibit a finesse of workmanship which
was barely emerging by 1964 and 1965. In 1968, given the chairs made in 1963,
one would expect those made in 1967; yet Aaron might have lacked the talent
and imagination or the interest to continue along these lines, there might have
arisen a demanding need within himself to develop in some other direction, or a

particular consumer public to which he was appealing might have required other traits. The unusual notch in the upper center of the top slat in rocking and dining chairs (but absent in settin' chairs, which, owing to their use, must be as strong as possible) could not have been predicted early in Aaron's career; it is the result of Aaron's search for a unique quality serving as a personal trademark to differentiate his works from those of his predecessors, and it has been perpetuated because of its appeal visually to him and to some of his customers.

It has also been suggested, in regard to both origin and change, that "every group is constantly subjected to outside influences, but unless there is something there, the stimulus does not take;" the "sudden changes" in "decorative style" of a people's art such as pottery are "the result of general cultural instability working upon the mind of a sensitive individual."[41] Such a viewpoint tends to direct attention away from the immediacy of events, from momentary occurrences, and from the process of production which necessarily is dynamic; it is informed, too, by the notion that what the researcher calls folk or primitive art is conservative to the extent of being static as it slowly evolves in a single direction until external forces disrupt its equilibrium, causing cultural disintegration unless, or until, an artist within the group is able to pick up the pieces in triumph rather than in defeat. Change, whether good or bad (and usually what is called cultural change is disparaged as the harbinger of the decline of a people's art), is seen as originating from outside the system of production. This is not to say that interaction with people outside one's immediate area, and products made elsewhere to which one has access, do not affect production. In regard to chairmaking, new tools have occasionally introduced a degree of standardization (welcomed by many craftsmen), but they have also expanded the variety of articles produced and altered the characteristics of these objects, and they have satisfied growing demands for the products. Customers from outside the immediate area often have somewhat different values requiring fulfillment, thus creating a wider variety of products and encouraging new objects, designs, and traits if the craftsman is willing,[42] but sometimes he is not. Focusing on culture change generally, and attributing the specific behavior of particular individuals to the impact of culture, direct observation to the realm of externalities, thus ignoring or diminishing the significance of the dynamics generated uniquely within each event.

To bring to a close this survey of chairmaking in southeastern Kentucky, I would repeat that my research was directed toward finding a way of analyzing the things that people make and do. Special emphasis has been placed on the individual and on the actual behavior of producers, for without the individual and his skills and activities there would be no objects for study. I have excluded from discussion the museum specimens that some other researchers work with, but most aspects of the method presented here are as applicable to the study of objects as to the study of object makers; investigation of living human beings who are making and using things adds a dimension lacking in research for many decades; and observations of contemporary craftsmen offer insights for understanding objects made long ago about which little is now known.

"Anyone who has known the shattering experience of being involved with a real work of art easily becomes intolerant of all exploitation of cheap effects and is very ready to maintain that there is only one art, indivisible and incapable of being diluted, and beside which all else is devoid of significance or value.

"The true character of art," continues Arnold Hauser, "is not to be understood from either folk or popular art; it reveals its nature only upon the highest level of creative activity." [43]

It is my hope that this study provides some indication of the way in which "the true character of art" may be understood among many people representing different levels of socioeconomic and educational attainment and engaging in a variety of activities; that we may learn much about those aspects of human behavior labeled art, folk art, and creativity by setting aside the terms art, folk art, and creativity in favor simply of studying the things that people make and do in daily life. The primary effect of what has been called art is that of giving pleasure: to the person who makes or does something taken to be ordered and balanced and harmonious, to the percipient who empathizes with that individual in his satisfaction at having mastered the necessary techniques to produce a pleasing form, and to anyone who finds enjoyment in using an object that resulted from the skillful control of tools and materials and form. If the object produced is taken to be spiritually or intellectually elevating, or if it brings a shattering emotional experience to the percipient-user, then the individual's life is enriched owing to the deeper meaning felt in the form and design, but this fact in itself does not distinguish art from nonart, nor does the absence of this effect in one percipient render the object, the skill, or the activity less significant or valuable to others.

There is, indeed, only one art, not two or three or four, and it is to be found universally in human experience as an integral, not isolable, element of man's behavior. Presumably all manifestations of that process of human thought and action called art by many researchers will one day be fully, but also equally, studied and appreciated. Achieving this goal requires an inter-disciplinary approach in the best sense of that word, one that encourages the researcher to examine the actual behavior of individuals who make and do things, and of those who acquire and use things, in interaction with other people, and one that ensures a study of the whole man as a unique individual; it requires, too, a constant reexamination of the assumptions, concepts, and models employed by oneself and other scholars, for otherwise the method of analysis that one develops and promotes may not be very useful or satisfying to work with.

Notes

Chapter 1. A Strange Rocking Chair

1. See Paul S. Wingert, _Primitive Art: Its Tradition and Styles_ (Cleveland and New York, 1962), pp. 3-11. Wingert attempts to distinguish folk from primitive art, characterizing the former as "a unique and highly personalized, untutored art expression. This is not an early phase within a historical development, but is a 'sport,' in the biological sense of the word, that is, a spontaneous deviation from the norm" (pp. 4-5). Obviously I do not agree with Wingert; nor do I accept Douglas Fraser's proposition in _Primitive Art_ (New York, 1962): "Several other types of art are often confused with the primitive kind. One is folk or popular art. . . . In comparison with primitive art, which exists, so to speak, at the top of its culture, popular art betrays a consciousness of lower social and artistic status that amounts to an inferiority complex" (pp. 13-14).

2. See Joseph Jacobs, "The Folk," _Folk-Lore_, IV (1893), 233-238, wherein he suggests (pp. 235-236) that the "Folk is simply a name for our ignorance: we do not know to whom a proverb, a tale, a custom, a myth owes its origin, so we say it originated among the Folk." One of the most direct statements about folklore as survivals among "backward peoples" was made by C.S. Burne, _The Handbook of Folk-Lore_ (London, 1914), p. 2: "The study of this traditional lore began with the observation that among the less cultured inhabitants of all the countries of modern Europe there exists a vast body of curious beliefs, customs, and stories, orally handed down from generation to generation, and essentially the property of the unlearned and backward portion of the community."

3. For information on these artists see Jean Crawford, _Jugtown Pottery: History and Design_ (Winston-Salem, 1964); Ruth Bunzel, _The Pueblo Potter: A Study of Creativity in Primitive Art_ (New York, 1929); Robert Thompson, "Abatan: A Master Potter of the Egbado Yoruba," in _Tradition and Creativity in Tribal Art_, ed. Daniel P. Biebuyck (Berkeley and Los Angeles, 1969), pp. 120-182; and Adrian A. Gerbrands, _Wow-Ipits: Eight Wood-carvers of New Guinea_ (The Hague, 1967).

4. See, for example, some of the comments in "What Is American Folk Art? A Symposium," _Antiques,_ LVII (1950), 355-362; or remarks by Arnold Hauser in _The Philosophy of Art History_ (Cleveland and New York, 1963); or statements in most of the works on "country furniture," such as Ralph and Terry Kovel, _American Country Furniture, 1780-_

<u>1875</u> (New York, 1965); Henry Lionel Williams, <u>Country Furniture of Early America</u> (New York, 1963); Albert Sack, <u>Fine Points of Furniture: Early American</u> (New York, 1950); and James Lazeare, <u>Primitive Pine Furniture</u> (Watkins Glen, 1951).

In his presidential address, "American Folklore after Seventy Years: Survey and Prospect," delivered to the American Folklore Society in 1958 and published in <u>Journal of American Folklore,</u> LXXIII (1960), Wayland D. Hand admitted (p. 4) that "the folklore of material culture is one of the most neglected fields of American folklore. This work has fallen largely to museum people, who follow it as a collateral interest; and the society has been notably backward in supplying leadership in this important field." It is indeed unfortunate, given the increasing preoccupation of students with the ethnic arts generally, that there are available for perusal so few detailed ethnographies or monographic studies consisting of substantive material for analysis organized by means of specific hypotheses. At present, folk art study lacks an adequate methodology and data base.

"There are now many museum exhibits and many big books devoted to 'folk art.' There is material to study, but no theories have been developed to enable that study," complains Henry Glassie in "Folk Art," in Richard M. Dorson, ed., <u>Folklore and Folklife: An Introduction</u> (Chicago, 1972), p. 257. In his introductory remarks, however, Dorson notes (p. 41) that a "basis for theory is laid in a nine-hundred-page doctoral dissertation by Michael O. Jones . . . [who] elaborates a complex theoretical model for the study of handmade items of material culture intended for utilitarian purposes. The model considers the local economics of production and distribution, the psychological types of the artists, external influences of taste and demand affecting the folk community, the ecological factors controlling the raw materials, and the traditional techniques manipulated by the artist. Jones seeks to take into account every element — historical, individual, cultural, traditional, aesthetic, economic, environmental — entering into the folk art process." In the present work, however, it is the individual artist who receives the closest attention; other factors are treated rather cursorily owing to limitations of space. Still, it is hoped that some of the gaps in our knowledge of making and doing things in daily life will be filled by this monograph.

Among the better-known ethnographies containing at least some information on creativity and aesthetics, especially in regard to material art in North America, which is of particular interest to me, are Bunzel, <u>The Pueblo Potter</u>; Lila M. O'Neale, <u>Yorok-Karok Basket Weavers</u> (Berkeley, 1932); John Adair, <u>The Navaho and Pueblo Silversmiths</u> (Norman, 1944); Dorothy Jean Ray, <u>Artists of the Tundra and the Sea</u> (Seattle, 1961); and John Robert Vincent, "A Study of Two Ozark Woodworking Industries" (M.A. thesis, University of Missouri, 1962). Vincent's work differs from the present volume in lacking biographical data about producers, information on responses to the objects, and an examination of production as art, but his report and mine might be compared if the student wishes to investigate the technology of making things by hand. Of interest, too, is Henry Glassie, _Pattern in the Material Folk Culture of the Eastern United States_ (Philadelphia, 1968), which is distributional in intent and descriptive in nature. Among other works, the student should be familiar with Franz Boas's analysis in _Primitive Art_ (New York, 1955), and the essays reprinted in Carol F. Jopling, ed., _Art and Aesthetics in Primitive Societies_ (New York, 1971), as well as the original essays in Biebuyck, _Tradition and Creativity in Tribal Art_. The Festival of American Folklife, held annually in early July at the Smithsonian Institution, gives evidence of the increasing interest in the ethnic arts in America (see catalogues from previous festivals). Finally, it should be noted that _Pennsylvania Folklife_, formerly _The Pennsylvania Dutchman_, contains much material, especially of a technological nature, for examination by the interested student; Don Yoder, editor of _Pennsylvania Folklife_, has initiated a new series of annual publications entitled _American Folklife_; in recent years _Keystone Folklore Quarterly_ has published several articles on objects and their making; and the interested student should be familiar with Don Yoder, "The Folklife Studies Movement," _Pennsylvania Folklife_, XIII (1963), 43-56; should examine some of the works listed by Robert Wildhaber in "A Bibliographical Introduction to American Folklife," _New York Folklore Quarterly_, XXI (1965), 259-302; and should note some of the selections in Dorson, _Folklore and Folklife_, especially the essays by Henry Glassie, Warren E. Roberts, Don Yoder, J. Geraint Jenkins, Robert Wildhaber, and E. Estyn Evans.

5. I have suggested some techniques of data gathering and a framework for dealing with modes of behavior often called folk art in "Two Directions for Folkloristics in the Study of American Art," _Southern Folklore Quarterly_, XXXII (1968), 249-259, as well as in other essays, but I wish to approach the problem somewhat differently here by enlarging upon my recent remarks in "The Well Wrought Pot: Folk Art and Folklore As Art," American Folklore Society meeting, Austin, Texas, November 16, 1972.

6. Boas, _Primitive Art_, p. 155. Three and a half decades before Boas's remarks Joseph Jacobs had noted ("The Folk," p. 235) that "Artistry is individual" and "we must search for the individual among the folk, at least for the initiative." See also Phillips Barry, "The Part of the Folk Singer in the Making of Folk Balladry" (in _The Critics and the Ballad_, ed. MacEdward Leach and Tristram P. Coffin [Carbondale, 1961], pp. 59-76), who proclaimed (p. 76): "Let it be literally cried from the house tops that the folk singer is a personality, an individual, and most of all a creative artist."

7. Alfred C. Haddon, _Evolution in Art: As Illustrated by the Life-Histories of Designs_ (London, 1895), pp. 332-333.

8. Ernst Grosse, _The Beginnings of Art_ (New York, 1897), pp. 9, 12, 314. See also A. Lane-Fox Pitt-Rivers, _The Evolution of Culture and Other Essays_ (Oxford, 1906), esp. the introductory comments by Henry Balfour.

9. The phrases quoted are, in order of appearance, from Pitt-Rivers, _The Evolution of Culture_, p. 4; Haddon, _Evolution in Art_, p. 324; Herbert Barry, III,

"Relationships between Child Training and the Pictorial Arts," in Jopling, Art and Aesthetics in Primitive Societies, pp. 64-72 (although such references to "homogeneous societies" are prolific in the literature and by no means limited to this article); and Roy Sieber, "The Visual Arts," p. 442, in The African World: A Survey of Social Research, ed. Robert A. Lystad (New York, 1965), pp. 442-451, 555-556 (but Sieber is only one of many authors who summarize primitive art in this way.

10. Grosse, Beginnings of Art, pp. 12, 50.

11. Haddon, Evolution in Art, p. 4.

12. Ibid., p. 332.

13. I shall be using both "aesthetics" and "taste," but not synonymously. Key ideas in understanding the nature of the aesthetic attitude, according to Thomas C. Munro (The Arts and Their Interrelations [Cleveland, 1967], p. 98), are that attention is directed to an object as a perceptual form or as a form suggested to one's imagination, which is what other researchers have tended to call "psychic distance"; and that emotional involvement fixes apperception temporarily with great intensity, which includes fusion with the object and is the opposite of establishing psychic distance, and which also includes associations generated by the work of art which help to maintain one's desire to "savor the emotional qualities aroused by the images and meanings." "Aesthetic," however, is not a sufficiently comprehensive term to embrace all the responses to objects (particularly those things serving in some measure a practical purpose), many of which rightly involve the factors of other kinds of association and of the context of manufacture and use as conditioners of judgments; thus, the term "taste" is sometimes used to examine more broadly attitudes and preferences. Modifying somewhat remarks by Russell Lynes (The Tastemakers [New York, 1954], pp. 339-340), it might be said that taste is conceived of as either good or bad (depending on one's predilection), that it is not constant or universal, and that factors influencing standards of preference or excellence include not only aesthetic sensibility but also the nature and purpose of the object created to which one is responding, personal values deriving from one's experiences and goals and interactions with other individuals, one's sensitivity or ability to apperceive, and one's training in the evaluation of the objects that are judged. While the aesthetic experience may be universal in human life, particular standards of preference vary considerably and require more than apperception of form and evaluation of the object on its own terms; taste is not necessarily objectively arrived at by the individual who gives voice to his standards. Keeping this discussion in mind, we have some guidelines for more penetrating investigations of responses to things that are made, responses that are not examples of the aesthetic as commonly conceived but are much broader in scope and nature. Thus, additional insights might have been presented by Harold K. Schneider in "The Interpretation of Pakot Visual Art" (in Jopling, Art and Aesthetics, pp. 55-63) if he had gone beyond the strictures imposed by use of the concept of "aesthetic" in order to take into account the association of ideas — not regarded as

part of the aesthetic in its allegedly pure form — evident in the native's response to European possessions which he claimed to be "the prettiest things he had ever seen because he had never seen anything like them before" (p. 60). Many of the reactions reported by Daniel J. Crowley in "An African Aesthetic" (in ibid., pp. 315-327) could also be investigated to great advantage by not conceiving of them as examples of the aesthetic, and by then considering the kinds of experiences and associations, having nothing to do with the aesthetic experience per se, which influenced the natives' standards of preference. For example, Crowley notes (p.324) that "young men and boys were outspoken in their dislike of heavy raised welts or broad pyrography made with heated nails" as found on some of the masks, "even though these were in our eyes perfectly balanced with the style and mass of the mask." Crowley's response was apparently wholly in the nature of an aesthetic experience — he took the masks as perceptual forms and evaluated the lines in terms of their balance in relationship to the whole object — but, while the natives no doubt did the same thing, Crowley's informants preferred other kinds of lines probably because of negative associations with scarification, engendered perhaps by what they conceived to be their own "backward" behavior in contrast with what they had seen in the cities and among whites. Thus, "They like only carefully incised narrow lines that had not been picked out with color or burning, possibly reflecting the growing dislike of cicatrization, tattooing, and teeth filing as marks of the bush. Even so," wrote Crowley, "girls whose abdomens had not been cicatrized were considered infinitely less desirable sexually than those who had beautified themselves by this ordeal." Cicatrization of the abdomen has sexual connotations (and uses), however, and is not regarded strictly as "art" in the sense of decoration only; nor are responses to it by men purely "aesthetic." Dislike of pronounced scarification and preference for less obvious incisions on masks, apparently contradicted by the desire to have a woman with cicatrization on the abdomen, make sense only when the researcher deals with responses in terms of likes and dislikes, preference and excellence, rather than strictly the aesthetic, as Crowley implicitly, but not completely, attempts to do.

   14. As Glassie noted in Pattern (p. 16), although he was concerned with the distribution of objects by types and subtypes, it is "necessary to know not only what an object is and what its history and distribution are, but also what its role in the culture of the producer and user is, and what mental intricacies surround, support, and are reflected in its existence." This is precisely the kind of information that has not been presented in studies of folk art (including films).

   15. Robert A. Georges, "Toward an Understanding of Storytelling Events," Journal of American Folklore, LXXXII (1969), 316.

   16. Carpenter's remarks are appended to Herta Haselberger's essay, "Method of Studying Ethnological Art," Current Anthropology, II (1961), 362. In "A Structural Approach to Esthetics: Toward a Definition of Art in Anthropology," American Anthropologist, LX (1958), 702-714, Warren d'Azevedo also stresses (p. 712) "art viewed as activity and

process manifested in social relations with its locus in the producers of art."

17. For Nootenboom's comments see Haselberger, "Studying Ethnological Art," p. 372. For alternative views elevating the object to supreme importance, however, see P. Jan Vandenhoute's comments (ibid., p. 375), and Robert Plant Armstrong, The Affect-ing Presence: An Essay in Humanistic Anthropology (Urbana, 1971); for a critique of this approach see my review of Armstrong's book in Western Folklore, XXXI (1972), 215-217.

18. Georges, "Understanding of Storytelling Events," p. 328.

19. Kenneth L. Ketner, "What Is the Story?" a paper read at the American Folklore Society meeting, Los Angeles, California, November 13, 1970.

20. Two works have influenced my conception of art: Munro, The Arts and Their Interrelations, pp. 316-318, 326 ff., and esp. pp. 107-109; and D. W. Gotschalk, Art and the Social Order (New York, 1962), pp. 28, 60, and esp. pp. 93-94.

21. This characterization of art would seem to take into account the responses of the Pakot and others who have no equivalent for the word "art" but who do single out "special" objects for appreciative comment. See Schneider, "The Interpreta-tion of Pakot Visual Art," Man, LVI (1956), 103-106, reprinted in Jopling, Art and Aesthetics, pp. 55-63.

22. On medicine see my monograph, Why Faith Healing? (Mercury Series, Canadian Centre for Folk Culture Studies, Ottawa, Ontario, 1972); on gossiping see James West, "Plainville, U.S.A.," in Abram Kardiner, ed., The Psychological Frontiers of Society (New York, 1959), p. 303. Another mode of expressive behavior worth investi-gating is that of traditional gardening or landscaping; see E. N. Anderson, Jr., "On the Folk Art of Landscaping," Western Folklore, XXXI (1972), 179-188.

23. See Carpenter's comments in Biebuyck, Tradition and Creativity in Tribal Art, p. 204.

24. Beatrice Blackwood's remarks are appended to Haselberger, "Studying Ethnological Art," p. 360.

25. Patricia B. Altman in the catalogue Ceramics: Form and Technique, prepared by the Museum and Laboratories of Ethnic Arts and Technology, University of California, Los Angeles (n.d.), p. 10.

26. Georges, "Understanding of Storytelling Events," p. 323. See also J. Barre Toelken, "The 'Pretty Language' of Yellowman: Genre, Mode, and Texture of Navaho Coyote Narratives," Genre, II (1969), 199-235.

27. Haselberger, "Studying Ethnological Art," p. 342.

28. See Ralph Altman's comments in Biebuyck, Tradition and Creativity, p. 184.

29. Mamie Harmon, "Folk and Primitive Art," in Funk and Wagnall's Standard Dictionary of Folklore, Mythology, and Legend, ed. Maria Leach, II (New York, 1950), 898. The tendency to conceive of folk art as the (rather debased) imitation of elite art is apparent in the writings of many contributors to "What Is American Folk Art? A Sym-posium," Antiques, LVII (1950), 355-362, and to "Country Furniture: A Symposium," Antiques, XCIII (1968), 342-371; and it is evident in many other works as well, including

Kovel and Kovel, _American Country Furniture_; Williams, _Country Furniture of Early America_; Lazeare, _Primitive Pine Furniture_; Sack, _Fine Points of Furniture_; Hauser, _Philosophy of Art History_; Nina Fletcher Little, _American Folk Art_ (Colonial Williamsburg, 1969); and comments by Nina Fletcher Little, Erwin O. Christensen, and others in Helen Comstock, _The Concise Encyclopedia of American Antiques_ (New York, 1958).

30. Richard M. Dorson, _Bloodstoppers and Bearwalkers_ (Cambridge, Mass., 1952), p. 9.

31. Alan Dundes, "The American Concept of Folklore," _Journal of the Folklore Institute_, III (1966), 230. See the criticism of such conceptions as Dorson's and Dundes' in the paper, "ICEN – An Alternative: A Re-Evaluation of the Concept 'Group,'" presented by Beth Blumenreich and Bari Lynn Polonsky at the American Folklore Society meeting, Austin, Texas, November 18, 1972.

32. For example, see James Walton's comments appended to Haselberger, "Studying Ethnological Art," p. 377. Walton quotes a statement by Fox-Strangways that "'Folk' means 'all human beings.' You are a member of the folk, so am I."

33. Ellen J. Stekert, "Folklore Research in Urban Environments," a paper read at UCLA, January 18, 1973.

34. Ketner, "What _Is_ the Story?" p. 6.

35. Gotschalk, _Art and the Social Order_, pp. 93-94. Note, too, the remark by Phillips Barry ("The Folk Singer in Folk Balladry," p. 61) that "the folk-singer, however much he be keeper of a tradition, is never for a single moment dominated by it. He learns his songs and in his interpretation of them does exactly what he pleases with them." Barry also writes (_ibid._, p. 76): "Let it be literally cried from the house tops that the folk singer is a personality, an individual, and most of all a creative artist. In the name of good science and good sense, let us have done once and for all with calling folksong and folk balladry artless." Unfortunately, however, most commentators seem to equate creativity with major innovation; and in respect to singing many researchers who are text oriented dwell upon the relative stasis of song texts and fail to perceive the creative aspects of performance and singing.

36. Allen H. Eaton, _Handicrafts of the Southern Highlands_ (New York, 1937), p. 5.

37. Dan Ben-Amos, "Toward a Definition of Folklore in Context," _Journal of American Folklore_, LXXXIV (1971), 13, 14.

38. Jacobs, "The Folk," p. 237.

39. Burne, _Handbook of Folk-Lore_, p. 1. This conception of "folk" and "lore" is not limited to Burne or to the time of her writings; it is still quite common among folklorists, including some of those engaged in what is called "folklife studies."

Chapter 2. The Bookcase Masterpiece

1. For examples of the techniques of data gathering see some of the works cited in my article, "The Study of Traditional Furniture: Review and Preview," _Keystone Folklore Quarterly_, XII (1967), 233-245. See also Gladys A. Reichard, _Navajo Shepherd_

and Weaver (New York, 1936); Kenneth S. Goldstein, A Guide for Field Workers in Folklore (Hatboro, Pa., 1964), esp. p. 108 ff.; John Collier, Jr., Visual Anthropology: Photography as a Research Method (New York, 1967); Thomas C. Munro, Toward Science in Aesthetics (Indianapolis, 1956), passim but esp. pp. 43-46, 53, 57, 59, 79; and L. L. Langness, The Life History in Anthropological Science (New York, 1965). A particularly neglected area of research is the relationship between personality and folklore, despite the fact that Goldstein has suggested (Guide for Field Workers, p. 121) that one of the "most important contributions which the field worker can make to folklore studies is the gathering of data for use in personal life history documents."

Results of the techniques I used were not always what had been anticipated in advance. Some of the photographs of objects shown to people to elicit their criticism, because of the angle of the shot or the distance or the composition, had an effect on the viewer which the actual object might not have had. I found, too, that few individuals who were not themselves engaged in craftwork were interested in or willing to undertake my tasks. It was also apparent that only a few of the objects were thought to be, or had ever been considered, something special or worth close inspection and extensive comment. What became clear is that chair-making is not considered an art form, although certain chairs are "pretty" and command attention; that fitness for use is of primary concern; that there is no codified system of exclusively aesthetic criteria although there are obviously standards of excellence and preference, and of composition and construction, which tend to vary from one individual to another and which are not often verbalized as clearly stated principles; and that there is little interest in the object for its own sake but as a tool, a device, used to solve a very practical problem. Nor was there much interest in or concern for the individual who produced the objects.

2. The stages in construction in this type of craft are reviewed by John Robert Vincent, "A Study of Two Ozark Woodworking Industries" (M.A. thesis, University of Missouri, 1962).

3. The sources of ideas vary among producers, although it is unlikely that the essential processes differ fundamentally from the manner in which artists in the Western elite tradition gather their ideas for execution. Whether the artist is conscious of the process or not, there must be some accumulation and selection of material from past experiences and reorganization of that data into the conception of a work of art. Sometimes, however, the conceptualization allegedly takes the form of a flash of sudden inspiration, and the artist cannot discern the ultimate origins of the idea. Ruth Bunzel (The Pueblo Potter: A Study of Creativity in Primitive Art [New York, 1929], p. 50) notes that the Pueblo potters "all speak of sleepless nights spent in thinking of designs for the pot to be decorated in the morning, of dreams of new patterns which on waking they try and often fail to recapture, and above all, the constant preoccupation with decorative problems even while they are engaged in other kinds of work." And Franz Boas (Primitive Art [New York, 1955],

p. 157) *suggests that many Indians called their designs "'dream designs,' and claim that the new pattern actually appeared to them in a dream."* These are only ostensible sources based on the unconscious absorption of ideas that precipitated in the artist's mind as a sudden, ecstatic conception; perhaps the artist does cite as the immediate source a dream, an intense emotional experience, or the intercession of a spiritual being, and divine inspiration may well be a precipitating factor, but the process of generating ideas is more complex than these assertions would suggest. The actual sources of ideas are diverse but include at least the following: adaptation of ideas from other living craftsmen, drawing ideas from objects made by other peoples, accepting suggestions from the consumer, taking advantage of accidental inventions or discoveries during the manipulation of raw materials, and experimenting to some extent with the materials at the time of manufacture. See also Alan P. Merriam, *The Anthropology of Music* (Chicago, 1964), pp. 166 ff.

4. Bunzel, *Pueblo Potter*, p. 49; Ruth Bunzel, "Art," in Franz Boas, ed., *General Anthropology* (Boston, 1938), p. 554; Boas, *Primitive Art*, pp. 156-157; George C. Mills, *Navaho Art and Culture* (Colorado Springs, 1959), p. 131.

5. Nina Fletcher Little, Janet R. MacFarlane and Louis C. Jones, and E.P. Richardson, "What Is American Folk Art? A Symposium," *Antiques*, LVII (1950), 360, 361; for a discussion of this problem see my paper "Folk Art: Planful or Impulsive?" read at the annual meeting of the Southern California Academy of Sciences, Los Angeles, May 6, 1972.

6. Stith Thompson, "Folktale," *Funk and Wagnall's Standard Dictionary of Folklore, Mythology, and Legend*, ed. Maria Leach, I (New York, 1949), 408, cited by Daniel J. Crowley, *I Could Talk Old-Story Good: Creativity in Bahamian Folklore*, Folklore Studies, vol. 17 (Berkeley and Los Angeles, 1966), p. 1.

7. See Basil Bernstein's review of Iona and Peter Opie, *The Lore and Language of Schoolchildren*, in *British Journal of Sociology*, XI (1960), 178-181.

8. Phillips Barry, "The Part of the Folk Singer in the Making of Folk Balladry," in *The Critics and the Ballad*, ed. MacEdward Leach and Tristram P. Coffin (Carbondale, 1961), p. 61.

9. See my paper "'S.J.O.C.P.F.M.': The Importance of Folklore in American Studies," given at annual meeting of southern California chapter of American Studies Association, Fullerton, April 16, 1971; specific examples of lines are from two former students in two folklore classes at U.C.L.A. in 1970 and 1971.

10. John Quincy Wolf, "Folksingers and the Re-Creation of Folksong," *Western Folklore*, XXVI (1967), 106.

11. Stith Thompson's remark, from *Funk and Wagnall's Standard Dictionary of Folklore*, I, 498, is quoted by D.K. Wilgus, *Anglo-American Folksong Scholarship since 1898* (New Brunswick, 1959), p. 285. There are other examples of what has been conceived of as variability within "small-group culture." Two singers (as reported by Roger D. Abrahams, "Creativity, Individuality, and the Traditional Singer," in John A.

Burrison, ed., _Creativity in Southern Folklore_, Vol. III of _Studies in the Literary Imagination_ [Atlanta, 1970], p. 13) who are of the same age and from the same "Appalachian-Ozark type of rural enclave" nevertheless "differ considerably on virtually every other feature and represent in the fullest sense the variety available within this apparently restrictive tradition" (which suggests that the tradition is not so restrictive as Abrahams assumed or that the women do not belong to the same group or that the construct group needs reexamination by the author). John M. Roberts (_Three Navaho Households: A Comparative Study in Small Group Culture_ [Cambridge, Mass., 1951], p. 83) has suggested that "every small group defines an independent and unique group-ordered culture." Some years before Roberts's study appeared, Ruth Benedict (in introduction to _Zuni Mythology_, Vol. I [New York, 1935]) stressed, in respect to folklore, the freedom of expression within "the fixed limits" permitted Zuni storytellers. "It is obvious," she wrote (p. xxxvii), in a direct challenge to scholars employing the historic-geographic method in diffusion studies, "that where such freedom in handling incidents is expected of a good storyteller, it will often become impossible to trace with assurance a tale's genetic relationship with tales of other peoples."

Chapter 3. It All Ended Up the Wrong Way

1. "What we wish to insist upon is that it is not enough to study the tunes," wrote Phillips Barry; "the singers also should be studied and the reason for their individual preferences established as far as possible on psychological grounds," which is the goal of the present study in respect to chairmakers rather than singers. See Barry's article, "The Part of the Folk Singer in the Making of Folk Balladry," in _The Critics and the Ballad_, ed MacEdward Leach and Tristram P. Coffin (Carbondale, 1961), pp. 59-76. For studies approaching what Barry had in mind, see Ellen J. Stekert, "Two Voices of Tradition" (Ph.D. dissertation, University of Pennsylvania, 1965), and Anne Murase, "Personality and Lore," a paper read at annual meeting of the Southern California Academy of Sciences, Los Angeles, California, May 6, 1972.

2. The literature on grief is extensive, but a few works of particular interest are J. M. Tanner, ed., _Stress and Psychiatric Disorder_ (Oxford, 1960); Katherin J. Bordicks, _Patterns of Shock_ (New York, 1965); Herman Feifel, _The Meaning of Death_ (New York, 1959); and Robert Fulton, _Death and Identity_ (New York, 1965). It seems to me that the behavior of most of the storytellers and singers mentioned by Henry Glassie ("'Take That Night Train to Selma': An Excursion to the Outskirts of Scholarship," _Journal of Popular Culture_, II [1968], 1-62) could be interpreted from the point of view of grieving over a loss rather than as a result of freedom from ordinary responsibilities or dissatisfaction with one's own culture, which are Glassie's main explanations.

3. That day may have arrived. A Midwestern newspaper recently published a syndicated wirephoto of President Nixon and a member of the House of Repre-

sentatives between whom stand Charley (in long hair, beard, and overalls) and a seven-slat rocking chair with a curved wood seat, extensive ornamentation, and fancy, hand-carved slats with one or more words incised on each. (Unfortunately, the photograph is not clear enough to make out most of the words, though it looks as if Charley's name is on the second slat from the top.)

4. There are few studies of the relationship between personality and art style in folk or primitive art. Initial attempts include Richard M. Dorson, "Oral styles of American Folk Narrators," in Folklore in Action, ed. Horace P. Beck (Philadelphia, 1962), pp. 77-100; Richard M. Dorson, "The Art of Negro Storytelling," in Negro Folktales in Michigan (Cambridge, Mass., 1956), pp. 19-30; Robert Thompson, "Abatan: A Master Potter of the Egbado Yoruba," in Tradition and Creativity in Tribal Art, ed. Daniel P. Biebuyck (Berkeley and Los Angeles, 1969), pp. 120-182; and Adrian A. Gerbrands, Wow-Ipits: Eight Woodcarvers of New Guinea (The Hague, 1967). For a brief critique of the latter two works see my review in Western Folklore, XXXI (1972), 138-141. Other works on individual artists include Edward D. Ives, Larry Gorman: The Man Who Made the Songs (Bloomington, 1962); Roger D. Abrahams, ed., A Singer and Her Songs: Almeda Riddle's Book of Ballads (Baton Rouge, 1971); Daniel J. Crowley, I Could Talk Old-Story Good: Creativity in Bahamian Folklore, Folklore Studies, Vol. 17 (Berkeley and Los Angeles, 1966); Ruth Bunzel, The Pueblo Potter: A Study of Creativity in Primitive Art (New York, 1929); J. Barre Toelken, "The 'Pretty Language' of Yellowman: Genre, Mode, and Texture in Navaho Coyote Narratives," Genre, II (1969), 199-235; David Bynum, "Themes of the Young Hero in Serbocroatian Oral Epic Tradition," Publications of the Modern Language Association, LXXXIII (1968), 1296-1303; Loman D. Cansler, "He Hewed His Own Path: William Henry Scott, Ozark Songmaker," in John A. Burrison, ed., Creativity in Southern Folklore, Vol. III of Studies in the Literary Imagination (Atlanta, 1970), 37-63; Cecelia Conway, "Ben Owen, Master Potter, Moore County, N.C.: A Traditional Potter with an Artist's Integrity," paper read at American Folklore Society meeting, Austin, Texas, November 16, 1972; Loman D. Cansler, "Walter Dibben, an Ozark Bard," Kentucky Folklore Record, XIII (1967), 81-89; James Dow, "He Says, 'I've Heard of You,' and I says, 'No Doubt': Status-Seeking through Storytelling," paper read at California Folklore Society meeting, Fullerton, April 16, 1971, and published in New York Folklore Quarterly, XXIX (1973), 83-96; Henry Glassie, Edward D. Ives, and John F. Szwed, Folksongs and Their Makers (Bowling Green, Ohio, 1970); and Michael and Carole Bell, "The Elderly Artist: Some Comments on Psychic Need as an Impetus to Creativity," paper read at California Folklore Society meeting, Fullerton, April 17, 1971.

Chapter 4. Make It Look Older, More Antique

1. Despite Paul Bohannan's assertion to the contrary in "Artist and Critic in

an African Society," in Marian W. Smith, ed., *The Artist in Tribal Society* (London, 1961), pp. 85-94: "I was wrong in my field work because, Western fashion, I paid too much attention to artists, and when the artists disappointed me I came away with nothing" (p. 94). In the Western elite art tradition it is the critic's task to verbalize the artist's aims and the success or failure of his works; if a recognized group of critics is lacking, and if a codified system of artistic and aesthetic principles is not found, it is the artist who is most sensitive to his tradition. Besides that, personality is an important factor in the proclivity or ability of an individual to articulate critical responses.

2. Ruth Bunzel, "Art," in Franz Boas, ed., *General Anthropology* (Boston, 1938), p. 510.

3. Meyer Schapiro, "Style," in A. L. Kroeber, ed., *Anthropology Today* (Chicago, 1953), p. 311.

4. Robert Thompson, "Abatan: A Master Potter of the Egbado Yoruba," in *Tradition and Creativity in Tribal Art*, ed. Daniel P. Biebuyck (Berkeley and Los Angeles, 1969), p. 158.

5. *Ibid.*, pp. 181, 166 and n. 65, 158, 161, 168.

6. Ralph Altman's remarks are appended to Herta Haselberger's article, "Methods of Studying Ethnological Art," *Current Anthropology*, II (1961), 357. See also the remarks by Beatrice Blackwood, p. 360; Adr. G. Claerhout, p. 364; William Fagg, p. 366; Douglas G. Fraser, p. 368; Gene Weltfish, p. 378; and Frank Willette, p. 380.

7. Some of these factors have been briefly considered in my article, "Two Directions for Folkloristics in the Study of American Art," *Southern Folklore Quarterly*, XXXII (1968), 249, 259

Chapter 5. Like Somebody Hugging You

1. Information on the economics of craftwork, especially the way in which this factor affects the nature of the product, may be found in John Robert Vincent, "A Study of Two Ozark Woodworking Industries" (M.A. thesis, University of Missouri, 1962).

2. See D. W. Gotschalk, *Art and the Social Order* (New York, 1962), pp. 87-169, and the analysis of form by Franz Boas in *Primitive Art* (New York, 1955), pp. 17-63.

3. C. G. Jung, *Psychological Types, or the Psychology of Individuation*, trans. H. Godwin Baynes (London, 1964), p. 480. For insights into Jungian psychology, see Carlos C. Drake, "Jungian Psychology and Its Uses for Folklore," *Journal of American Folklore*, LXXXII (1969), 122-131. Other, basically psychological interpretations of folk or primitive art on a group level include such works as George C. Mills, *Navaho Art and Culture* (Colorado Springs, 1959); J. L. Fischer, "Art Styles as Cultural Cognitive Maps," *American Anthropologist*, LXII (1961), 79-93; and Vytautas Kavolis, "The Value-Orientations Theory of Artistic Style," *Anthropological Quarterly*, XXXVIII (1965),

1-19. The most pertinent work for my study is "Chairs and Their Owners," a paper read by Professor Francis Henninger at the first meeting of the Popular Culture Association, East Lansing, Michigan, April 7-8, 1971. Henninger suggests certain propositions about the relationship between culture and the design of different parts of chairs; for example, he says in his abstract that "when seats and backs are raked backwards they cause the sitter to assume a more relaxed, less aggressive position. It is a 'listening' position, suited to a society with democratic bases which expects knowledge and decisions to be produced by the mutual effort of cooperating conversants."

4. Other information on chairmaking is available in Vincent, "Two Woodworking Industries;" the anonymous articles, "An Old Chair Maker Shows How," Foxfire, III (1969), 11-16, 53-55, and "Cash Crop in North Carolina," Mountain Life and Work, XLIV (1968), 14-17; Jonathan Williams, "The Southern Appalachians," Craft Horizons, XXVI (1966), 35-67; John Cummings, "Slat-Back Chairs," Antiques, LXXII (1957), 60-63; Allen H. Eaton, Handicrafts of the Southern Highlands (New York, 1937); Irving Phillips Lyon, "Square-Post Slat-Back Chairs: A Seventeenth Century Type Found in New England," Antiques, XX (1931), 210-216; L. J. Mayes, The History of Chairmaking in High Wycombe (London, 1960); and the short article on a West Virginia craftsman entitled simply "Authentic," Mountain Life and Work, XL (1964), 45-48.

5. Jung, Psychological Types, p. 480.

6. See Mary S. Herrick, "A Chenango County Coffin," New York Folklore Quarterly, VIII (1952), 135-136.

7. Jung, Psychological Types, p. 500.

8. See Michael Owen Jones, "Traditions of a Kansas Farmer" (M.A. thesis, Indiana University, 1966), p. 345.

9. This is my interpretation of the behavior of the artists surveyed by Henry Glassie, "'Take That Night Train to Selma': An Excursion to the Outskirts of Scholarship," Journal of Popular Culture, II (1968), 1-62. "These creators," writes Glassie (p.52), with whom I would take issue, "may have been freed to do so by an elimination of their customary responsibilities (as in the case of sudden bachelor Tab Ward) or have been forced to do so because of a dissatisfaction with their own culture brought about by a comparative knowledge of other cultures (as in the case of our friend Dorrance Weir)." For information about the other artists, see the film, "The Art of Theora Hamblett" (University of Mississippi Extension, Oxford, Mississippi), and Edward E. Ives, Larry Gorman: The Man Who Made the Songs (Bloomington, 1962).

10. See the comments by Archie Green in the booklet that accompanies the record album, Sarah Ogan Gunning, "Girl of Constant Sorrow."

11. This judgment is based on the depiction of a few chairs on the porch of Charley's house in the Midwest in a small Polaroid print Charley sent me in 1970. The picture, slightly out of focus, was taken at a long distance from the house.

Chapter 6. It Takes Half a Fool to Make Chairs

1. Culture change has often been disparaged as a harbinger of decline of a people's art tradition, particularly if the subject in question is folk or primitive art. I question, however, the assumption of Henry Glassie (Pattern in the Material Folk Culture of the Eastern United States [Philadelphia, 1968], p. 237) that "there is little place for material folk culture in our world. It cannot last." For a critique of various comments on culture change and folk art see my "Culture Change and the 'Folk' Arts," Southern Folklore Quarterly, XXXVI (1972), 43-60, a review of recent books by Adrian A. Gerbrands, Daniel P. Biebuyck, and Carol F. Jopling in Western Folklore, XXXI (1972), 138-141, and especially my review of Adrian A. Gerbrands, ed., The Asmat of New Guinea: The Journal of Michael Clark Rockefeller (New York, 1967), in Southern Folklore Quarterly, XXXIII (1969), 361-366.

2. On new developments in folk art see three essays by Nelson Graburn: "The Eskimos and 'Airport Art,'" Trans-Action, IV (Oct., 1967), 28-33; "L'Art et les processus d'acculturation," Revue internationale des sciences sociales, XXI (1969), 491-503; and "Art and Pluralism in the Americas," a paper presented at the 39th International Congress of Americanists, Lima, Peru, August 6, 1970. Usually, however, "culture change" is disparaged; see, for example, Louis Harap, Social Roots of the Arts (New York, 1949), pp. 130-133, 140; Arnold Hauser, The Philosophy of Art History (Cleveland and New York, 1963), p. 331; Guillermo de Zendegui, "The Crisis in Folk Arts," Americas, 18 (1966), 29; and comments by Adr. G. Claerhout, T. Barrow, William Fagg, and Frank Willett appended to Herta Haselberger's article, "Method of Studying Ethnological Art," Current Anthropology, II (1961), 341-384. Only Ralph Altman (ibid., p. 356) is willing to admit that the "study of tourist art in the widest sense of the term might contribute to the understanding of the process of accultura-tion, artistic innovation, of the personality of the artist, et al." Some of the most frequent changes that occur in art as a result of urbanization and industrialization are surveyed by me in "Culture Change and the 'Folk' Arts." It should be pointed out that the investigator himself is often a factor in bringing about changes, whether he wants to be or not; some researchers are even advocating active participation in helping craftsmen market their goods. See, for example, Rayna Green, "Folklorists and Craft Revival," a paper read at meeting of American Folklore Society, Austin, Texas, November 16, 1972; Nelson Graburn, "The Marketing of Canadian Eskimo Art," a paper presented at meeting of Northeastern Anthropological Association, Ottawa, Ontario, May 8, 1970; and Nelson Graburn, "Eskimo Carvings and Coops: The Anthropologist as Innovator" (unpublished MS).

Chapter 7. The Beauty Part and the Lasting Part

1. Understandably, there are numerous examples of the tendency of an investi-

gator to rely on his own system of categorization; two fairly recent instances are *The Asmat of New Guinea: The Journal of Michael Clark Rockefeller*, ed. Adrian A. Gerbrands (New York, 1967), p. 23; and Hans Himmelheber, "Personality and Technique of African Sculptors," in *Technique & Personality in Primitive Art*, ed. Hans Himmelheber, Robert Redfield, and Melville J. Herskovits (New York, 1963), pp. 84-85.

2. See Sieber's comments in *Tradition and Creativity in Tribal Art*, ed. Daniel P. Biebuyck (Berkeley and Los Angeles, 1969), p. 202.

3. The quotation comes from Bernhard Berenson (who does not appreciate folk art), *Essays in Appreciation* (London, 1958), p. 144. See also "Country Furniture: A Symposium," *Antiques*, LVII (1950), 355-362. It was Berenson (*Essays*, p. 143) who wrote: "I am convinced that popular art is always a deviation from professional individual art, never a spontaneous upsurging from the dumb dull masses of new ways of feeling, seeing and expressing with the voice, the pen or the pencil."

4. Robert Thompson, "Abatan: A Master Potter of the Egbado Yoruba," in *Tradition and Creativity in Tribal Art*, ed. Biebuyck, pp. 175, 182, 121-122.

5. David Pye, *The Nature of Design* (New York, 1964); D.W. Gotschalk, *Art and the Social Order* (New York, 1962); Thomas C. Munro, *The Arts and Their Interrelations* (Cleveland, 1967); Thomas C. Munro, *Toward Science in Aesthetics* (Indianapolis, 1956); and R.M. MacIver, *Social Causation*, 2d ed. (New York, 1964). I have also found useful Alan P. Merriam's *The Anthropology of Music* (Chicago, 1964), as well as his *A Prologue to the Study of African Arts* (Yellow Springs, 1962), and his "The Arts and Anthropology," in *Horizons of Anthropology*, ed. Sol Tax (Chicago, 1964), pp. 224-236.

6. This conception of art is a modification of that presented by Munro (*Arts and Their Interrelations*, pp. 107-108). He makes the point (*ibid.*, pp. 97, 98, 102) that the aesthetic is not sharply delineated from the practical, but see also Raymond Firth, *Elements of Social Organisation* (London, 1951), pp. 155-182; MacIver, *Social Causation*, p. 275; and Edmund Carpenter's comment in *Tradition and Creativity in Tribal Art*, ed. Biebuyck, p. 203. For a discussion of this subject, see Mikel Dufrenne, "The Aesthetic Object and the Technical Object," in *Aesthetic Inquiry*, ed. Monroe C. Beardsley and Herbert M. Schueller (Belmont, Calif., 1967), pp. 188-198; attempts to distinguish between technical and aesthetic objects are often of little use, since most art serves a practical purpose and most tools have been regarded as aesthetic by some people. The distinction between technological and cultural orders was expressed by MacIver, *Social Causation*, pp. 275-290, and no doubt it obtains in the minds of MacIver and other researchers; such a demarcation is more of an intellectual construct than a fact of artistic production.

7. For the "native" conception of art, see also Harold K. Schneider, "The Interpretation of Pakot Visual Art," originally published in *Man*, LVI (1956), 103-106, and reprinted in Carol F. Jopling, ed., *Art and Aesthetics in Primitive Societies* (New York, 1971), pp. 55-63. Also note the comments by Biebuyck, Ralph Altman, and Carpenter

in _Tradition and Creativity in Tribal Art_, ed. Biebuyck, pp. 6, 184, 203.

8. The socioeconomic relationship between producers and consumers is described by William Morgan Williams, _The Country Craftsman: A Study of Some Rural Crafts and the Rural Industries Organisation in England_ (London, 1958).

9. These terms are modifications of those used by Eric R. Wolf, _Peasants_ (Englewood Cliffs, 1966); George M. Foster, "The Dyadic Contract: A Model for the Social Structure of a Mexican Peasant Society," _American Anthropologist_, LXIII (1961), 1173-1192; and E. E. LeClair, Jr., "Economic Theory and Economic Anthropology," _American Anthropologist_, LXIV (1962), 1179-1203.

10. Raymond Firth (_Primitive Economics of the New Zealand Maori_ [New York, 1929], pp. 172-173) makes the observation that "economic production enlists decorative art in the service of promoting industry, and in return provides it with a rich field for experiment and display." Somewhat more fully, he claims that "the high regard for art, the increased valuation attaching to the economic product when tastefully adorned, has an important stimulus to effort and to reinforce the social sentiment which clusters around industry. Moreover . . . this redounds to the advantage of art, since the sphere of economic production affords a wide field for the exercise of talent."

11. See, for example, J. M. Tanner, ed., _Stress and Psychiatric Disorder_ (Oxford, 1960); Katherin J. Bordicks, _Patterns of Shock_ (New York, 1965); Herman Feifel, _The Meaning of Death_ (New York, 1959); and Robert Fulton, _Death and Identity_ (New York, 1965). Most of the creative expression alluded to by Henry Glassie ("'Take That Night Train to Selma': An Excursion to the Outskirts of Scholarship," _Journal of Popular Culture_, II [1968], 1-62), including Weir's song, can be interpreted according to the mode of analysis I am proposing.

12. See Gotschalk, _Art and the Social Order_, pp. 28, 60, 93-94.

13. H. G. Barnett, _Innovation: The Basis of Cultural Change_ (New York, 1953), pp. 208-212.

14. See Jane C. Goodale and Joan D. Koss, "The Cultural Context of Creativity among Tiwi," in June Helm, ed., _Essays on the Verbal and Visual Arts_ (Seattle, 1967), pp. 160-174; and Jerome Bruner, "The Conditions of Creativity," in H. E. Gruber, G. Terrell, and M. Wertheimer, eds., _Contemporary Approaches to Creativity_ (New York, 1963), esp. pp. 12-16.

15. For a discussion of the phases of creativity in art generally, see Gotschalk, _Art and the Social Order_, pp. 54-83, and Munro, _Arts and Their Interrelations_, pp. 315-324. For individual and small-group culture, see John M. Roberts, _Three Navaho Households: A Comparative Study in Small Group Culture_ (Cambridge, Mass., 1951); David Bidney, _Theoretical Anthropology_, 2d ed. (New York, 1967), esp. pp. xi-xli; and Roger D. Abrahams, "Creativity, Individuality, and the Traditional Singer," in John A. Burrison, ed., _Creativity in Southern Folklore_, Vol. III of _Studies in the Literary Imagination_ (Atlanta, 1970), p. 13.

16. Gotschalk, _Art and the Social Order,_ pp. 56, 57, 72, 76 ff.; Munro, _Arts and Their Interrelations,_ p. 326; and Arnold Hauser, _The Philosophy of Art History_ (Cleveland and New York, 1963), pp. 232 ff. Most investigators of primitive art have contended that the artist has the image completely in mind before he approaches his materials, and that he then transforms that fully conceived mental image into an object by transferring it to the materials. No human being is so skilled. Research on the subject has gone little beyond the most obvious aspects of the objective or overt phase of creativity. Nevertheless, see the comments by Ruth Bunzel, _The Pueblo Potter: A Study of Creativity in Primitive Art_ (New York, 1929), p. 49; Ruth Bunzel, "Art," in Franz Boas, ed., _General Anthropology_ (Boston, 1938), p. 554; Franz Boas, _Primitive Art_ (New York, 1955), p. 156; and George C. Mills, _Navaho Art and Culture_ (Colorado Springs, 1959), p. 131.

17. Gotschalk, _Art and the Social Order,_ pp. 70 ff.

18. Gotschalk (_ibid.,_ pp. 58 ff.) also refers to the second phase as the "subjective phase." Munro (_Arts and Their Interrelations,_ pp. 315 ff.) refers to it as the "psychic phase." Either way it is the same thing and it cannot be separated in reality from the "objective" or "overt" phase.

19. See Merriam, _Anthropology of Music,_ pp. 165-184.

20. Pye, _Nature of Design,_ pp. 30 ff.

21. Some of the reasons for convention in art are suggested by Hauser, _Philosophy of Art History,_ pp. 372, 408, and Munro, _Arts and Their Interrelations,_ pp. 342-349. Most significant is Munro's remark (p. 342): "There is no artistic creation out of nothing; _ex nihilo nihil fit._ The comparatively original part of an artist's work consists, not in thinking up completely new ideas, but in working out a few variations on one or more of the styles he inherits. . . . If his contribution, large or small, is accepted and imitated, it becomes part of a tradition. By such gradual increments the traditions of art and of civilization develop."

22. Ideas about the creation and replication of prime objects are from George Kubler, _The Shape of Time: Remarks on the History of Things_ (New Haven and London, 1962), pp. 39, 43, 70, 71, 76, 78.

23. Munro, _Arts and Their Interrelations,_ p. 386.

24. The conception of taste defined here is a modification of Russell Lynes's ideas as presented in _The Tastemakers_ (New York, 1954), pp. 339-341. For other studies of taste and aesthetics, see Irvin L. Child, "Personal Preferences as an Expression of Aesthetic Sensitivity," _Journal of Personality,_ XXX (1962), 456-513; C.S. Ford, E. Terry Prothro, and Irvin L. Child, "Some Transcultural Comparisons of Esthetic Judgment," _Journal of Social Psychology,_ LXVIII (1966), 27-33; M. Lawler, "Cultural Influences on Personal Preferences in Design," _Journal of Abnormal and Social Psychology,_ LXI (1955), 690-692; Robert H. Lowie, "A Note on Aesthetics," _American Anthropologist,_ XXIII (1921), 170-174; John Messenger, "Reflection on Aesthetic Talent," _Basic College Quarterly,_ IV (1958), 20-24; Daniel J. Crowley, "An African Aesthetic," in Jopling, ed., _Art and Aesthetics,_

pp. 315-327; and Robert Ferris Thompson, "Esthetics in Traditional Africa," Art News, LXVI (1968), 44-45, 63-66. Much of what is called the aesthetic, however, seems to be standards of taste. I find myself agreeing with W. A. McElroy ("Aesthetic Appreciation in Aborigines of Arnhem Land: A Comparative Experimental Study," Oceania, XXIII [1952], 81-94), who concludes (p. 94) that "the present research finds little or no evidence for the existence of interracial 'good taste' based upon inherited predispositions."

25. On disciplined versus naive aesthetic experience or judgments, see Gotschalk, Art and the Social Order, pp. 159-161.

26. James West, "Plainville, U.S.A.," in Abram Kardiner, The Psychological Frontiers of Society (New York, 1945), p. 307. On the concept of aesthetic see Munro, Toward Science in Aesthetics, esp. p. 98; Gotschalk, Art and the Social Order, pp. 3 ff.; and Merriam, Anthropology of Music, pp. 259-276.

27. In regard to Proffitt's feelings toward his song, see Sandy Paton's remarks in the booklet accompanying the album Frank Proffitt Memorial Album, Folk-Legacy FSA-36; "Lord Lovel" is on side 1, band 2. Richard Nevins's remarks about the Ward brothers are from jacket notes on the album Fields and Wade Ward, Biograph Records RC-6002A.

28. Merriam, Anthropology of Music, p. 269. The six factors in the Western elite concept of the aesthetic were set forth and examined by Merriam (ibid., pp. 259-276).

29. See Bunzel, Pueblo Potter, p. 54, but see also pp. 8, 53, 87; Philip J. C. Dark, "The Study of Ethno-Aesthetics: The Visual Arts," in Helm, ed., Essays on the Verbal and Visual Arts, p. 143; and George C. Mills, "Art: An Introduction to Qualitative Anthropology," Journal of Aesthetics and Art Criticism, XVI (1957), 2, 5.

30. These concepts of type and style are developed from comments by Meyer Schapiro, "Style," in A. L. Kroeber, ed., Anthropology Today (Chicago, 1953), p. 287, and Henry Glassie, Pattern in the Material Folk Culture of the Eastern United States (Philadelphia, 1968), p. 8.

31. See Jean Lipman's comments in "What Is American Folk Art? A Symposium," Antiques, LVII (1950), 359; and Erwin O. Christensen, American Crafts and Folk Arts (Washington, 1964), p. 2. See other contributions to the symposium in Antiques, as well as Louis Harap's remarks in Social Roots of the Arts (New York, 1949), pp. 130-133, 140; Hauser's statements in The Philosophy of Art History, p. 331; and even Richard M. Dorson's comment in American Folklore (Chicago, 1959), pp. 180-181.

32. See the criticism of this model by MacIver, Social Causation, pp. 101 ff.; Thomas C. Munro, Evolution in the Arts (Cleveland, 1957); and Kubler, The Shape of Time.

33. See Glassie, Pattern in Material Folk Culture, pp. 228-230; John Robert Vincent, "A Study of Two Ozark Woodworking Industries" (M.A. thesis, University of Missouri, 1962), chap. ii.

34. Hauser, Philosophy of Art History, p. 294. For critiques see MacIver, Social Causation, pp. 226 ff., and Alan Dundes, "The Devolutionary Premise in Folklore Theory,"

Journal of the Folklore Institute, VI (1969), 5-19. For a critique of Dundes's article see Elliott Oring, "The Devolutionary Premise: A Point of Order," presented at California Folklore Society meeting, Sacramento, April, 1972.

35. Charles F. Montgomery, in "Country Furniture: A Symposium," *Antiques,* XCIII (1968), 355.

36. The clarification of this point came to me in a letter from Charles F. Montgomery, April 18, 1968.

37. Ralph and Terry Kovel, *American Country Furniture, 1780-1875* (New York, 1965), p. v.

38. Henry Lionel Williams, *Country Furniture of Early America* (New York, 1963), p. 16.

39. Glassie, *Pattern in Material Folk Culture,* pp. 228-230.

40. The proponents of evolution include Munro, *Evolution in the Arts* (in which he posits a "multiple dialectic"), and Hauser, *Philosophy of Art History,* as well as Thompson, "Esthetics in Traditional Africa." MacIver (*Social Causation*), however, is critical of this explanation of social and cultural change.

41. See Bunzel, *The Pueblo Potter,* p. 88.

42. For specific examples of these changes in other traditions of art and technology, see Carlos C. Drake, "The Traditional Elements in the Cooperage Industry," *Keystone Folklore Quarterly,* XIV (1969), 81-96; Darrell D. Henning, "Maple Sugaring: History of a Folk Technology," *Keystone Folklore Quarterly,* XI (1966), 239-274; Bunzel, *Pueblo Potter, passim;* Jean Crawford, *Jugtown Pottery: History and Design* (Winston-Salem, 1964), *passim;* and Ralph Rinzler, "Cheever Meaders: North Georgia Potter," in Austin Fife, Alta Fife, and Henry Glassie, eds., *Forms Upon the Frontier* (Logan, 1969), p. 77.

43. Hauser, *Philosophy of Art History,* p. 282. Boas (in *Primitive Art*) stressed the importance of perfection of form, which to him seemed to be the essence of art; it is to Boas that I am indebted for the basic idea with which I end this chapter. That any art tradition is worth investigation should be apparent; primitive art, however, had suffered much the same fate as folk art until a few decades ago. Now neither researchers nor laymen would deign to charge primitive art with crudity or inferiority (note that Hauser [Ibid.] does not mention primitive art at all), although suspicion lingers about designating this art as "primitive." The esoteric quality of primitive art was bound to save it from disgrace, whereas the art in the commentators' own society lacked this charming mystery, or so they have thought. As a consequence, even distinguished researchers succumb to discrediting the nonacademic or nonelite art in their very midst. (How easy it is in a crowded room to brush aside one's relatives and embrace the exotic stranger!)